Jean Lipman-Blumen, Ph.D., Harvard
Graduate School of Arts and Science,
is ARCO Professor of Public Policy and
Professor of Organizational Behavior,
Claremont Graduate School, Claremont,
California.

She is co-editor with Jessie Bernard of
*Sex Roles and Social Policy: A Complex
Social Science Equation.*

Dr. Lipman-Blumen is the president of
LBS International Ltd., a woman-owned
and woman-managed consulting firm that
engages in social and behavior science
research, policy analysis, and organizational consulting. The firm also offers
workshops and training programs in management, achieving styles, and other
gender-related issues.

PRENTICE-HALL
FOUNDATIONS OF MODERN SOCIOLOGY SERIES

Alex Inkeles, Editor

GENDER ROLES AND POWER

JEAN LIPMAN-BLUMEN
Claremont Graduate School

Prentice-Hall, Inc., Englewood Cliffs, New Jersey 07632

Library of Congress Cataloging in Publication Data

LIPMAN-BLUMEN, JEAN.
Gender roles and power.

Includes index.
1. Sex role.   2. Power (Social sciences)   I. Title.
HQ1075.L57   1984   305.3   83-24725
ISBN 0-13-347518-2
ISBN 0-13-347500-X (pbk.)

To Jessie Bernard—
my mother, my sister—
and my children

© 1984 by Prentice-Hall, Inc., Englewood Cliffs, New Jersey 07632

Printed in the United States of America

10 9 8 7 6 5 4 3 2 1

ISBN 0-13-347518-2
ISBN 0-13-347500-X {pbk}

Prentice-Hall International, Inc., *London*

Prentice-Hall of Australia Pty. Limited, *Sydney*

Editora Prentice-Hall do Brasil, Ltda., *Rio de Janiero*

Prentice-Hall Canada Inc., *Toronto*

Prentice-Hall of India Private Limited, *New Delhi*

Prentice-Hall of Japan, Inc., *Tokyo*

Prentice-Hall of Southeast Asia Pte. Ltd., *Singapore*

Whitehall Books Limited, *Wellington, New Zealand*

CONTENTS

PREFACE

This book has taken me on an odyssey, a long journey in which I visited islands of research and knowledge, as well as relationships past and present. New aspects of history, psychology, philosophy, political science, economics, and sociology were the stopping points along the way. Taking longer than I (or my patient editor) ever envisioned, this exploration of the sex-gender system in many disciplines, historical periods, and cultures offered me more material than could possibly be condensed into a two-hundred page book. Mementoes of this extended journey—in the form of sections mapping sex roles onto gender roles throughout the life cycle, weighing the speculations of archaeologists and historians of ancient civilizations, exploring the history of gender-divergent educational systems from Athens and Sparta to the present day, describing entrepreneurial enterprises of the eighteenth-century Northern French bourgeoisie, and examining power relationships between mistresses and their maids—remain (fortunately, for the weary reader) filed away in the dark recesses of my files.

The central organizing metaphor of the book—the sex-gender system as the blueprint for all other power relationships—provided a prism through which I could examine anew research findings, other knowledge, and relationships. It helped me to understand phenomena that previously seemed inscrutable, random, or even simply absurd. My hope is that it will offer a similar lens to the reader.

Acknowledgments

Where do I begin to acknowledge the legion of colleagues, friends, and family members who have contributed to this book? First, of course, I am indebted to Alex Inkeles, not only for his patience and support during the long gestation of this book, but also for the standards of intellectual excellence he has imparted to me, beginning with my early days as his graduate student at Harvard. Bernadette Inkeles was a continuous source of optimism and support at every point in this long odyssey.

Next, Jessie Bernard has served as the "compleat feminist scholar"— the one with whom I argued many points about sex and gender roles, to whom I frantically turned as my human archive when gremlins impertinently stole a critical footnote from my files, and the one who both encouraged and flogged me to continue at moments when I would have gladly abandoned my typewriter and the nagging issues of sex and gender roles. At various points, she read and critiqued early versions of the manuscript.

I am also indebted to the Center for Advanced Study in the Behavioral Sciences, Palo Alto, California, where I spent 1978–1979 as a Fellow in Residence, with the support of the National Endowment for the Humanities, The Spencer Foundation, and the Rockefeller Foundation. That was an important year, in which I had time to read and mull over ideas that only later fit together into what I hope is a coherent vision.

One of the wonderful surprises involved in undertaking such a project is the discovery of many individuals whom I have yet to meet face-to-face, but who spent time and energy ferreting out references, citations, and statistics, as well as discussing ideas over the telephone. Among these very special invisible colleagues I count both Paul Richards and Louis Savary.

The many versions of this book have been typed by various dedicated people: Jo Thornton, Sharon Fisher, and Randy Arnold. At one point, Randy Arnold helped me to cut the book, and she labored long and hard tracking down footnotes and other material that the gremlins refused to return. My colleague Susan Schram worked with me in the final days of manuscript preparation, systematically checking and rechecking sections with a dedication that defies recompense.

Other feminist colleagues and students, female and male, were a constant source of encouragement in this exciting but arduous effort. Nancy Schlossberg, Muriel Cantor, Sol Levine, Harold J. Leavitt, Georgia Strasburg, and Seymour Rubenfeld all made special contributions. Support also came from unexpected quarters: non-feminists. For example, Jack and Francis Thornton, my marvelous typist Jo Thornton's husband and father-in-law, who worked as her proof-readers, encouraged me to continue, insisting I had opened their non-feminist eyes.

Finally, my own family members have probably taught me more than any scholarly research could have about the double helix of sex and gender roles. The family in which I grew up and the family I have tried to raise remain two oases of love, humor, patience, and encouragement. Parents and children usually cannot escape these relationships. Siblings can. So I owe a special debt of love and gratitude to my sister, who has never failed to be there.

Jean Lipman-Blumen

CHAPTER 1
SEX ROLES, GENDER ROLES, AND POWER

Men's and women's roles are currently caught in the vortex of a darkening social storm, which threatens to spark changes in their relationships as individuals and as groups. Occasional lightning flashes allow us only the briefest glimpse of the different shapes toward which these roles are evolving and the underlying power struggle they symbolize.

Less than a decade ago, "sex roles" and "gender roles" were still obscure sociological concepts, confusing not only to the general public, but to academicians as well. Only social scientists, and very few of them, bothered to distinguish between *sex roles*, that is, behaviors stemming from biological sexual differences, and their constant companion, *gender roles*, those socially created behaviors assigned differentially to women and men. Fewer still attempted to describe how biological sex roles and socially generated gender roles are braided together into a structured set of relationships known as the *sex-gender system*. Today the concepts of sex roles, gender roles, and the sex-gender system have become familiar lightning rods, attracting unprecedented attention, from concern to calumny.

The debate and confusion marking these concepts flow from three primary sources: (1) the imprecise way the terms are used (much like Humpty Dumpty's words, they mean whatever one chooses them to mean); (2) the complexity with which biologically based sex roles and culturally constructed gender roles are intertwined in a sex-gender system[1]; and (3) the increasing recognition of the fundamental power relationship between women and men that the sex-gender system expresses. How do we deal with this confusion?

DEFINING SEX ROLES AND GENDER ROLES

In everyday life, the terms *sex role* and *gender role* are used interchangeably, obscuring important differences and underlying issues. To reduce the first source of confusion, we shall try, wherever possible, to distinguish between them, recognizing (and asking the reader to remember) that in real life they are virtually inseparable. We shall use the better-known term, *sex roles,* to refer specifically to behaviors determined by an individual's biological sex, such as menstruation, pregnancy, lactation, erection, orgasm, and seminal ejaculation. At the same time, we should not forget that even biologically determined phenomena do not escape the influence of cultural attitudes, norms, and values. For the moment, let us think of *values* as those things the society labels desirable or good, and *norms* as socially approved standards of behavior.

Although we may try to tease out the essence of biologically based sex roles from the more complex sex-gender system, ambiguities and contradictions remain. For example, even though bearing children is a physiologically determined aspect of the female sex role, not all women can, or choose to, bear and nurse infants. Similarly, not all men opt to engage in procreation. And from a strict chromosomal, hormonal, and anatomical perspective, some individuals are neither male nor female.

Gender roles, on the other hand, are socially created expectations for masculine and feminine behavior. Exaggerating both real and imagined aspects of biological sex, each society sorts certain polarized behaviors and attitudes into two sets it then labels "male" and "female." Gender roles are social constructions; they contain self-concepts, psychological traits, as well as family, occupational, and political roles assigned dichotomously to members of each sex. For example, the traditional female gender role includes expectations for females to be passive, nurturant, and dependent. The standard male gender role incorporates alternative expectations—behavior that is aggressive, competitive, and independent. Women as mothers, nurses, and teachers, men as doctors, generals, and legislators are part of this pattern.

On one level, the culturally created polarities of gender roles are simply one more set of opposing concepts (such as day and night, hot and cold, up and down) by which human beings have sought to understand the world in which they live. On another level, the more complicated meaning of the polarities represented by male and female gender roles is signaled by their resting on more than purely physical bases. Why gender roles, without any biological basis, include "opposite" behaviors and traits for females and males is a question we shall explore throughout this book.

One example of how socially defined gender roles represent cultural elaborations of biological sex roles might be useful here. Obviously, bearing children is biologically possible only within the female sex role. That the female assignment of nurturing and rearing is not biologically inevitable is seen from the fact that some men, as well as women who have never given birth, have reared children. Theoretically, then, childrearing could be part of either gender role. Still, in most societies childrearing is assigned to females and becomes central to the female gender role, with the result that childrearing is treated *as if* it were a biological imperative for females.

To recapitulate, gender roles encompass all those cultural expectations associated with masculinity or femininity that go beyond biological sex differences. Gender roles represent a more complex conceptualization than sex roles. As such, gender roles involve that intricate blend of social and psychological behaviors, attitudes, norms, and values that society designates "masculine" and "feminine."

THE DOUBLE HELIX OF THE SEX-GENDER SYSTEM

In all societies, gender roles and sex roles intertwine in a dynamic double helix that feminist theorists have labeled the sex-gender system. The threads of sex and gender roles are so intricately interwoven that most observers believe the current patterns have always existed. The threads of sex and gender roles are tied to filaments of age, class, religion, race, and ethnicity, as well. This elaborate social knot is the second source of confusion in the current sex-gender role debate.

Before recent scholarly examination, the complexity of the sex-gender double helix was taken as proof of its inevitability. This rather myopic view ignores several critical factors, particularly cross-cultural and historical variations in sex-gender systems, as well as the influence of individual choice. Although biological sexual differentiation occurs in all societies, gender roles differ cross-culturally; that is, what men do in one society, women may do in another. Even within the same culture, men's and women's roles may vary from one historical period to another. In the Soviet Union today, for example, street sweeping is an occupation associated with the female gender role, whereas in the United States it is a job performed mostly by men. And before the Industrial Revolution transformed the Western world, women had clearly recognized economic roles, but by the mid-nineteenth century, European and American women were relegated to *Kinder, Kuche,* and *Kirche* (children, kitchen and church).

This shortsighted view also ignores the degree to which personal choice shapes the sex-gender system. Men and women can choose how they will enact at least certain aspects of both sex and gender roles. For example, most men and women can decide whether or not to become parents. And after childbirth, most mothers can opt to nurse or bottle-feed their babies. These illustrations suggest that human choices influence even biologically based sex roles. Of course, social pressures to select traditional roles may color these "choices."

Nonetheless, despite individual, cross-cultural, and historical variation, the sex-gender system exhibits a remarkably recognizable structure. Sex and gender are everywhere combined in systems that generally channel females and males into ostensibly complementary roles, requiring mutually exclusive tasks that reap vastly different rewards. For purposes of analysis, wherever possible we shall separate the sex-gender system into its two major factors: gender roles and sex roles. We shall try to disentangle the distinct contributions that sex and gender make to the sex-gender system. In addition, where feasible, we shall acknowledge the differences *within* gender groups that are linked to other characteristics, such as age, class, ethnicity, and race.

THE POWER RELATIONSHIP
SYMBOLIZED BY GENDER ROLES

The third major source of concern and confusion about the sex-gender system is the growing recognition that sex and gender roles express an important power relationship between females and males, one which serves as the model for all other power relationships. (We shall return to this point as a major theme of this book.) The relative roles and positions (statuses) of women and men in society, their different responsibilities and privileges, and their unequal control over societal resources point to a major power difference between them.

Throughout history, the power differential between men and women has been attributed, with varying weights, to biology and environment. Few deny the possibility that the sex-gender system, with its underlying power dynamic, was originally set in motion by important genetic differences between men and women. Disparities in size and strength, as well as women's childbearing and lactating capacities, formed the cornerstone of the sex-gender system. The primitive and physically difficult environment in which it originated made the system reasonably "functional" for those times. Few, however, notice that patterns initially established on these grounds still persist long after the circumstances have changed. This persistence stems mostly from the underlying power relationship, which continues to provide the dominant group with advantages it is understandably reluctant to relinquish.

Much—perhaps too much—attention has been devoted to the fact that while women became pregnant and bore and nursed children, men protected them from danger, built shelters, and provided food. Women's genetically based, but time-limited, physical dependency was linked to male dominance. Only now are anthropologists beginning to correct the historically unbalanced picture in which women's contributions to food production and shelter were considerably minimized.[2] The active versus passive, independent versus dependent dichotomy generated by this primordial picture led to sexual stereotypes from which civilization is still struggling to emerge.

Considerable contrary evidence that social training can overcome traditional sex typing is largely ignored. Psychological and physiological data on sex-linked traits suggest that the degree of overlap between the sexes is as important, or more important, than the average differences between them.[3] Researchers report, for example, that 40 percent of females may exhibit greater assertiveness than males, and a similar proportion of males exhibit more interdependence, and possibly dependence, than females.[4] But this evidence has not captured either the scientific or the popular imagination.

The differences between male and female continue to hold center stage. The fact that differences exist often seems more important than their specific nature. This concern with differences points to an underlying phenomenon: the existence of differences suggests that one member of the relationship is more, has more, deserves more of what is defined as desir-

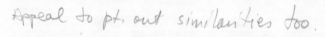

Appeal to pt. out similarities too.

able in that society. This differentiation provides one rationale for the veiled power relationship linking women and men.

Once such social arrangements are established, those who have become accustomed to the greater privileges and power find it both natural and imperative to defend the status quo. Later generations accept the structure as "given." Those who benefit the most and have come to believe that they truly deserve the dominant position naturally guard it vigorously. The scientific community, itself a major beneficiary, starts with this assumption and inevitably reconfirms what it already believes. Even when the original conditions that gave rise to the social structure have changed, institutional arrangements perpetuate the system. The advantaged group deliberately and unwittingly sees to it.

THE BLUEPRINT FOR ALL POWER RELATIONSHIPS: GENDER ROLES

Some observers have noted that the current structure of the sex-gender system represents a centuries-old power relationship—often a power struggle—that persists despite the erosion of its original social bases. The major premise of this book goes one step further to suggest that the cultural (and hence mutable) aspects of this power relationship—that is, gender roles—provide the blueprint for *all* other power relationships. Gender roles are the model for power relationships between generations, socioeconomic classes, religious, racial and ethnic groups, as well as between imperial powers and their colonies, and between less developed and post-industrialized societies. Power is the infrastructure of the sex-gender system. As a result gender roles are carefully guarded, or otherwise changes in this primal power relationship might spread to all other established power relationships. In Western society, the relationship between men and women has been defined as the earthly replica of that between God and humans. This divine link cloaks gender roles in inviolable sanctity. As long as gender roles maintain their proper power balance, all other power relationships based on this model are safe.

Gender roles do not, of course, exist in isolation. Private and public gender roles influence one another and in turn affect the entire range of social roles. The gender power relationship itself is influenced by events and changes in the larger society. Later we shall examine the interpenetration between private and public gender roles, as well as between gender roles and other social roles. It is a complex and endless dialectic; small wonder that attempts to redefine gender roles and the power relationship they symbolize meet serious resistance.

Great effort is devoted to preserving these polarized differences, which symbolize the power differential between male and female gender roles in most societies. Tasks are assigned to one group or the other; rarely to both. Of course, what men do in one culture, women may do in another; however, in all societies, men's activities, privileges, responsibilities, and resources are more highly valued than women's. They represent the desiderata of life.

Allotting certain tasks to women and complementary ones to men creates a structural interdependence between the sexes. Such interdependence itself is neither undesirable nor an inevitable precondition for inequality. In fact, when both parties to an interdependent and complementary relationship have equal control over valued resources, there is no impediment to their equal power. The crux of the problem is that every society values men's contributions and resources, their activities, privileges, even their responsibilities, more highly than women's. This greater valuation of males stems from and points to the serious power difference between women and men.

A DEFINITION OF POWER

Before and since Machiavelli, power has carried numerous definitions. For our purpose, we shall use *power* to mean the process whereby individuals or groups gain or maintain the capacity to impose their will upon others, to have their way recurrently, despite implicit or explicit opposition, through invoking or threatening punishment, as well as offering or withholding rewards. When power is firmly established, the explicit use of punishments and rewards is hardly necessary. The knowledge that one controls such social resources is usually sufficient to evoke compliance from the less powerful. We need only examine most societies' military establishment to see this phenomenon at work. The military often fulfills its mission simply by being, its implied threat of punishment sufficient to quell nonconformity.

Control over resources, particularly institutional resources, is a vital aspect of power relationships. Those resources most closely linked to the key values of the society are particularly important since they represent contributions to the social process. Individuals or groups who can make or deny such contributions may command the compliance of those who lack comparable resources, or those whose resources are denigrated or ignored by the society. The result: control over differential resources leads to power relationships.

The more powerful control society's major institutions, as well as the social, economic, and political resources that flow from these institutional structures. Social institutions continually validate the judgments and values used in their creation and preservation. The validation is more than symbolic; it entitles the powerful to deploy institutional resources to reward those who comply and help, as well as to punish those who resist. In this way, powerful societal decision-makers have the resources to impose their will recurrently on others who lack such assets. Power breeds more power, and ideologies, as we shall see, facilitate the process.

The More Powerful and the Less Powerful

Before proceeding, let us caution the reader that, for convenience, we occasionally shall abbreviate "the more powerful" and "the less powerful" to "the powerful" and "the powerless." Nonetheless, we think in "more powerful" and "less powerful" terms because we assume that few individuals or groups are totally lacking in resources that could be redefined or negotiated for power.

In most power relationships, nevertheless, one can usually distinguish between the more and the less powerful, although they may change places over time. Without the ruled, there can be no ruler. And the ruled must, for reasons we shall explore, be willing to be ruled—at least apparently, and at least for the moment.

SOME OBSERVATIONS ON POWER

In this book, we shall examine sex and gender roles within the context of power. Here, we make several observations about power relationships whose applicability to the sex-gender system we shall then explore in later chapters.

1. The uncertainty of life is the basis of the human need for power and control. Because the future is unforeseeable, we experience a sense of existential helplessness and anxiety. Neither our fortune nor our fate is ultimately within our control. Uncertainty and awareness of the inability to control even one's own life and environment are the essence of the human condition. We respond by seeking ways to relieve this sense of helplessness and anxiety, this feeling of not being in control.

2. Several common solutions are applied to this human dilemma in Western society. One is to entrust ourselves to an all-powerful, unseen, and thus irrefutable force or deity. In this way, some people feel safe in an uncertain world. A second solution is to entrust ourselves to institutions that appear more powerful than we are, thereby shedding the burden for our sense of safety and acknowledging our dependence and subordination. A third solution involves submission to a benign human ruler, often a benevolent despot. Still another strategy is to seek control over something, anything, but preferably *someone*, thereby creating the illusion of our own power. The adage "a man's home is his castle" captures the notion that the individual, frail within the larger world context, can feel strong and in control if he or she can exert power over those who are even less powerful. Rather than permitting an escape into dependence and subordination, this solution leads the controlled and the controller into belief in the latter's power and right to dominate.

The first solution—religious belief—is a general one open to all. The comforts derived from religion are too well known to require any additional comment here. As we shall see, this course is followed more actively by women than by men the world over, with international statistics attesting to women's greater church-going activity and religiosity.

Many people need more tangible evidence of safety and control over uncertainty than religion provides. They turn to concrete institutions and other people. Women, for reasons we shall explore, have chosen, and been chosen, to entrust themselves to men and the institutions men run. This choice, while not necessarily relieving women's sense of helplessness, often produces a feeling of security. It also inevitably acknowledges their dependent, subordinate role in the gender-power relationship.

The fourth solution—controlling others—is the one men commonly choose, although women who control others, be they children, husbands, or workers, also sense their own enhanced security and confidence through such arrangements. Power over others fosters the illusion of controlling one's own destiny as well. By convincing the controlled, the controllers also convince themselves.

3. The differentiation of sex and gender roles symbolizes a power relationship in which each group labors repeatedly to exert its will over the other. The more powerful group asserts its demands; the less powerful seeks ways to circumvent or subvert the more powerful group's wishes. When the dominant group controls the major institutions of a society, it relies on *macromanipulation* through law, social policy, and military might, when necessary, to impose its will and ensure its rule. The less powerful become adept at *micromanipulation,* using intelligence, canniness, intuition, interpersonal skill, charm, sexuality, deception, and avoidance to offset the control of the powerful.

4. No group willingly relinquishes power. The powerful try to maintain their ascendancy by various means.

5. Power is exerted through the use or control of resources. Each gender group cultivates and protects its own resources, while simultaneously seeking to devalue, deny, ignore, diminish, capture, or decimate the resources of the other. The process continues despite the vast difference in the amount or quality of the resources controlled by the two groups. Numerous means—institutional, political, and personal—may be utilized to offset the opposing group's power-generating resources.

6. The powerful and the powerless take the social structure for granted. They rarely recognize the degree to which institutional arrangements, laws, customs, and practices, rather than individual talent, are responsible for the advantages the powerful enjoy and the disadvantages the powerless endure. Both the rulers and the ruled, the dominant and the dominated, accept their condition as the inevitable result of innate ability and predispositions. The dominant group attributes its success to its competence, without perceiving that the competition is rigged. It is, therefore, not surprising that the dominant feel they deserve to rule. From this perspective, men's vigorous resistance to even the smallest diminution of their power becomes more understandable.[5]

7. Those in charge feel they bear great burdens for the society by protecting and controlling the less powerful. Looking through the large end of the social telescope, powerful males have difficulty detecting the details or the importance of the contributions made by females and less powerful males. It all looks so inconsequential. This view of the world through the eyes of the powerful justifies the structural arrangements. It offers those in charge what economists call "disincentives" to share control or societal burdens, even when this monopoly costs men dearly in health and longevity.

8. Power relationships are encased in the *social stratification system* of a society, the system that assigns individuals and groups to different niches or social levels. Within the larger stratification system, women and men are

bound together in a sex-gender system through sexuality, marriage, and procreation. The sex-gender system increases the difficulty of their living apart. Other unequal groups often live separately from one another, but not most women and men. Segregation is not even a choice for the sexes as it is for racial, political, religious, or other social groups locked into power relationships. Women who live with men, essentially segregated from other nonrelated women, are prevented from recognizing the sources of their powerlessness, a recognition other groups have learned in the ghetto.[6] Some women, even today, do not glimpse this unequal power relationship.

9. Growing awareness of the imbalance and disadvantage in a power relationship increases when the less powerful live and/or work separately from the dominant group. The ghetto breeds an understanding of the dissimilarity between those inside and those outside its boundaries. For individuals or groups to live together within a power relationship, there must be an acceptable rationale. Either the power relationship must be explained in terms of genetic imperatives (biological predetermination) or recast and disguised as desirable, even preferable, to other states of being. As long as the powerless live too close to the powerful to have a clear view of their condition, the powerless (a) will identify with the powerful, (b) feel they derive some greater advantage living within, rather than outside, the power relationship, (c) and thus, remain.

10. The less powerful group—in this case, females—allows itself to be dominated as long as it believes that some combination of the following conditions exists:

a. The dominant group is more knowledgeable and capable.

b. It has the interest of the weaker group at heart.

c. The dominant group controls valuable and otherwise unattainable resources.

d. The disparity in resources is so overwhelming that efforts to change—even by physical force—are doomed to failure.

e. The weaker group, if it behaves properly, can vicariously share the dominant group's power.

Not until the powerless learn the message the ghetto teaches only too well (that their impotence is neither simply individual nor inevitable), will they demand change. Until that time, they will accept their weaker role in a power relationship, first, as inevitable; second, as the result of their own inadequacy; and/or third, as the best available situation under the circumstances.

11. Once the powerless recognize that their self-interest lies in joining with similarly disenfranchised people, they can unite to demand change. But the barriers to unification with other powerless individuals or groups first must be surmounted.

Later, we shall describe how women, living at home with fathers or husbands, rarely recognize themselves as part of a group suffering discrimination, although many acknowledge their individual anguish. For some women, entry into the gender-segregated labor force evoked their first awareness that most women held lower-paying jobs than their male co-workers, despite the same or more education, experience, and talent. This and similar observations led many women to understand their predicament as a group phenomenon, the plight of the powerless, not simply as individual bad luck or inability. They began to recognize that the "personal" was often "political." Only then could they begin to organize in their own behalf to attack the structural bases of their powerlessness.

12. The unification of the powerless represents a major threat to the powerful who:

a. Try to convince the powerless that their condition is a genetic given and/or the best of all worlds.

b. Insist they will protect the powerless and let them share vicariously the powerful's resources.

c. Failing that, strive to set the powerless against each other through competition for resources.

d. Convince the powerless, mainly through stereotypes, that other similarly powerless groups are too contaminated to permit association (thus, minority groups, even weak minority groups, are kept from joining forces with other powerless groups, and the powerful remain in charge).

e. Attempt to coopt the leaders of the powerless by offering them a taste of individual power in unimportant domains, buying them off by pandering to their self-interest, and leaving their abandoned powerless followers without leaders.

13. Societies continue to socialize their members to patterns of behavior long after those patterns have ceased to be relevant to society's survival. Sociologists call the result *culture lag*. Socialization techniques groom each gender group to behave in clearly differentiated ways, teaching women that achievement (power) is attained passively and vicariously through relationships, and teaching men that it is realized actively and directly through action. The polarized forms of behavior persist, taught by one generation to the next. Although members of the younger generation initially revolt against their socialized roles, over time they fall into line behind their parents, taking their places as the current adult generation.

14. Ideologies or belief systems give meaning to social life. They remain viable until changing conditions seriously challenge them. At that point, a revised ideology, which redefines the value placed on the "advantages" offered by the dominant group, helps to free the less powerful from the powerful's grip.[7] When a new ideology helped women to perceive that male assistance and protection, clothed as chivalry and paternalism, served to dominate women, keeping them from independence and self-reliance, they began to reject this "privilege" (a privilege like the protective legislation that barred women from the more desirable jobs). Thus, a new ideology began to loosen the hold of the more powerful male group.

15. A revised ideology that offers an explanation not only of what is, but also what might be, is important and probably necessary for a powerless group to rally together. It suggests a purposeful plan of action to effect change. Such an ideology must link together the present and the future by identifying all manifestations of the power relationship, so that one small concession by the powerful will not be taken as adequate change. The suffragettes of the early 1900s, for example, failed to realize that getting

the vote was only the first move in the power struggle, and as a result, their efforts were prematurely defused.

These fifteen points listed above are the central observations about power whose applications to gender roles we shall explore in this book. From our perspective, how the gender power relationship came to be is less critical than how, why, and in what form it is maintained in modern Western society. Why do women in the last two decades of the twentieth century still find themselves the primary child caretakers and homemakers and men the primary leaders and governors of institutions and nations? What are the underlying dynamics of the gender power relationship? How and why is the power relationship between women and men changing? How has it worked at other times and in other places? What will it look like in the twenty-first century? These are some of the questions we shall undertake to answer.

SUMMARY

Theoretically at least, sex and gender roles are distinguishable from one other, despite their inseparability in the sex-gender system we encounter in daily life. Sex roles are the behaviors and expectations based on physiological sex characteristics, whereas the behaviors and expectations associated with gender roles embody social and cultural definitions of masculinity and femininity.

The sex-gender system represents the core power relationship on which all other power relationships are patterned. As such, the relationship between men and women as individuals or groups involves a process in which each repeatedly attempts to impose his, her or their will on the other, either by threatening punishments or offering rewards.

NOTES

1. Linda Gordon, "Why Nineteenth-Century Feminists Did Not Support 'Birth-Control' and Twentieth-Century Feminists Do: Feminism, Reproduction, and the Family," in *Rethinking the Family; Some Feminist Questions,* ed., Barrie Thorne with Marilyn Yalom (New York: Longman Inc., 1982), pp. 40–53.

2. Michelle Zimbalist Rosaldo and Louise Lamphere, eds., *Woman, Culture, and Society* (Stanford, Cal.: Stanford University Press, 1974).

3. Eleanor E. Maccoby and Carol N. Jacklin, *The Psychology of Sex Differences* (Stanford, Cal.: Stanford University Press, 1974).

4. David C. McClelland, *Power: The Inner Experience* (New York: Irvington Publishers, 1975), p. 90.

5. William J. Goode, "Why Men Resist," in *Rethinking the Family: Some Feminist Questions,* ed., Barrie Thorne with Marilyn Yalom (New York: Longman, Inc., 1982), pp. 131–147.

6. Ibid.

7. Jean Lipman-Blumen, "Ideology, Social Structure, and Crisis" (paper presented at American Sociological Association, 69th Annual Meeting, Montreal, Canada, August 25–29, 1974).

CHAPTER 2
THE GENDER POWER RELATIONSHIP: ITS EXISTENTIAL AND INSTITUTIONAL FOUNDATIONS

THE EXISTENTIAL FOUNDATIONS OF POWER RELATIONSHIPS

To understand the gender power relationship, it is first necessary to understand why most relationships tilt toward a power balance. Power is the imperfect human response to the existential uncertainty of life. Recognizing that even the events of the next moment are unpredictable and therefore uncontrollable and that, as mere humans, we can be swept instantaneously into the void generates immense anxiety.

We seek to reduce this existential anxiety by creating for ourselves and others the illusion that we really are in control. Several strategies exist for constructing this mirage of control over our own destinies.

Strategy 1: Protection by an Omnipotent Force

We can entrust ourselves to the guardianship of a benevolent omnipotent force, usually sacred but occasionally secular. For some, this is a comfortable way to reduce their sense of powerlessness. This strategy, of course, entails the paradox that the anxiety stemming from powerlessness is reduced only by acknowledging one's own feelings of powerlessness and committing oneself to the care of a more powerful force. Nonetheless, belief in a deity who protects and rewards them for obeying a strict moral code offers some individuals a sense of control over their destinies. Major religions, as well as smaller cults, grant their followers security and safekeeping from existential uncertainty, provided they follow certain precepts.

When religious faith entails participation in a church, the individual reaps the added security of a tangible, sacred institution that provides a framework for dealing with the anxiety generated by the "human condition." The church as an institution not only offers the believer a link to a protective spiritual deity; it also specifies the norms, values, and rituals that guard daily life against painful uncertainties. If religious faith protects us from the awareness that we do not control our own destinies, it also demands that we acknowledge our relative powerlessness and the omnipotence of whatever god we choose.

This acceptance of an omnipotent sovereign creates the first condition of a power relationship. In fact, the relationships between human beings and their deities are the quintessential power relationships. The belief that the gender relationship is the earthly replica of that divine relationship creates the sacred aura around the sex-gender system and the power relationship between the men and women. Both the Old and the New Testament insist that the domestic union is modelled upon the divine relationship.

Leadership roles in the church, as in other social institutions, carry a mandate for control over followers. For the church leader, the role of earthly representative of a deity implies control over others, or at least some discernible links to the unknowable—a powerful position indeed. Positions of leadership, whether sacred or secular, convince both leader and followers of the leader's power to protect (or punish) the powerless, as we shall see.

Both men and women have sought to quell their existential anxiety through religious faith and participation in the church. Women, however, have earned a reputation for greater religiosity than men. This image of women as more religious and moral stems in part from their greater church attendance, documented through time and across cultures. Women's predominance in church activities remains evident today. But despite their alleged inclination toward religious faith and activity, until recently women were rarely counted among church leaders. This pattern of subordination is one we shall meet again and again. Only in this last decade, in the wake of the resurgent women's movement, have women begun to penetrate the barriers to church leadership—that closely guarded citadel of male institutional power.

If it were only within the institutional domain of the church that women were denied leadership roles, we probably would dismiss it as a single allocation of more and less powerful roles. But that women are the followers and men the leaders in the entire spectrum of social institutions attests to the critical nature of this power relationship between the genders.

Strategy 2: Submission to Secular Institutions

The subordination/dominance pattern of the gender relationship in all social institutions is particularly significant in light of the second major strategy for reducing existential anxiety: submission to secular institutions that provide the context for the major expression of social life.

The gender power relationship evident in all social institutions (with men invariably controlling and women being controlled) results in a pervasive power imbalance throughout society, for it is within these social institutions that roles are enacted and life is conducted. Men more often than women have sought security in large-scale bureaucracies. This is quite understandable, since their fate within bureaucratic institutions has been more positive than women's. Women have been sequestered mostly within the smaller-scale secular institution of the family.

Like sacred institutions, secular institutions promise security and order through clearly drawn structures (usually hierarchical and often bureaucratic) tied to a unifying ideology, with norms, values, and sanctions. Institutional rules (or what sociologists call *norms*) are designed not only to achieve certain values the institution upholds, but also to create an atmosphere of institutional control—an important surrogate for the devoutly desired but elusive individual control. These institutions hold out the promise of stability, order, and predictability of life that individuals, try as they may, cannot seem to create for themselves.

Secular institutions accomplish this rather remarkable feat through their ideology and structure, with roles predictably differentiated by gender and age, as well as by intelligence, race, ethnicity, wealth, beauty, strength, and other criteria. Here too, the familiar pattern of male leadership and dominance, interwoven with female followership and subordination, is evident. Whatever secular institutions we examine—the occupational system, the economic, political, or legal systems, even the family—the power relationship between women and men is clear and unvarying.

Strategy 3: Submission to a Benign Human Ruler

The third strategy for coping with the existential dilemma is to put ourselves under the benign protectorate of another more powerful individual, someone who will rule us with wisdom and understanding. The secular models for this benign protector are the parents of our childhood, although we know from domestic violence reports that even parents are not always able to lead without abusing their power. The tradeoff for this protection is usually unquestioning followership. As any adolescent can attest, such tradeoffs may seem less attractive over time, particularly when the less powerful begin to glimpse their own potential strength and the clay feet of their ruler.

Often, the choice of the individual protector is not entirely our own. Rather, it is structured by the relationships and institutions in which we find ourselves. For example, children have no choice regarding which particular people become their biological parents. Even in the world of work, the job usually comes tied to a specific boss, like it or not. In other cases, like the selection of political leaders, we seem to have somewhat more choice. Even then, however, our options are limited by the available candidates.

Some individuals seem to emerge as natural choices to be our protectors. Those who control our social institutions are obvious possibilities. So are other individuals whom we believe to be stronger, smarter, wealthier, wittier, or more powerful than ourselves. Many times the definition of certain others as stronger, smarter, or better than ourselves is one we are trained (or in sociological jargon *socialized*) to accept from early childhood. Within each of the multiple social roles we enact, there are clear cultural expectations regarding who is the leader, who the follower, who the more powerful, who the less powerful. Children and parents both understand the enormous power difference between them. So do workers and bosses. Until the civil rights movement, blacks were trained to believe in the stereotype of whites' "natural" dominance, higher IQ, and "more desirable"physical characteristics. Until quite recently, the majority of American men and women also accepted as "natural" the dominance of males and the subordination of females. Raised from childhood to believe that little boys are stronger and smarter than little girls, both genders grow up to adult roles that reflect the power difference between men and women. Women, who learn at their fathers' knees that men will protect them, may find it difficult to reject this strategy. This third solution—placing oneself under the protection of a stronger, smarter, more powerful individual—may increase the protected one's sense of security. The benefits it brings to the protector are evident in the fourth solution.

Strategy 4: Control over Others

The fourth general strategy for coping with the anxiety generated by inability to predict or control the future is to control something or someone else. This is a characteristic male strategy. Through this strategy, protectors convince themselves, along with their wards, that the protectors are in control—of the people, things, or situations they protect, as well as of their own lives. And although this invincibility is often illusory—particularly with respect to controlling their own destinies—it does, in fact, provide protectors with considerable power over others.

Being in control rests on the power to make decisions—to decide, what and who is good or bad, deserving or undeserving, valuable or worthless, brilliant or dull, desirable or unappealing. This power to define and label is an awesome right—indeed, one Adam exercised in his first week on the job. Defining and labeling people and things enables one to rank-order values, norms, statuses, and roles, with their associated behaviors and attitudes—the building blocks of society. Those who make such value judgments, sorting people and things into layers of not-so-good, good, better, and best, then fashion and control social institutions perpetuating those decisions.

This solution—controlling other people and/or things—is commonly selected by men and denied to women. Often, women are coerced into supporting their own denial of control. Women have often unwittingly joined in this denial with men they trusted to protect their interests, only to discover that even men who sincerely had women's "best interests at heart" did not really understand those best interests. But regardless of who actually controls, the fact that one individual or group becomes the dominant one and the other the dominated creates a power relationship. And regardless of the benign intentions, here are the seeds that inevitably blossom into serious power struggles.

POWER AS A PROCESS

Many observers of power understand that it is neither an attribute of the powerful nor a commodity. Rather, power is a *process* characterized by subtle and obvious but constant negotiation and renegotiation between the more and the less powerful. It is moved along by decisions about who and what can and will prevail. We see the hallmarks of such negotiation in a nod, a raised eyebrow, a smile, a kiss, a frown, a speech, a petition, a signed contract, a diplomatic pouch, a military battle. The process of power entails negotiations and decisions about which party has the right to decide, to label, to create value hierarchies, to control social institutions, to allocate resources, to reward and punish, to influence important events. This process is not contained simply within the thought processes of the rulers. It must be validated and agreed to by the ruled. Validation is vital to the implementation of the ruler's decisions. Barring brute force, the ruled's consent is a necessary condition for the rulers' continuing control over the society's institutions. Men cannot rule without women's consent.

Power, then, is a process that includes decision-making, negotiating, and acquiescing or validating, as well as ruling. At the very least, the ruled must consent to the ruler's decisions. This interaction between the ruled and the rulers illuminates the underlying relationship between them. The negotiating process in which both ruled and ruler collaborate is a power relationship, one we see in daily transactions between men and women, parents and children, bosses and workers, as well as diplomats of larger and smaller nations.

Students of power have often observed that the ruled, the so-called powerless group, may not realize their own strength in these negotiations. We shall explore this observation later within the context of the gender power relationship. For now, let us simply say that the long, dark shadow cast by existing institutional structures, justifying and justified by ideology, obscures the less powerful's vision of their own strength. As a result, the less powerful tend to accept the decisions of those they perceive as more powerful and thus help, willingly or unwillingly, to maintain the existing balance of power. The less powerful—in this case, women—agree that the more powerful—that is, men—should continue to control the major institutions of the society, at least until the powerful make an extraordinarily bad decision. Or until the ruled become powerful enough to assert their own will, to take control of the institutions.

These are some of the most common ways in which individuals deal with the anxiety arising from human frailty and uncertainty. Although they address the problem of existential anxiety, including the need to feel secure in an insecure and unpredictable world, these strategies also lead us into power relationships, either as dominant or subordinate partners. These solutions generate the existential bases of the most fundamental power relationship among human beings—that between men and women, as individuals and as groups. The gender power relationship, the model for every other power relationship among human beings, is enacted within the context of all social institutions. In fact, it is this very institutional context that increases the power of the rulers and limits the potential of the ruled.

THE INSTITUTIONAL FOUNDATIONS
OF POWER RELATIONSHIPS

Power relationships have institutional foundations as well. The gender power relationship leads the way. First, as we shall see, the nature of institutions enhances the dominant group's power, while simultaneously diminishing the potential of the subordinate group. Second, social institutions are held together by ideologies, or belief systems, which assure us that the explanations of life that they symbolize—including the contradictions intrinsic to all power relationships—are valid. Third, institutions accumulate massive resources, which those in control use to consolidate their position. Fourth, contributions to society, to institutions, and even to individual relationships depend upon control over resources, both institutional and individual. Those very contributions, however, are evaluated by those who control social institutions, because the power to define, label, and evaluate is an intrinsic component of the dominant role. Fifth, the doctrine of "separate spheres," designed to justify the power and resource differential of women and men, rests on separating two institutional domains: the private domain and the political.

The Reflexive Nature of Social Institutions

The reflexive nature of social institutions is at least partly responsible for their capacity to enhance the ruler's power and limit the chances of the subordinate group. But just what do we mean by *reflexive?* Institutions are reflexive in that they give the original institutional structure additional and enduring legitimacy by validating the judgments and assumptions used in the initial design. Even more crucially, they spread the mantle of legitimacy over the decisions and activities of those who control and perpetuate these institutions through time. So within each institution there is a reflexive phenomenon, a looping back upon itself, a reinvesting of the institution with its own rationale, assumptions, and values, that over time enlarges its claim to legitimacy.

As institutions continue to validate themselves, their hierarchical structures become entrenched. The relative positions of roles and the groups permitted to occupy those roles rigidify. Gender roles, with men dominant and women subordinate in every institution, are frozen into their reciprocal power positions. The reflexive quality of institutions has thus played an important part in legitimating the archaic power balance between the genders.

Such validation is more than symbolic, however, since social institutions amass impressive reservoirs of resources, resources that are available to those in charge. Those in control then use these resources to consolidate and maintain their position. They use status, prestige, promotions, and money, or shame, ostracism, and a host of other resources to reward those who comply as well as to punish those who resist their authority.

The ability of the rulers to impose strict controls on less powerful individuals and groups within institutions is enhanced by the second strategy we described for dealing with existential anxiety: the propensity of individuals to entrust themselves to a seemingly omnipotent institution. Individuals who submit themselves to powerful institutions to reduce their existential fear are predisposed to be compliant institutional members. They rarely require their institutional commanders to invoke punishments. Their own reasons for being there and the weight of the institutional structure work together to quiet any reservations they may have; that the institutional resources belong to those in command seems perfectly reasonable.

As a result, those who make the major institutional decisions about society are in a strategic position. They have virtually unlimited access to society's resources. This access allows them to impose their will on other individuals and groups who not only lack comparable resources, but who, as victims of the existential human condition, seek refuge in powerful social institutions. Resources, particularly institutional resources, play a critical role in all power relationships, as we shall see; the gender power relationship is no exception.

THE INSTITUTIONAL FUNCTION OF IDEOLOGY

Social institutions and the resource-distribution networks they generate are kept in place by ideologies. *Ideologies*, or belief systems, assure us that the explanations of life that the institutions symbolize—including who is entitled to power—are correct. Such explanations or ideologies about the unknowable future and the incomprehensible, even contradictory, present offer believers a sense of comfort and safety. They promise relief from anxiety. In this way, ideologies provide strategies for getting on with the business of life. They offer interpretations, even justifications, for the contradictions we confront daily: for why one group constitutes the powerful, another the powerless; for why some people live in mansions and others in ghettos; for why mothers are praised for performing the most valuable social duty, but reap no tangible rewards; for why children may be desired, but are still abused.

In addition to providing explanations for life's contradictions, institutional ideologies suggest several approaches for dealing with existential paradoxes: accept them as proof of a better life in the hereafter; accept them because they are rooted in human nature; accept them as necessary for the "collective good"; accept them because they are traditional and unchangeable. This is the message woven into the very fabric of our major ideologies.

Minor or new ideologies that offer alternative interpretations do exist among smaller groups and social movements. In times of crisis, they rise to a level of public awareness and acceptability and offer serious possibilities for restructuring institutional arrangements. Crises, partly through sanctioning new ideologies, create genuine opportunities to change power relationships.

Control of institutions leads to several results for both rulers and ruled. First, for the rulers there is the comforting illusion that by controlling the destiny of others, they are demonstrating control over their own fate. The ideologies supporting institutions also convince all concerned that the leaders, by virtue of their innate characteristics, are worthy of their powerful positions.

For those who are denied control over these institutions, living in their shadow is preferable to living unprotected. To deny the ideology and revolt against these institutions and their rulers is to invite wrath and punishment. If, in addition, the ideology insists (1) that the ruled lack the qualities for dominance; (2) that those in charge are both benevolent, all-knowing, and predestined to rule; and (3) that to deny their leadership is blasphemy, then those who live at the will of the powerful may as well surrender to the inevitable. Only when these ideologies are shown to be imperfect or false, when they no longer provide the explanatory handles that individuals need to live, are they likely to lose their hold. Only then can those who have accepted, been lulled and comforted, and thus ruled by these ideologies begin to believe it is possible to deny the ideologies, the institutions they justify, and those in charge. Only then can the tender sprouts of new ideologies grow through the cracks in the major institutional ideologies. Only then can new understandings of the possible relationships between men and women emerge. Until then, institutions and the resources they generate and distribute remain largely at the disposal of male rulers.

SUMMARY

The gender power relationship is sustained by strong existential and institutional bases. Facing the inevitable uncertainties of living, human beings choose among a variety of strategies for dealing with the anxiety this generates. Both individual men and women are practitioners of each strategy we have outlined: submission to an omnipotent force, an institution, or another powerful individual; or taking control over institutions, people, and situations. However, certain strategies seem more congenial to men, others to women. Historical conditions, institutional arrangements and practices justified by ideology, access to resources, norms, values, even stereotypes, all channel men into dominant and women into subordinate positions. Only through a continual process of negotiation, using resources contributed to the social good as power chips, can the power relationship be changed, as we shall see in the next chapter.

CHAPTER 3
RESOURCES AND CONTRIBUTIONS: MAINTAINING THE GENDER POWER RATIO

In the power process, each party to the negotiations acts to increase its control. Each reacts to its "opponent's" efforts to restructure the power balance. Acting and reacting, each seeks to hold, or better yet increase, its ground. The resources that each can marshall are crucial to the outcome.

THE IMPORTANCE OF RESOURCES

The bargaining that lies at the heart of the power process involves promises of contributions to the welfare of the opponent, as well as to the society at large. So the power relationship between women and men is determined by their differential control over resources and the contributions they can make.

Since, as we have suggested, the group already in charge of the major institutions has access to massive resources, how can those lower down in the hierarchy, with fewer resources, have any real impact on the dominant group? More specifically, how can women, as individuals or as a group, ever impose their will on the powerful men who control society's institutions?

Each gender group has its own special set of resources, which it uses in the gender power struggle. Males, drawing on their institutional reserves, have a large array of resources—political, economic, technological, legal, educational, and occupational. In addition, men often have greater physical strength—at least greater upper body strength—than women. Although less important now than in pretechnological times, physical strength remains symbolically significant. At the institutional level, physical strength is represented by military might. Perhaps this underlies the great resistance to women's inclusion in the military services.

Only recently have women been able to count at all on institutional resources. Even so, these resources have been limited, as has the number of women with real access to them. More often, women have had to rely on their individual resources, including intelligence, wit, beauty, sexuality, youth, and potential parenthood. More and more, women now count among their resources educational and occupational achievement, and a few, now as always, rely on inherited wealth. As more women enter the political and corporate arenas, political and corporate clout are also becoming key resources.

This listing of gender-linked resources makes it apparent that men, even now, have the advantage at the institutional level, women at the individual level. Socialized from an early age to approach the world from these two very different vantage points, men and women engage in the gender power relationship with notably distinct styles.

Males learn early that they are expected to view their natural aggression as a resource to move them toward targeted goals in the public arena. They are trained to act with unabashed competitiveness, and by competition and aggression to accomplish their goals. They must act for themselves and for others in the major arenas of life. They also learn that teamwork is a highly approved strategy for success, one that is consistent with the ideology of the large-scale institutions within which they must succeed.

Women's personal resources are designed for a smaller stage—in interpersonal relationships with lovers, husbands, or children, and within the confines of domestic life, not public institutions. According to women's upbringing, aggression and competition, territory already claimed by men, are socially inappropriate (that is, "unfeminine") resources. They are taught to interact more gently, to help, nurture, and charm.

Beauty and sexuality have been women's traditional resources for success. Using such assets, women were groomed to compete for success not *with* men, but with one another *for* men, and indirectly *through* men—father, husbands, lovers, sons, and patrons—for all of life's rewards. That beauty, sexuality, and charm have often brought women greater social and even economic rewards than intelligence and hard work can be seen by a simple fact: Wives of prominent men usually have far greater resources at their disposal than do the majority of successful professional women. In fact, such access to resources allows high-status wives to make valuable societal contributions. Public recognition of women's vicarious achievement through successful husbands is evident in their appearance on the list of "most admired women." Every year, wives of political leaders routinely outnumber women whose achievements stem solely from their personal ability and efforts. Gradually, however, women who have achieved success on their own are becoming more visible.

Women and men have both been socialized to believe that women are more moral, more gentle, more empathetic, more nurturant than men. These feminine resources are truly fine strengths, they are told. Women have been raised with the belief that beauty and charm, gentleness, morality, nurturance, and empathy are more desirable traits, on a higher plane, than male aggressiveness, competition, and brute strength. These "feminine" characteristics are necessary for those who give and nurture life, women are taught. Women see that they are set apart, as the life bearers, the nurturers, the gentler, better, more moral breed.

That these allegedly "better" feminine characteristics are not useful as resources outside the home is truly curious. Women are trained to exercise these better characteristics within the limited stage of interpersonal relationships, particularly within the home. Thus, the exchange value of women's personal resources, only recently recognized as valuable by corporate managers and politicians alike, has been seriously limited. Even so, women acting collectively and individually have demonstrated their ability to offset, and sometimes to undermine, the institutional control established by men. We shall examine instances of such action later and also examine the ways in which women, acting together, can augment their resources and enhance their negotiating position in the gender power struggle.

CONTRIBUTIONS AND POWER

Potential contributions are the lifeblood of the negotiation process. Each party's potential contribution, the value of that contribution, and its renewability are critical to the outcome of the negotiation. The contributions themselves are based on availability and control of valued resources.

Public leaders, who govern institutions that generate massive resources, have the advantage, as we have seen. Marx's insight into the importance of control over the means of production speaks directly to this issue. Marx's point, enlarged to cover production of goods and services, laws, education and employment opportunities, religion, politics, and military force, allows us to understand the significance of such control.

Despite their importance, large-scale institutions that deal with public issues are not the only wellsprings of valuable resources; they do, however, provide resources that are more likely to be perceived and counted as valuable. In the private arena, the family as an institution also produces crucial resources—the next generation, for one. But somehow these "means of reproduction" fail to bring women recognition, status, and power. Although women's biological contributions tend to entrap them, the resources contributed by women are still important. Otherwise, why the struggle for control over the means of reproduction—that is, women's reproductive capacity? Otherwise, why the serious policy debate about the right to contraceptive information and devices, as well as access to abortion? Otherwise, why are men willing to fight in court and Congress to gain control over women's bodies and their sexual and reproductive functioning? In this case, folk wisdom gives us a clue to the meaning of social behavior. "Keep them barefoot and pregnant" summarizes one strategy for subordinating women. Simply seize control of the means of reproduction. Simply deny appropriate rewards and recognition to this—the most basic, but hardly the only—societal contribution of women.

Within the sex-gender system, the behaviors and attitudes comprising gender roles are evaluated as contributions to the maintenance of society. These contributions may be used as bargaining chips in the power negotiations between women and men, both as individuals and groups. Each contribution is tied to some agreed-upon reward. The game, however, is slightly rigged, since men traditionally have had the power to define and label, to set valuations on contributions, to sort them into hierarchies. This, in turn, enabled men to determine what sociologists call *the reward structure;* that is, who gets rewarded for what, in what coinage, and in what amount. So in a classic Catch-22 pattern, the control of institutions, which produce and distribute broad-scale decision-making authority, prestige, money, and other resources, is highly valued. Other kinds of contributions do not reap comparable rewards. Even the reproduction of the next generation, which perpetuates society, or the tending of human relationships, that social glue which keeps society together, is of lesser value.

TWO SPHERES, DIFFERENT CONTRIBUTIONS

The notion of men's and women's "separate but equal" spheres—popularized in the nineteenth century and clinging to life even now—has been used to justify the different contributions and reward structures that exist in each sphere. Assigned to the public domain, men not only control social institutions; they also design social policy, wage war, create culture, and support and protect women and children through their labors in the public arena. They perceive their contributions as important and their roles as often burdensome—but (they hope) not thankless. Authority, autonomy, obedience, love, and personal services are the thanks they expect in return from women, children, and less powerful men. These contributions by men presumably keep the external world (what Kenneth Boulding calls the "economy")[1] in order.

According to the two-spheres concept, women have their own sphere of control: the private domain, the internal world (or what Boulding calls the "integry"). Here, women bear and raise children, and nurture them, men, and other women. Here too, women preside over and deal with their own and their families' psychological and emotional tensions, dulling pain and friction, particularly that imposed by the "heartless world" beyond the home, described by Christopher Lasch.[2] Women organize and administer social and interpersonal activities, nurse the sick, tend the old, provide round-the-clock personal and domestic service, including meals, clothes, and sleeping and studying quarters, not to mention sexual pleasure. Women too often feel that their contributions, while important, are burdensome to them. They too expect to be thanked in the coinage of love and respect and, at least since the Industrial Revolution, with economic support.

Earlier versions of gender-role ideology, which described "women's sphere" and later "women's two roles," served in certain historical periods as adequate explanations of the power relationship between the sexes.[3] The Industrial Revolution banished women and children from factory jobs, sending women home to take charge of the household. It also framed an ideology of separate spheres for women and men that largely overlooked one important fact: Women worked more hours than men, often at more difficult tasks, but their labors produced no revenue or capital. Women became locked into unpaid service roles—service to family, church, and community—from which they have never totally broken free.

Later, as women entered the paid labor force, the ideology of the two roles maintained the rationale for women's ongoing domestic service in the home. Even when women moved into the twentieth-century labor market, the service notion inherent in the two-role ideology prescribed service roles as the only appropriate paid employment for respectable "feminine" women. The low pay of traditional feminine service jobs in the labor market was another carryover from women's unpaid domestic and community service roles.

Feminist theorists have argued that, although women earn no wages for doing so, they contribute to the economy in at least two other critical, but little noticed, ways. First, as we have indicated, by bearing children they produce the next generation of laborers. Second, by tending to the emotional, physical, and social needs of their husbands and later their working-age children, women restore the vitality of the labor force. Of course, women also contribute their labors directly to the marketplace through their own occupational roles—a major and growing female contribution since World War II. According to some, this has been the most important social change of the twentieth century.

No one would deny the importance or the burden of the contributions made by both women and men as individuals and as groups. Society undoubtedly needs most of these tasks to be performed, although not, some would argue, by the exact division of labor we ordinarily see. These valuable contributions are some of the bargaining chips that men and women, as individuals or groups, use in their negotiations with one another. But the rigged nature of the game—that is, men's disproportionate authority to write the rules, set the evaluations, and control massive institutional resources—denies women's contributions their full value and reward.

Throughout recorded history, the public evaluation of both genders' contributions has favored men; women's legacy to life outside the home rarely caught public attention. Feminist historians are busy uncovering material that promises a more complete picture of the female contribution to society. Nonetheless, it seems clear that both women and men bring various, if different, resources to the larger society in which they live and to the power relationship between them. Men's historical contribution to society—running the social institutions that order our lives—is an undeniably important service. Society recognizes its worth and rewards men with honor, status, and economic return, all negotiable for public and private power.

Feminists would argue that women's contributions are less valued than men's by every societal measure. Childbearing, nursing, and child-rearing are acknowledged ritualistically in the litany of services valuable to the society, but women are not rewarded with the main public value of most societies—economic and public status.

Women's rewards are measured in private coinage—praise, love, reverence—currencies with surprisingly little economic leverage or public power. Feminist scholars would argue that instead of rewarding women's unique and powerful contribution of producing new life by more options, society has turned this valued contribution into a weapon against women. Not too surprisingly, society has dealt with women's instrinsically powerful ability to bring forth new life by converting it into a mechanism for limiting women's power in the external world. Children are used to encumber women, much as the Lilliputians immobilized Gulliver. Women's other contributions of nurturance and service are similarly unrewarded by resources translatable into power. But, as we shall soon see, women do in fact use their own resources in ways that shape society.

How much of this division of labor and rewards is inevitable or necessary? And if not inevitable or necessary, how and why does the pattern persist? Clearly men and women must cooperate in the procreative process, either in the bedroom, or more recently, in the laboratory. And women, at least some women, must be willing to bear children. Beyond that, the division of labor by gender is potentially interchangeable. Researchers can find no genetic obstacle to men bottle-feeding babies and caring for children. Similarly, no genetic basis has been demonstrated that disallows women from controlling the powerful institutions of society. Indeed, we have examples to the contrary: Queen Elizabeth I, Queen Victoria, and in modern times, Queen Elizabeth II, Golda Meir, Margaret Thatcher, and Indira Gandhi. But the public and private division of labor persists, along with the differential evaluation of men's and women's contributions.

A nagging question remains: Why are women's contributions so little valued, so poorly rewarded? Some observers argue that women's contributions are virtually invisible. Believing in their own competence and genuinely suffering under the unshared burdens of institutional control and decision-making, the dominant group (here, powerful males) fails to notice the contributions of less powerful men and women. So dominant males often attribute women's success to the wrong causes. This skeptical attitude toward women's contributions perpetuates men's reluctance to share the burdens and the rewards of societal control. Cynicism and skepticism toward women's contributions strengthen the existing institutional disincentives for men to reevaluate their own and women's capacities and contributions. Even the threat of ulcers, heart disease, high blood pressure, and early death are not sufficient to make the powerful loosen their grip on the institutional sources of power.

Women who have labored long and hard in the occupational system rarely receive the same rewards as men. Even those unusual women who experience the quick rise up the corporate ladder that their male peers take for granted may be punished for their success. Their male mentors may suffer by association, a clear warning to other men not to help women outside a family or social setting. The Bendix Corporation fiasco, in which Harvard Business School graduate Mary Cunningham rose meteorically to a key vice presidency but then resigned when her success was attributed to an alleged personal relationship with Bendix President William Agee, offers many possible interpretations. Agee's subsequent fall from corporate grace is a lesson to would-be male mentors. The contributions of even— perhaps particularly—the most brilliant women are suspect. Women who have been punished by the fallout from men's skeptical attitudes toward female equality often decide that remaining in a subordinate role in hetero-sexual power relationships is their "best bet." Other female witnesses to such examples learn to "keep their place." The moral is not lost on poten-tially sympathetic men either.

SUMMARY

The definitions and evaluations of men's and women's contributions to the gender power relationship, as well as to the total social context, tend to maintain the existing institutional arrangements. That those in charge of major social institutions have been granted the authority to define and evaluate these contributions seriously rigs the game. Nonetheless, the power process continues—a dialectic of negotiation and renegotiation in which institutional and personal resources are the bargaining currencies. The process through which those with more and those with fewer re-sources constantly adjust their power relationship is the subject to which we now turn.

NOTES

1. Kenneth Boulding, "The Grants Economy," *Michigan Academician,* 1 (1969), 3–11.
2. Christopher Lasch, *Haven in a Heartless World* (New York: Basic Books, 1977).
3. Alva Myrdal and Viola Klein, *Women's Two Roles: Home and Work* (London: Rout-ledge and Kegan Paul, 1956).

CHAPTER 4
MACRO-MANIPULATION, MICROMANIPULATION: THE CULTIVATION AND POACHING OF POWER

At first glance, "the war between the sexes" seems an outmoded concept in the late twentieth century. No doubt we should abandon it for its failure to capture the subtlety and complexity of the power relationship that we recognize in the modern sex-gender system. But a tug and pull persists between men and women, both as individuals and groups, with the power balance continually under tension.

In a previous chapter, we questioned the "biological imperative"— that is, the notion that gender roles are biologically determined. We suggested that short of biological procreation, gestation, and lactation, most behaviors and attitudes associated with male and female gender roles are flexible. In fact, most could be part of the female or the male gender role. And we find that is often the case when we survey gender roles in different societies and at different points in history.

THE BODY POLITIC AND THE BODY PERSONAL

Why, then, if nature is not the overriding reason, are men's and women's gender roles so different? Why does gender role differentiation persist in its current form throughout most of the world? Is it simply because women provide comforting and valuable unpaid services that men are reluctant to relinquish? Or is it perhaps because gender roles are the blueprint for all power relationships and are rigorously maintained because any change would signify that this ultimate stronghold of clearly demarcated power is unstable? This is a question we shall approach from numerous sides.

Most societies have some system of social stratification that indicates the relative rankings of various groups. A stratification system implies that some groups are above and others below in the pecking order. What is the basis for deciding who falls where? And what means, if any, exist for moving from one status level to another?

In many societies, the conditions of birth are the original determinants of status. The family's social status, based on lineage, wealth, and occupation, provides the individual with a lifetime identity. Birth order within the family also affects the individual's status. For example, the firstborn male may inherit the family fortune through primogeniture, and later-born brothers must seek their own livelihoods.

There is still another key criterion—gender. With a few monarchical exceptions, in all strata in virtually all societies, women rank below men of the same class, even within their own families. Why does this happen? To some degree it is related to the notion of spheres—public versus private—which we began to explore earlier. One way of understanding the separation and differentiation of women's and men's roles is to recognize men's control over the body politic, and women's over the body personal, as well as the interpenetration of these public and private domains.

Decisions made in the public sphere, commonly called "public policy," have a clear impact on private lives. This is another way of saying that male-controlled public institutions as well as the laws and policies that regulate them, have a strong, direct influence over other men's and women's private lives. Public decisions have enormous potential for widespread impact because they involve large institutions and the people who live within them. These public decisions, usually made by men, can change the very structure and substance of social institutions.

In a democracy, one might argue, women's right to vote offsets men's pervasive public control. Women's population advantage should ensure this outcome. Students of the political process also remind us that women are going to the polls in greater and greater numbers, particularly in the United States, where their voting preference—labeled the *gender gap*—is beginning to worry politicians. Nevertheless, in the United States neither female nor male voters have ever elected a woman president or vice president. Nor have they ever sent more than a small handful of women to the Congress in any one session, although female legislators are growing in numbers at all governmental levels. The vast majority of public laws that spell out American public policy are crafted and voted on by male-majority state and national legislatures. Male legislative domination also exists in most national assemblies around the world. In addition, the guidelines and informal practices that implement these legislative initiatives are generated in government departments and agencies where the top administrative posts are held mostly by men.

Despite this seemingly overwhelming power imbalance, women, even without legislative might, often manage to make their own will prevail, even with regard to social policy. True, men impose their view of the world on women through affairs of state. But women, through domestic, local, national, and even international action, do offset this influence, imprinting men's lives with women's will.

In all power relationships, the parties seek to impose their will on one another through decisions and related behavior; so it is with women and men in their power relationship. But this is hardly a matched contest. When the male-dominated institutions of society are pitted against the female-dominated interpersonal actions of separate individuals, it is barely a contest at all.[1] Still, as we shall see later in this chapter, women have managed to offset, even subvert, men's control over the body politic by their own control over the body personal or domestic. And on numerous occasions, women have thwarted male-crafted public policy by collective political and legal action.

THE INTERPENETRATION OF PUBLIC AND PRIVATE DOMAINS

This tug of war between men and women locked in an endless power struggle often involves an interpenetration of the public and private arenas. The doctrine of the two spheres, described previously, proposes that men contribute to the social good by taking charge of the public sphere, and women through the private domain. The most ardent feminist could not deny that even the advances women made in the 1970s have not totally changed this general picture.

Despite the clear demarcation between the two domains, decisions in each sphere influence events in the other. Any casual observer of politics knows that laws created in the public arena limit behavior in the private sphere. It is less obvious, but true nonetheless, that private, interpersonal events shape public happenings as well. For example, at the highest level of public decision-making, the Supreme Court legalized abortion, freeing thousands of women from the danger of illegal abortions. At the interpersonal level, in the privacy of their bedrooms, women's individual decisions to limit the number of children they will have affect not only their immediate families, but also the body politic. Women's contraceptive behavior influences the demographic shape of the nation, as well as every industry from infants wear to higher education. This interpenetration of public and private decision-making occurs endlessly in numerous other areas of social life.

From one perspective, historical circumstances carved out men's and women's spheres of dominance. Traditionally, each group seemed to go about its business without much attention to events in the "other world." Some sociologists even argue that men and women live in totally different worlds.[2] But actions taken within those separate spheres have a fallout far beyond their recognized limits. In the public arena, men make choices and decisions that enhance their own and/or their group's position in the society. In the private domain, and increasingly in the public domain as well, women act to offset men's advantage and adjust the power balance.

Most power relationships, however, are played out in a zero-sum situation: When one side goes up, the other must go down. Public decisions and action inevitably influence not merely other public actors, but those in the private sphere as well. Private, individual, and interpersonal decisions similarly have a real, if more subtle, impact on the public domain. The dialectic between macromanipulation and micromanipulation balances and rebalances the gender power struggle.

MACROMANIPULATION AND MICROMANIPULATION: PUBLIC AND PRIVATE POLICY

Major societal decisions (macrodecisions) and private, interpersonal decisions (microdecisions) are inextricably linked to the gender power struggle. Thus, it is not surprising that powerful males often engage in macromanipulation (sometimes called "the formation of public policy") to control major societal decisions. Women react with micromanipulation (interpersonal policy) to dominate domestic action, as well as to offset the oppression of macromanipulation. More recently, growing numbers of women have sought to engage in macromanipulation through the ballot box and public action. But the majority remain locked into the micro level.

If men monopolize the authority to define, evaluate, and reward, women—whose participation is essential to the power process—develop their own ways of dealing with this unequal power relationship. Living as the less powerful provides daily lessons in survival strategies. (Is this perhaps why women and other seemingly powerless groups can emerge as leaders in crisis periods, when new survival strategies are most highly valued?) Many women have come to understand that by forging social policy, laws, and social practices to control power relationships even further, the powerful are practicing macromanipulation. Women recognize that, through society's macrostructures, the dominant group attempts to control or manipulate power relationships and all the transactions that such relationships entail. The dominant group's ability to make and break the rules is central to its control.

Through their long history as the subordinate group, women have learned how to survive in a world fashioned by the dominant group's definitions, rules, rewards, and punishments. The only realistic response of many women to such overwhelming institutionally based macromanipulation is micromanipulation, the use of interpersonal behaviors and practices to influence, if not control, the power balance.

Restricted to micromanipulation, women, as well as other powerless groups, become well versed in interpreting the unspoken intentions, even the body language, of the powerful. They learn to anticipate their governors' behavior, to evoke as well as smother pleasure, anger, joy, and bafflement in their rulers, to charm, to outsmart, even to dangle the powerful over the abyss of desire and anguish. By the various interpersonal strategies of micromanipulation, women have learned to sway and change, circumvent, and subvert the decisions of the powerful to which they seemingly have agreed. They know when to observe the rules the dominant group has created. Women have also mastered how to "obey without obeying" those rules they find overly repressive. When necessary, they cooperate with men to maintain the mirage of male control. True, a growing minority of women have also consciously rejected the tools of micromanipulation in favor of a more direct assault. The majority, however, continue to operate primarily at the interpersonal level.

Learning Micromanipulation

How, we might ask, is micromanipulation learned? As children, dependent upon powerful adults, we all spend many years learning the underside of power relationships, including the techniques of micromanipulation. Most adult males graduate into life situations where they no longer use such skills and knowledge, preferring instead the challenge of more direct (read "adult" and "masculine") exercise of power through macromanipulation. Most men tune down, if not totally out, their own interpersonal monitoring system, setting aside the knowledge and skills they too learned from infancy. Only the most perceptive male leaders are canny enough to preserve these skills and knowledge and weld them to strategies of macromanipulation. Machiavelli, as well as some contemporary politicians and corporate managers, understood that this combination of macromanipulation and micromanipulation is an irresistible formula for leadership, the veritable lion and fox combined.

Women, rarely provided the opportunity to sharpen their skills of macromanipulation, hone the interpersonal strategies of micromanipulation. Put in charge of not-yet-verbal infants, they have daily practice in interpreting the tiniest nonverbal cues. But a paradoxical outcome occurs: The special advantages, even the genius, of micromanipulation become denigrated as the domain of women and children. Seldom given the opportunity to knit micro- and macromanipulation together, women frequently must rely on micromanipulation alone to thread their way through the gender power relationship.

How, we may ask, can women as subordinates use micromanipulation to offset the seemingly insurmountable odds of the dominant group's macromanipulation? How, in fact, can they make their contributions, already devalued by the dominant group, count for anything? Why is it that the powerful, in this case men, do not simply overwhelm women and enforce their will through the sheer physical force they command—as individuals, as lawmakers and enforcers, as military officials?

On occasion, men do force their will on unwilling women; rape and wife-battering statistics tell us that story only too clearly. Most of the time, however, using such force is a last resort, signaling to the less powerful that the more powerful are running out of other negotiating chips. Moreover, if what the powerful want from the powerless is love, affection, obedience, and production—either in the form of new human life, personal goods and service, or economically marketable commodities and services—they know they cannot get these by force. The truly oppressed produce little; they are too worn down.

Love, much like power, is an interactive process. Only among the deranged, and rarely then, do absolute force and despotism produce love. Thus, even those men who could enforce their will on women through physical force or the social might of institutions know it is quite useless in the long run. And although some men would be willing to use such means on other men's women or women as a group, they usually are less tempted to try such strategies on their own daughters, wives, and mothers—despite occasional hostile fantasies.

WOMEN'S ROLE AS MORAL GUARDIANS

While men have served as guardians of the body politic, women guarded the body personal, particularly individual and social morality. Degler and others have suggested the ways in which women's private control of morality has acted to counterbalance men's public power.[3] By setting private moral standards, women occasionally have offset, even diminished, the institutional power men used against them in interpersonal relationships. For example, a virtuous wife could shame an educated, powerful husband into abandoning licentious conduct.

Women's roles in social movements—from social purity, to abolition, to prohibition, to civil rights, to nuclear freeze—may be seen as efforts to extend their private moral power to the public arena. Women's moral authority, however, has never become a legitimate part of social institutions beyond the family. It did not, for example, lead women in great numbers to formal roles as judges or legislators. As late as 1983, only 3 percent of national legislators and 7.2 percent of all federal judges were women, and it is not coincidental that even in the early 1980s the single female member of the Supreme Court is still seen as a rarity.

WOMEN'S EFFORTS TO EXERCISE PUBLIC POWER

Nonetheless, women have occasionally, and more so recently, ventured into the public arena to "set things right." Women's activities against slavery, alcohol, prostitution, and poverty have had a recognizable impact on society.[4] Their efforts frequently have resulted in legislation. More often, women managed to push through legislation primarily because men, failing to take the "weaker sex's" efforts seriously, did not oppose them.

Legislation resulting from women's concern for morality and justice may slip through initially unnoticed or discounted. Eventually, when men recognize that the new law changes power relationships, they move to repeal it. The Prohibition Movement of the early twentieth century offers a clear example of women utilizing their moral resources for public influence over the behavior of men. Some would interpret the repeal of the prohibition legislation as the response of the male power structure to women's efforts to constrain male behavior.

The Equal Rights Amendment (ERA) offers a more recent example. Early attempts to pass the ERA, which would prohibit sex discrimination, sailed to easy victory. This early success occurred before the ERA came to the serious attention of those whose power base would be diminished. Subsequent organized efforts by women's groups to make the ERA the Twenty-seventh Amendment to the U.S. Constitution met fatal resistance.

The opposition was fueled by impressive economic resources from several key male power centers, despite national opinion polls indicating popular approval for the measure. The challenge to women's push for legal equality could be interpreted as a dawning recognition that granting women constitutionally guaranteed equal rights would permanently impair the male power position. And even when such a move had the support of the majority of American men and women, the male power establishment, with the help of those female groups who feared they would lose the "protection" their subordinate position offered, managed to deny 51.3 percent of the American population legal equality. The reintroduction of the Equal Rights Amendment by the Democratic Speaker of the House in the opening session of the 98th Congress follows another familiar pattern: Men, whose own purposes would be well served (in this case a Democratic desire for a political victory by attracting the female vote) by a coalition with women, ostensibly supporting a female cause. The gender power struggle continues.

EXERCISING INTERPERSONAL POWER: WOMEN'S CONTROL OVER FERTILITY

The Impact of The Pill

Until recently, men's impact on women's lives appeared, and often was, greater than vice versa, at least at the collective level. Men's control of legislative, financial, educational, religious, health, and occupational institutions determined much within society. The conditions of life and technological development favored men's stronger power position, a position maintained despite their declining population advantage. As long as sexuality led almost inevitably to maternity, the reins that kept women tied to hearth and home were short and stout.

The technological breakthrough of the Pill, which gave women virtually complete control over their sexuality and parenthood, introduced major changes in the power contest between men and women. But the struggle for control was exceedingly subtle. Now women, who previously controlled male sexual behavior as well as their own through the fear of pregnancy, were no longer intimidated by such consequences. It seemed women finally were in control of their bodies. They could determine whether and when they chose to become mothers, a role that almost inevitably restricted them to the private sphere.

Although the Pill permitted women control over parental status, achieving control over sexual conduct was far more elusive. Their refusal to engage in sexual activity came to mean not conformity to the norms of respectable womanhood, but exertion of female will in a power situation. Men responded by labeling uncompliant women "frigid" or "gay," attempting in this way to provoke the compliance they could not produce before. Women's increasing awareness of and desire for sexual satisfaction were interpreted by some as feminist muscle flexing. Some bewildered psychiatrists further escalated the conflict by blaming male impotence on women's new sexual expectations. These circumstances led radical feminists to argue that the sex act itself is inevitably a demonstration of the power struggle between the sexes.

The Pill was simply one index of more pervasive social changes. Other technological advances were transforming the ability to communicate, travel, manufacture, educate, legislate, cure, and reproduce. Science, politics, religion, and economics contributed to changing conditions that expanded the action possibilities for men and thus inevitably for women. The gender power relationship has been affected by these external conditions, but the conditions themselves have been fostered and controlled by men. Biological differences, once the basis for determining distinct spheres of activity, began to require reinterpretation. If men could walk on the moon, couldn't women venture beyond the home? To do so, women had to control their own fertility. They had to determine when and how often they would become mothers. By controlling this important decision, women could choose to continue their education and eventually enter the paid labor market, two critical factors in accumulating resources. They might even seek political and military roles.

Declining Fertility Rates

Although the struggle to determine control over sexuality and parenthood was carried out at the interpersonal level, evidence of women's increasing power began to appear in declining fertility rates. Fertility rates are intimately linked to other socioeconomic and technological factors, only some of which mirror this underlying struggle. Educational attainment, the age at which women marry, women's participation in the labor force, their residence in rural or urban areas, technology, decreased infant and maternal mortality rates, as well as legislative changes are among the many factors besides improved contraception that influence fertility rates.

Beginning around 1960, these and other factors created a shift in marriage and childbearing patterns. The long-term trend toward early marriages and childbearing began to falter, depressing the fertility rates of women in the childbearing ages. This trend continued during the 1970s, so that the fertility of American women reached a point even lower than the previous fertility low of the mid-1930s, during the Great Depression. In the early 1970s, the annual number of live births continued to plummet, increasing somewhat after 1974. The total fertility rate,[5] however, began a decline in the early 1970s that continued unabated, except for a slight increase in 1977. The rise in the total number of births during those years in which the fertility rate was decreasing is accounted for not so much by changes in the power relationship, but by increased numbers of women of childbearing age. Thus, in 1970, the actual number of births was 3,731,386, and the total fertility rate was 87.9. By 1980, the number of live births had dropped to 3,598,000 and the total fertility rate had also fallen to 69.2

Since 1973, the total fertility rate, a statistic used to predict whether the future population will shrink or expand, has dipped below 2100, the level at which births and deaths balance one another. In ways not yet widely recognized, women had begun to influence the future population size, and thereby the society's future. The recent rapid drop in the total fertility rate is interpreted by some demographers as a postponement, rather than a permanent rejection, of childbearing, although there is some evidence that sentiment against unlimited reproduction continues to grow both in the United States and abroad.[6] Zero population growth is unlikely to be achieved before the year 2000, even if the current low birth rates continue.[7] But women's determination of their own fertility levels represents their increased control over the future of society—an influence that recent anti-abortion activity, perhaps not coincidentally, seeks to stem.

Still other measures of fertility patterns offer us a view of American women's decision to have fewer children. The number of children ever born to women in different age groups is one such measure. By 1970, women 18 to 44 years old had had an average of 1.9 children each. This average dipped to 1.8 children per woman by 1980. For women at both ends of the childbearing spectrum, the average number of children ever born was lower in 1978 than in 1970. For example, women 20 to 24 years old averaged 0.7 children per woman in 1970, compared to 0.6 in 1978. And women 35 to 39 years old averaged 3.0 children in 1970, but by 1978 only 2.7. These data suggest that, as individuals, women have negotiated implicit or explicit childbearing agreements that provide them with some measure of control over their lives.

Fertility Rates of Groups with Different Resources

The number of children women have differs for women in different groups: married and unmarried, married at different ages, in or out of the labor force, non-college or college-educated. In a sense, we may view these groups as having differential levels of resources in the power game.

Fertility Rates among the Unmarried

An especially striking illustration of the resource component in power, here power over childbearing, is the situation among women with the least resources—unmarried, particularly teenage unmarried, women. The decline in fertility rates we have just described masks an increase in fertility rates among unmarried women.

The birth rate among unmarried women first began to climb in 1965, with a rate of 22.2 births per 1000 unmarried women. In the next five years, births outside marriage continued to rise by an annual 3 percent average. By 1970, these births peaked at a rate of 25.7,[8] and by 1977, 15.5 percent of all children were born to unmarried mothers (compared to 4 percent in 1950).[9] This rise affected both white and black women, and teenage pregnancies accounted for much of the increase. Between 1965 and 1970, the rate for teenage pregnancies outside marriage rose an average of 6 percent annually, while the marital birth rate for women 25 to 44 years old witnessed a 2 percent average decline. In 1977, 48 percent of all nonmarital births were attributed to teenage mothers, and 39 percent of teenage births occurred among unmarried young women, a group with exceptionally limited resources.[10] Among both white and black women, teenagers contributed comparatively more to nonmarital births than older women.

Women, particularly teenage women, having children outside marriage increase their responsibilities, while simultaneously limiting their ability to augment their resources through education and employment. For both married and unmarried women, early motherhood reduces their chances of independence based on increased earning power. Why, we might ask, in a time of improved contraceptive technology and availability, are young, unmarried women having more babies than ever before? Is this again a reflection of the struggle for power between men and women? Or is it a struggle for self-determination among women? Does the possibility of public assistance based on motherhood represent desirable adult status? Does it provide resources and quasi-independence for very poor young women? What happens when public assistance programs are slashed?

Fertility and Age at First Marriage

Getting married very early, before one has the opportunity to develop educational, occupational, and economic assets, limits resources for both men and women. It is particularly detrimental to those women who begin their families soon after marriage. For women in each childbearing age group, the earlier they married, the more children they had. Again, both factors—early marriage and more children—contributed to their lack of resources and their dependence on others, primarily men. In 1978, among women 40 to 48 years old, those who had married between ages 14 and 17 had an average of 3.9 children each; those who married between ages 30 and 34 averaged 1.8 children per woman.[11]

Marrying young is associated with early and frequent motherhood, both because many young marriages occur in response to an existing pregnancy, and also because there are more childbearing years still available to these women. But this pattern of early age at first marriage, often accompanied by early parenthood, reduces the potential lifetime resources of young women. If also affects young men, although the economic results are somewhat less severe for males. It is therefore not surprising that young marriages have the greatest likelihood of ending in divorce, another blow to resource accumulation and power.

Fertility, Education, and Employment

Education and employment are two major avenues for developing resources. Education and labor-force participation also are linked to childbearing patterns. In general, the more highly educated a woman is, the more likely she is to have a smaller number of children. U.S. Census figures for 1978 reveal that among women 35 to 39 years old, those who had not gone beyond the eighth grade had given birth to an average of 3.8 children per woman, compared to 2.1 children each among women who had graduated from college or gone beyond.

A woman's entry into the labor force is similarly connected to childbearing patterns. The more children a woman has, the less likely she is to be in the labor force. Not so for men. Again, the number of children ever born per 1000 women is a convenient measure of different patterns. Among women 20 to 24 years old who were in the labor force in 1978, the number of children born per 1000 women was 668, compared to their unemployed age-mates' rate of 1297 per 1,000. Among women 40 to 44 years old, employed women also had fewer children than their unemployed age-mates (3081 vs 3433), but the gap was narrower.

As more women exercise their options for high educational attainment and labor force participation, both of which tend to be associated with delay in marriage, the number of children these women have will decline. And the fewer children women have, the more likely those women are to be regular members of the paid work force. With such a pattern, women will increase their overall opportunities for resources.

All available evidence suggests that women increasingly expect to lead lives that include more education, more and better jobs, more money, and fewer children. Data on women's expectations for family size suggest that they now expect to have fewer children than women did even at the beginning of the 1970s. In fact, fewer women than in earlier decades are expecting to have three, four or more children. During the 1970s, American women anticipated a family that included about two children each. For example, married women ages 18 to 29 expected to have slightly more than two children each. By 1978, a larger proportion of married women in these age groups expected to have between 0 and 2 children, an expectation that fits with apparent declines in actual births. Moreover, the number of young wives expecting to remain childless or have only one child has steadily increased.[12]

In interpreting these patterns, still other factors must be taken into account. For example, these figures do not yet reflect the impact of recent unemployment rates, inflation, and reduced income levels—factors that traditionally suppress the birth rate. Another source of uncertainty is that the current population of females of childbearing age, born in the post-World War II baby boom, is larger than usual in relation to the total population. Ordinarily, that would lead to a second baby boom as these women produced their own families. But this outcome will be influenced by numerous factors: improved contraceptive technology, delayed first marriage, later first children, increased environmental (particularly population) concerns, rising cost of living, higher unemployment, and changing attitudes toward women's roles.

Taken together, all these conditions represent factors that impinge on women's power through control over their own lives, particularly their status as mothers. The fact that women now choose to marry later than they did in earlier periods suggests that they have sources of support other than a husband's wages, a condition underscoring their growing strength in relationships with men. And with each added choice—to continue their education, to enter the labor force, to limit family size—they increase their resources for independence and power in relation to men.

THE CULTIVATION, PROTECTION, AND POACHING OF POWER

According to our observations about power (see Chapter 1), each group or party in a power relationship attempts to exert its will over the other through the use and control of resources. Each cultivates and protects its own resources while simultaneously seeking to capture, devalue, or diminish the resources of the other. So it is with men and women. We have described the ways in which men, by exerting public power, and women, by exercising mostly private influence, seek to control not only their own lives and destinies, but those of others as well. Wherever possible, each gender cultivates and protects its resources from inroads by the other. This history of gender relationships may be read as a power exercise between women and men in which men and women create, nourish, and stockpile their own resources, resisting attempts by the other group to capture or reduce those resources. At the same time, each gender group makes both frontal and more circuitous attacks on the other's resources.

At times, domains previously under the exclusive control of one group have become the object of the other gender's poaching. Sometimes, this results in the poachers taking control. For example, early male dominance of the secretarial role eventually gave way to female dominance—also an illustration of how a powerful male role loses its status once women establish control.

Those domains under women's control are often ignored by males, at least until they become potentially lucrative or powerful. Tending to childbirth offers an excellent case of a power domain, once the preserve of women that gradually came under male control. In earlier periods, pregnant women turned to female relatives and midwives for assistance in childbirth and confinement. Midwives were outside the control of the all-male medical profession, and their responsibility—childbirth—was considered appropriate only for women attendants.

As the medical profession developed an appreciation of its own growing authority and the possibilities for power, wealth, and control in attending pregnant women, male physicians began to encroach on the midwives' turf by offering supposedly better care, more knowledge, science (often in the form of destructive obstetrical instruments), and rationality. Midwives resisted this takeover but gradually had to acknowledge defeat. The full brunt of the medical profession's power shunted them aside.

Childbirth, once a domestic, noisy, happy, painful, all-female celebration, was transformed into a sterile hospital procedure, quiet, painless, unconscious, and male-controlled. Moved from their own homes to the protective halls of nineteenth-century hospitals, women died in greater numbers than ever before from puerperal fever until sterile hospital procedures were introduced. Semmelweis, who introduced the techniques, was virtually driven mad by his medical colleagues for demonstrating that the unwashed hands of male obstetricians were the very source of puerperal fever. But male control continued. Only recently have midwives rejoined the struggle to attend childbirth, this time by demanding admission to hospital labor rooms.

When power domains move in the other direction, from male to female control, they often have already begun to lose their value or power. Norwegian sociologist Harriet Holter observed that women are allowed to enter decision-making bodies of society only when those groups are becoming, or have already become, obsolete or powerless.[13] (We should add maybe even dangerous.) When the role of schoolteacher carried authority and power as well as respect, it was not open to women. Only when the role diminished in power and status were women allowed into the ranks of educators. When the private secretary role held status and power, it, too, was reserved for males. As technology changed the secretarial role and typewriters came to play a central part in office tasks, the role became less powerful and also more open to women. Eventually, by the early twentieth century, women had virtually complete control of the secretarial profession—but the status and wages, not surprisingly, plummeted. As word processors transform the secretarial role into a high tech, better-paid position, another struggle between men and women may ensue.

When a previously safe and glamorous male power preserve becomes dangerous, women's chances for entering or dominating that domain often increase, despite ritualistic concern about the "weaker sex's" safety. Two clear examples support this point. First, the nursing profession admitted no women until the Crimean War, when Florence Nightingale was able to persuade the British Army that the wartime shortage of nurses could be solved by recruiting women. The second example is more recent. Women have faced insurmountable barriers in infiltrating the ranks of the U.S. Foreign Service, a cadre of powerful, high-status professionals. As late as 1970, less than 10 percent of all foreign service officers were women. The turbulence of the 1970s brought danger to diplomatic missions everywhere. Since that time, the desirability and glamor of the diplomatic role has dimmed, and simultaneously centralization of power diminished the already waning authority of diplomats. Not surprisingly, the most recent figures reveal that women now constitute 30 percent of the new entrants to the diplomatic corps.[14]

The cultivation, protection, and poaching of power between the genders continues. In the process, resources are distributed and redistributed. Negotiations proliferate. Women, with historically less power and fewer resources, have commonly used more subtle means to offset masculine power. With women labeled the moral guardians of society, private female condemnation of moral or sexual excess could diminish the self-esteem, and thus the interpersonal power, of even the most educated, brilliant, powerful, and wealthy male. As Euripides' *Lysistrata* suggests, sexuality itself has always been a resource whose use or denial could enhance a woman's personal and even political power. Sympathy, feeling, understanding—all scarce resources in the external world—were in long supply among women, who offered them to men in exchange for marriage, support, loyalty, and liaisons. Thus the power relationships were kept in equilibrium, adjusted and readjusted through the shifting conditions of history.

WOMEN STRUGGLE AGAINST INJUSTICE TO OTHERS, THEN TO THEMSELVES

Although the gender struggle has had a long, relentless history, women have only occasionally spoken out publicly on their own behalf. More often, women have acted to redress inequitable power relationships between other groups—between poor and rich, slave and master, majority and minority. In fact, as we shall see repeatedly, when women in the forefront of major social movements did try to address women's equality, they were forcefully reminded that the "women's issue" must wait until the "larger" social question was resolved. Abolitionists, socialists, Zionists, nationalists, civil rights workers all admonished women that they were selfish, elitist, or politically inept to press the women's question as an explicit or primary component of social justice and power relationships.

The 1960s and 1970s witnessed the rebalancing of power relationships throughout the world. Public attention increasingly became riveted on changing power balances. The civil rights movement of the 1960s made it clear to the women involved in that struggle that the gender power relationship would not be solved without direct action, without women speaking up on behalf of their own need for equality. As a result, in the 1970s women acted on their own behalf to adjust the gender power relationship in education, employment, politics, sexual behavior, and domestic responsibilities. Women entered institutions of higher learning in record numbers, pushed aside the barriers in blue collar jobs as well as in the traditional professions, and organized in the political arena.[15] These trends seemed to strengthen women's public power. At the same time, women's sexual behavior and tastes more nearly approached the male model, leaving women's role as moral guardian somewhat in question. The private power wielded by women through control of their own and men's sexual behavior began to wane. In the early 1980s vocal neoconservatism, coupled with serious economic constraints, joined to tighten society's control over women's sexual and economic behavior. The recent call for legal restraint of abortion is an obvious case. Despite access to abortion conferred by the Supreme Court in 1973, by the early 1980s women's right to control their bodies was being questioned anew. Serious efforts were mounted to overturn legal abortion.

Students of women's rights might wish to trace the historical dialectic between access to contraceptive measures and abortion and the larger economy, specifically the labor market. In periods marked by an expanding economy that require women in the labor force, a benign, if not an outright encouraging, attitude toward women determining their own fertility has prevailed. In periods of a tightening economy, on the other hand, women were urged, overtly and covertly, by restricted access to abortion and contraception, as well as by a groundswell of togetherness and familism, to have babies, to tend the hearth. What specifically, we might ask, is the relationship between women's fertility behavior, their labor-force participation, and the economy? In times of diminishing resources, are women being asked to relinquish their claim on the economic resources generated within the marketplace? Is access to abortion, women's right to control their fertility, one important avenue in the journey to gain the economic resources necessary to enhance their power position?

The recent retrenchment in affirmative action—primary political strategy of the 1970s for increasing women's (and other powerless groups') share of the societal pie—is another illustration of efforts to curtail women's access to resources and therefore to power. Women's attempts to gather resources and power are currently under attack from all sides. Reverse discrimination suits ask courts to rule *against* the selection of women on an affirmative action basis. The familiar phenomenon of urging women to set aside their own needs for the sake of the "greater societal good" is in evidence again. Some would call these signs of the times a backlash; others would recognize them as the familiar three steps forward and two steps back that have characterized American women's progress toward equality. Still others would identify these events as the very essence of the power process, the threads that weave together negotiation, resources, contributions, promises, and threats, and thus constantly adjust the gender power balance.

SUMMARY

Men and women, as individuals and groups, have maintained control over the body politic and the body personal, respectively. The interpenetration of the public and private domains, through macromanipulation and micromanipulation, keeps the gender power struggle in motion. Men and women, in their private and public lives, strive to maintain control over their own and each other's behavior. Sexual behavior, particularly, is often the focus of power poaching. Technology in the guise of the Pill, as well as the law interpreted in court decisions, have been two major factors in women's growing control over their bodies, their sexuality, their parental status, and their educational and economic opportunities. Control over the body personal has enhanced women's efforts to augment their economic resources and to share men's domination of the body politic. Economic downturns and vocal neoconservatism have created the current context for increasing efforts to limit women's ability to defer or limit maternity, as well as their labor-market participation, two critical forces that strengthen women's hand in the unending gender power struggle.

NOTES

1. Men influence and impose their will not only on women, but on weaker men as well. But the distinction that men of power make between less powerful men and women, both strong and weak, is very vague. In fact, weaker men are further weakened by comparisons with women, the officially designated powerless group. See Jean Lipman-Blumen, "Toward a Ho-

mosocial Theory of Sex Roles: An Explanation of the Sex Segregation of Social Institutions," *Signs,* vol. 1, no. 3, part 2, (Spring 1976), 15–31.

2. Jessie Bernard, *The Female World* (New York: The Free Press, 1981).

3. Carl N. Degler, *At Odds: Women and the Family in America from the Revolution to the Present* (New York: Oxford University Press, 1980).

4. William H. Chafe, *Women and Equality: Changing Patterns in American Culture* (New York: Oxford University Press, 1977); also William H. Chafe, *The American Woman: Her Changing Social, Economic, and Political Roles, 1920–1970* (New York: Oxford University Press, 1972).

5. The total fertility rate is a measure of the number of children a group of 1000 women would have during their entire childbearing period if they continued to experience the age-specific birth rates for that particular year.

6. Ellen Peck, *The Baby Trap* (New York: B. Geis Associates, 1971).

7. *The Washington Post,* May 25, 1975.

8. J. Sklar and B. Berkov, "Abortion, Illegitimacy, and the American Birth Rate," *Science,* 185:900–15.

9. Sandra L. Hofferth, Steven B. Caldwell, Linda J. Waite, *Teenage Motherhood: Social and Economic Consequences* (Washington, D.C.: The Urban Institute, 1979).

10. Ibid.

11. Examining the fertility patterns of women 40 to 48 years old enables us to see the size of their completed families.

12. U.S. Department of Commerce, Bureau of the Census, *Current Population Reports* Series P-23, no. 58 (Washington, D.C.: Government Printing Office, April, 1980), p. 18; U.S. Department of Commerce, Bureau of the Census, *A Statistical Portrait of Women in the United States: 1978* (Washington, D.C.: Government Printing Office, 1978).

13. Harriet Holter, *Sex Roles and Social Structure* (Blindern, Oslo: Universitetsforlaget, 1970).

14. *The Washington Post,* July 31, 1981.

15. Jean Lipman-Blumen and Georgia Strasburg, "U.S. Country Paper: The Educational Status of Women," prepared for the U.S. Office of Education and the U.S. Department of State for presentation at the U.N. Conference for International Women's Year, Copenhagen, 1980; see also Mary Lou Randour, Georgia Strasburg, and Jean Lipman-Blumen, "Women in Higher Education: Trends in Enrollments and Degrees Earned," *Harvard Educational Review,* vol. 52, no. 1 (Spring, 1982).

CHAPTER 5
WHY THE POWERLESS DO NOT REVOLT

Given that men control greater institutional resources than women, why don't they simply crush women into total submission and end the gender power struggle once and for all? Earlier we suggested two reasons why men use force infrequently against women. First, force is hardly an encouragement to love and affection. Second, if men want not only love but productivity, service, and work from women, those who are beaten down are incapable of such efforts. Additional important reasons exist for men's reluctance to coerce women's compliance. And still other factors—structural, attitudinal, and existential—lead women and men to join forces to protect the gender power balance.

MEN'S POWER POSITION AND THEIR NEED FOR WOMEN

What are these other key aspects of the power relationship itself that not only prevent men from using force, but predispose them to seek the apparent acquiescence, if not the enthusiastic endorsement, of women? One factor is the isolation that stems from the structural differentiation of gender roles. If sex and gender roles define men and women as unalterably different, with men alone perceived as the appropriate wielders of power, then men too are set apart, isolated in their lonely governing roles.

The existential condition—each individual's deep-seated awareness of his or her own human frailty and uncertainty—makes even the most renowned king seek approval of his decisions and beliefs, validation of his own existence. The common practice of princes surrounding themselves with fawning courtiers, of presidents, both national and corporate, of encouraging an entourage of "yes-men" is not simply the result of power's sweet nectar attracting obsequious bees. Of course, insincere and unrelenting rubberstamping eventually frustrates the powerful, who occasionally seek objective opinions, usually in vain. But the powerful conspire with the less powerful to validate their own decisions, their own view of life.

It is hardly surprising that men turn to women, both at home and at work, for emotional and moral validation. Thanks to gender roles defining women as society's emotional and moral arbiters, men's decisions in the public domain require recurrent validation and approval from women. Deprived of this legitimation of their experience and choices, men, as well as women, lose touch with reality and risk slipping through the looking-glass into the mad world of schizophrenia or megalomania. So men need women, defined by gender roles as more moral, emotional, and nurturant than men, to assure them that the choices they make as agents of power are good, even loveable. In those rare instances when women find themselves in seats of great institutional power, they too seek such reassurances.

THE STRUCTURAL BASES
OF MALE-FEMALE INTERDEPENDENCE

Another reason why men, as the socially dominant group, ordinarily do not choose to use visible force to gain women's agreement with their decisions is that they live together in families, domestically unsegregated. Women and men are both separated from their own gender groups, particularly those of different social, economic, racial, and ethnic backgrounds. And women who do not participate in the occupational world are even more segregated from other non-kin women.

The definition of separate but complementary roles (or "two spheres") created by the sex-gender system leads to a sexual division of labor within the home and the marketplace that spawns a structured interdependence between men and women. The rise of the nuclear family, with all its sociological, psychological, economic, and political correlates, increases men's and women's emotional intimacy and interdependence. This socially induced interdependence fosters cooperation between men and women. The physical and emotional enclosure we call the family provides the psychological and structural humidity and nutrients for the tendrils of emotional intimacy and vulnerability—be they affection, love, hatred, or simply familiarity—to take root.

That men and women live together in social and sexual intimacy within households, if not always families, increases the likelihood that they will look to one another for help and reassurance, as well as for emotional and economic support. These circumstances provide the soil in which emotional interdependence can grow. Feminists argue that women's economic dependence on men has more seriously devastating outcomes than men's emotional reliance on women. Researchers who cite the higher mortality and morbidity figures of divorced, widowed, and single men might dispute this view.

The fact that women and men live in mutual dependence within families or households patterned on a division of labor dictated by sex and gender roles also provides a structural basis for the maintenance of this arrangement. Their own structured social and sexual intimacy, coupled with their separation from other non-kin members of their own gender, keeps both women and less powerful men from joining forces with similarly situated members of their own gender group. Negative social class, racial, and ethnic stereotypes help to maintain these divisions within gender groups. The long-term nature of these living arrangements also reduces the likelihood that men will impose their decisions on women by brute force. It simply would not work in the long run. Men, as well as women, understand the folk wisdom of that old adage, "Softly, softly, catch a monkey." Thus, structural arrangements of intimate family living promote the growth of social, sexual, and affectional bonds that ease the power struggle between individual women and men.

Attitudinal Supports:
How Stereotypes Divide the Powerless

Although family living arrangements encourage interdependence and intimacy between the sexes, they tend to separate homebound women from other non-kin women; women in the labor force are less segregated from one another and more likely to join forces in their struggle for equality. Men's greater labor-force participation puts them in daily contact with other non-kin males. Moreover, men's—particularly powerful men's—membership in the ruling social group reduces their need for same-sex alliances, especially with men in less powerful positions. Even in terms of their dependence within the heterosexual union, men from the higher socioeconomic strata are less vulnerable than their mates; they almost always can attract other women with fewer resources to share their power and life style.

Thus, family living arrangements heighten the physical segregation of women who do not work outside the home. This physical separation of women from non-kin females of different socioeconomic, racial, and ethnic groups also provides the structural basis for inhibiting women from uniting to improve their power position relative to men. This structural basis for female segregation is strengthened by an attitudinal basis—negative stereotypes of other groups, including the women in those groups. Taken together, these factors limit the possibilities for women to create alliances with other women from different socioeconomic, racial, age and ethnic groups.

On one level, negative stereotypes of less powerful groups are fashioned by the powerful to maintain their own preeminence. Negative stereotypes depicting other groups as untouchables diminish the likelihood that women, the subordinate partners in heterosexual unions, will forsake this imperfect shelter for a potentially contaminating political or economic alliance with members of other stigmatized groups—particularly since whatever negative stereotypes describe a group as a whole are even more negatively applied to its women. Middle- and upper-class women (and less powerful men) are kept from alliances with their gender-mates from other socioeconomic, racial, age, and ethnic groups by the fear of contamination and loss of whatever limited advantages they currently have. Their working-class sisters, alternately disdainful and desirous of the life style of middle- and upper-class women, worry about the motivations of women above them in the social hierarchy. Rather than join those middle-class and occasional upper-class women who seek their help in reordering the power balance between male and female, working-class women suspect their motives as genocidal, elitist, and racist. The historical record often fuels their fears.

Add to this what women of all social classes, through the ages, have learned explicitly from their mothers and implicitly from their fathers: Given the barriers to women's own personal occupational and economic success, sexual competition among women for that scarce and valuable commodity—powerful men—is women's one dependable route to economic and social security. Until recently, when increasing occupational opportunities and greater acceptance of divorce and remarriage began to offer alternatives, the stage was elaborately set for fierce female sexual competition.

Working-class women, whose power chips have been the least valued by the dominant group, see access to resource-generating institutions as a cruel joke in which they repeatedly have been the victims of exploitative wages and health-jeopardizing work environments. Not surprisingly, they believe their best hope is entering the ranks of middle-class housewives, with whatever additional advantages their social telescope seems to magnify.

More affluent women have their own reasons for reluctance. They fear losing the vicarious status and power they now derive through their husbands' positions in the social hierarchy. Socialized from early childhood to achieve vicariously, first through their fathers and later through their husbands and sons, these affluent women are kept in line by control myths—another form of stereotype. Many of these women have been guided away from crucial enabling experiences—learning mathematics, science, finance, law—that would have broadened their personal options in the world beyond the family. Higher education may have radicalized some women, but it rarely gave them the critical tools to end their economic dependence on men.

More affluent women also have their own negative stereotypes of their less well-to-do sisters. They have been schooled to perceive their less affluent gender-mates as vulgar, ill-bred, ignorant, sexually promiscuous, lesbians, or welfare parasites. Belief in these stereotypes keeps all but a few of these vicariously successful women from joining women of less privileged socioeconomic, racial, and ethnic groups to reset the gender power balance. (We might note that less powerful men are prevented from uniting with other equally disenfranchised males across class, race, and ethnic lines by similar strategies.)

Other Rationales

Negative stereotypes about outsiders are not the only attitudinal basis for maintaining the strength of the heterosexual power relationship. For the powerless to go on living intimately with those who most directly limit their power, other strong rationales must exist. The weight of tradition predisposes both women and men to take the social structure for granted, including the entire panoply of institutional arrangements based on laws, customs, and practices, rather than on individual talent.

Most women and men accept the structural arrangements as natural, each group believing the stereotypes that keep the complementary gender-role dance in harmony. Males attribute their own success to competence, women's more limited success to innate female incapacities. Women, socialized from childhood to concur in this belief, usually do. Females, raised to be spectators at both the childhood playground and the adult institutional games in which men star, receive only rare opportunities to test their own skills. Many women, forced by the crises of widowhood, family illness, or divorce to test their abilities at traditional male activities, find they easily learn the requisite skills. Many discover their own unsuspected talent for these games.

Some women, valuing their deep-seated appreciation of the less competitive, more cooperative life styles and strategies learned within traditional female gender roles, would prefer to infuse institutional structures and practices with their own special perspective. Other women, radicalized by higher education and labor-force participation, express growing doubts about the "natural," much less the "inevitable," quality of the existing social structure. They have begun to reject the traditional institutional structures, on the grounds that "the only game in town" is rigged. No matter. The dominant group and the remaining powerless whom they "support" and "protect" continue to accept the institutional arrangements as givens.

Males controlling institutional arrangements see their position as deserved, and they resist, as sociologist William J. Goode tells us, all efforts to chip away at their power.[1] Powerful men's sincere belief that they are more intelligent and competent than women promotes their indignant resistance to efforts to redress women's unequal status. They continue to misinterpret such efforts, including affirmative action, as strategies to offer incompetent women and other minority group members an unfair advantage in gender-segregated economic and political institutions. Men's own structural advantage, embedded like the rabbit in the landscapes of children's picture books, is just as hard for them to detect. Over time, foreground blends into background. The less powerful who have identified the embedded rabbit as the structural arrangement known as "sex discrimination" find it nearly impossible to make the rabbit fade away into the background.

THE BLUEPRINT PROBLEM: A STRONG EXISTENTIAL FORCE

Still another factor helps to maintain the gender power balance. It offers one more clue to why men particularly, but not without women's witting or unwitting collusion, seek to keep the sex-gender system in "proper" balance—that is, with a clear power discrepancy between women and men. For simplicity, we shall call this the *blueprint problem.*

Earlier, we alluded to the importance of the interconnections among institutions. Everywhere in society, social institutions are composed of roles rank-ordered into a value and dominance hierarchy. The general pattern is repeated in all institutions: the family, the occupational system, the political and legal system, the religious system, the economic system. Men are situated in the highest stratum in every social institution, with women consistently located in strata below men of their own social group. As long as this key power relationship between men and women remains in the traditional balance, *all* institutions are protected from change.

This brings us to a major thesis of this book: The power relationship between men and women is at the very heart of the social fabric. Once it begins to unravel, so do all other power relationships. Hence, despite the fact that women may be the numerical majority in world population, they are subordinate everywhere to men of their own social group. Social science principles insist that variation in the political and economic systems of society will lead to variation in the relative importance and bargaining power of different groups. Nonetheless, in all known societies, despite differences in stage of development and political and economic structures, women's relative status and bargaining power are consistently less than that of men in their own cultures. Somehow, through structural arrangements and practices, legal mandates, customs, control myths, and a host of other social, psychological, political, legal, and economic phenomena, women are kept subordinate to men.

The need to maintain women's subordination at home and in the world at large is deep seated, since in some inchoate way both women and men understand that the power relationship between the genders is the blueprint for *all* other power relationships. Small changes in the gender power balance can be tolerated. Many unconsciously fear, however, that a major change, one in which women could negotiate the dominant role, would prove the undoing of all other power relationships modeled so carefully after this seemingly most stable and inevitable one.

This blueprint, itself presumably patterned after the divine relationship between God and humans portrayed in traditional Western religious systems, is then used to fashion all other power relationships. The blueprint itself becomes sacred. Its meaning becomes dangerous knowledge: that the Divine Echo, the gender power relationship, is the model of all power relationships in all societal institutions, the model that keeps all others in place. The awareness of this dangerous truth threatens every political power relationship.

The parallel between sexual and political dominance is seen in relationships among ethnic, racial, economic, and national groups. Western colonialism in Africa, Asia, and Latin America, not to mention the American slavery experience, was based upon the relationship between sexual and political power relationships. Numerous students of colonialism, including Ashis Nandy, suggest that the basic condition of colonialism is a psychological acceptance of the states of dominance/masculinity and subordinance/femininity by the rulers and ruled, respectively. In a trenchant politico-psychoanalytic analysis of British colonialism in India, Nandy argues that

> Colonial ideology in British India was built of the cultural meanings of two fundamental categories of institutional discrimination in Britain—sex and

age. . . . Colonialism . . . was congruent with the existing Western sexual stereotypes and the philosophy of life which they represented. It produced a cultural consensus in which political and socioeconomic dominance symbolized the dominance of men and masculinity over women and femininity.[2]

Eventually, both rulers and subjects accepted the notion of colonial rule as a "husbandly," "manly," or "lordly" prerogative. Nandy offers this as a description not of the micropolitics, but the macropolitics of colonialism. The notion of "protectorates" as unable to fend for themselves—less able, less educable, and more primitive than the colonial ruler—contains a metaphor too reminiscent of the female/male power balance to warrant dismissal as mere coincidence. The very language of colonialism evokes the domestic paradigm.

The inchoate awareness of the blueprint problem lies at the heart of seemingly disparate efforts to maintain the sex-gender system in its current balance. It is this barely conscious understanding that may be the connective tissue linking such apparently unrelated occurrences as opposition to the Equal Rights Amendment in the United States (where such legal equality would not be nonchalantly taken for granted); the unwillingness of Soviet husbands (whose wives have unusual equality in the work force) to share domestic chores within the family; and female clitoridectomies in Third World countries (where unbridled female sexual prowess allegedly would lead to a host of ills). Perhaps these are all last-ditch measures to ensure that the gender power balance stays at least symbolically tipped in men's favor.

Men and women share the dangerous knowledge that the gender power relationship, echoing the divine power structure of traditional religions, is the model for all other power relationships in every societal institution. It reinforces and is reinforced by the interconnectedness of social institutions. Men and women also share the fear of the unknown, the fear of what would happen if women, mobilizing and valuing their own resources, negotiated for the dominant position. What, indeed, would happen to the fabric of society if the key pattern were to change? Would every institutional power arrangement eventually shift? Probably.

WHY THE POWERLESS DO NOT REVOLT

It is not difficult to understand why the powerful want to stay in charge: a deep-seated, often unidentified fear that all institutional power relationships might unravel, structurally induced myopia, tradition, belief in their own superior talents, the negotiated power to define, label, and rank-order. These are seductive incentives for wanting to remain in charge, even though control brings serious burdens. But what do the powerless derive from this structured inequality? Why do they remain? Why do the less powerful, in this case women, continue to validate male decision-making and negotiate in ways that maintain their subordinate position?

First, and most significant to women as well as men, is the blueprint problem we have just discussed. Second, women and men alike are socialized from infancy to accept the traditional definition of gender roles. Both sexes believe in the gender definitions created by their forebears and inculcated by their parents and other adults through word and deed. They are repeatedly taught through *control myths* about the supposedly innate nature—that is, differentiation—of males and females.

Two control myths in particular keep women from renegotiating the power relationship to allow them greater access to institutional resources. First is the control myth that assures women that men are more knowledgeable and capable; second is the myth that men have women's best interests at heart (colonialism revisited).

That men are more knowledgeable and capable is a control myth of enormous influence. For example, despite females' early verbal and mathematical advantages over males, they are set on the "proper" track by control myths that guide them into nonquantitative, nonscientific, nonfinancial, nonlegal courses of study to enter service, helping, people-oriented occupations. Institutional arrangements and practices, also shaped by control myths, keep any curious or rebellious individuals from straying into the other gender's territory. Eventually the control myth about men's greater knowledge and capability becomes a self-fulfilling prophecy.[3] First we believe the definitions; then we act in accordance with them and, by so doing, we make them come true.

The second control myth—that men have women's best interests at heart, that men will protect these less knowledgeable, and therefore more dependent women—is also taught to men and women alike. For men, this means they believe they know better and more, and thus must take care of women and protect them from danger. Often, men see danger to women coming from other men, not themselves. And so they devise laws to protect women from those other men who would exploit and harm them. Protective legislation, notorious for protecting women and children not only from exploitation but from mobility-offering and high-salary jobs as well, was the joint accomplishment of women seeking protection and men who had their best interests at heart.

For women, the belief that men have their welfare at heart has several consequences. For one, they relax, let down their guard in the power struggle, and do not negotiate too hard. It seems pointless to antagonize a strong, wise, and especially a benevolent despot. Sexual and affectional ties to the benevolent ruler compound the issue. But believing in benevolent despots, even kindly rulers, means we believe that power is an *attribute* of a leader or ruler, a *commodity* that one has more or less of, rather than a *process* of decision-making and negotiation. But accepting the notion that men have women's and less powerful men's best interests at heart is to pin one's hopes on moral and ethical rulers.

However, Lord Acton warned us that "Power tends to corrupt, and absolute power corrupts absolutely." The lesson Lord Acton would have us learn is that those we grant unchecked power—power that need not be constantly renegotiated—cannot remain moral and ethical. Women and powerless men cannot relax and hand over the reins and burdens of decision-making about critical world events, even to those who might indeed have their best interests at heart.

Sometimes, of course, even those who sincerely want the best for women do not actually know what that "best" is. For example, those loving fathers and husbands who protected their daughters and wives from financial burdens often left their shielded widow and children in the hands of those other men—notoriously bankers and lawyers—who did, indeed, exploit their financial ignorance. Women know better than anyone else what constitutes their best interests, just as men are the most competent judges of their own welfare. To rephrase an old truism: "Until men walk in women's moccasins," their claims to know women's best interests are suspect—and vice versa.

The Overwhelming Odds

Still another reason why women, like other less powerful groups, tend to remain in the subordinate position in a power relationship is that they perceive the institutional resources that men have as unattainable for women, except through their relationships with men. The disparity is too great; it is too wide to be bridged. The odds are overwhelming.

In large part this perception is based on fact, since the majority of independently wealthy women have become so through inheritance or marriage. And even those relatively few women who have entered entrepreneurial and professional roles rarely receive the same rewards—money, prestige, position, or access to still more sacrosanct institutions—as men. The small number who do are usually featured on the women's page, rather than on the financial or front page of the newspaper. The woman physician who works full time at her profession rarely has even the economic advantages, much less the leisure time (another important resource), of the male physician's full-time housewife.

A keen awareness of this substantial disparity between men's and women's resources and the genuine inaccessibility of institutional resources to women has kept many gender power relationships intact. This is what keeps many discontented wives locked into the bonds of acrimony with spouses they would rather divorce. This trap traps the trappers, as well. Men too are caught by this arrangement. Wives who will never be able to earn enough in the labor force to support themselves, much less their children, may require lifelong, debilitating alimony payments. The awareness of this huge and seemingly irreducible disparity in resources has ignited the flame of fear among many women whose lives have been based on vicarious or derivative access to resources. Many of these women understandably oppose any movement for change, which they sense threatens to reduce their current, if tenuous, access to resources.

Women's belief in debilitating control myths often teaches them that their strengths are their weaknesses, as Chapter 7 explains in greater detail. Strong verbal skills (called "talking too much" in women, and "articulateness" in men) are keys to leadership roles in organizations. Women are taught to restrain their talking—that is, their displays of intelligence—in such settings, lest they make negative female stereotypes self-fulfilling prophecies.

Men too, from early childhood and throughout life, are indoctrinated with beliefs, expectations, attitudes, and values that limit their total role repertoire, including their sex and gender roles. Males, no less than females, are subjected to this pervasive socialization, through parents, teachers, peers, media, art, and religion—through a host of societal forces that create near mutually exclusive, but complementary, roles. In the next chapter, we begin to consider how socialization occurs, and how it leaves both women and men poised for the gender power struggle.

SUMMARY

Structural, attitudinal, and existential supports keep the gender power balance intact. Men, locked into their lonely decision-making roles, seek affirmation of their choices from women, defined as society's moral arbiters. Living together in households or families, men and women develop an intimate interdependence that encourages conscious and unconscious collusion between the genders to protect the power balance. Negative female stereotypes keep women from reaching across socioeconomic, racial, and ethnic boundaries to form power alliances with other women.

The gender power balance receives additional support from those who perceive it as the blueprint or model for all other power relationships. Its maintenance protects the stability of all other power relationships. Control myths that insist that men are more able than women but have women's best interests at heart contribute to the stability of male domination. Moreover, the disproportionate institutional resources that men control create overwhelming odds against which women feel it is futile to revolt.

This combination of structural, attitudinal, and existential forces operates to keep the gender power struggle on course. As we shall now see, male and female socialization to gender roles serves to reinforce this sex-gender helix.

NOTES

1. William J. Goode, "Why Men Resist," in *Rethinking the Family: Some Feminist Questions,* ed., Barrie Thorne with Marilyn Yalom (New York: Longman Inc., 1982).

2. Ashis Nandy, *The Intimate Enemy: Loss and Recovery of Self under Colonialism* (New Delhi: Oxford University Press, 1983), p. 4.

3. Robert K. Merton, *Social Theory and Social Structure,* rev. ed. (Glencoe, Illinois: The Free Press, 1957).

CHAPTER 6
SOCIALIZATION
FOR GENDER ROLES

WHAT IS SOCIALIZATION?

For the gender power struggle to persist, males and females must perform very different roles, linked to very different resources. Just how do they learn their distinctive parts so well? Sociologists use the concept of socialization to describe the fundamental processes by which individuals develop the attitudes, expectations, behaviors, values, and skills that coalesce into roles. Gender roles, like other social roles, are learned through socialization.

Very simply, *socialization* is that set of mechanisms and processes through which society trains its members to take their place as fullfledged social beings. Socialization includes both the systematic as well as the random experiences society generates to encourage people to behave in ways that protect the continuity of group life. Socialization occurs through explicit and implicit training by *agents of socialization*—parents, teachers, peers, and public figures. Exemplary individuals, known intimately or only as distant luminaries, serve as *role models*, with whom the developing members of society can identify.

Cultural Lag

Gender role socialization, managed primarily by adults raised under different social conditions, is inevitably geared to roles of a previous era. The result is *cultural lag*, a disparity between the expectations created by outdated socialization processes and the realities of an everchanging society. This disparity generates tensions that permeate all other roles gender roles touch. When social change is slow, these tensions remain within bounds. In times of rapid social change, however, general societal tensions, as well as those between the genders, escalate.

These tensions induced by the gap between socialization and actual reality perpetuate, even exacerbate, the power struggle between women and men.

Demographic trends—including marriage, divorce, fertility, and occupational patterns—provide a context for socialization within which boys and girls, later men and women, learn and relearn throughout life what is expected of them as members of distinct gender groups. Socialization to gender roles and the power dynamic they embody occurs through these and other social mechanisms and processes. For example, control myths based on ancient images of masculinity and femininity, which we shall examine later, are echoed in religion, media, and the arts. These prescribed gender images become part of the individual's self-concept. And they set the stage for the gender power struggle.

Through socialization, groups also develop characteristic collective self-concepts, seeing themselves and others like them as strong or weak, intelligent or dull, beautiful or ugly, important or inconsequential. In social interaction, members of the group project these self-concepts, to which others then respond. In this way, self-definitions that ascribe group characteristics or stereotypes to the self become self-fulfilling prophecies. These definitions of self, laced with values and expectations for the self and others, are carried into adult life. Because gender roles are diffuse, bleeding into all the other roles the individual enacts, these characterizations of self as male and female carry a potent impact. They help shape the individual's destiny as a member of society.

Socialization to specific and delimited roles involving skills rather than values and attitudes may be learned relatively quickly; for example, bank tellers are socialized within weeks. By contrast, socialization to more diffuse roles with complex sets of attitudes, values, and behaviors may take much longer. Gender roles, affecting all aspects of life and changing in content and meaning from one developmental stage to the next, undergo lifelong socialization.

SOCIALIZATION FROM BIRTH

The socialization for gender roles, as well as for class, age, and racial roles, begins very early. In fact, from the moment of birth, male and female infants receive different treatment, immediately setting them on two very different paths. Parents have expectations for their offspring based on their own acceptance of cultural stereotypes about the differences between females and males. Using these cultural definitions of sex differences, parents perceive and reinforce gender role differentiation in their sons and daughters.

These complex parental expectations are active from the moment the child is born; pink and blue blankets are only the symbolic tip of the socialization iceberg. Researchers Rubin, Provenzano, and Luria report that both mothers and fathers perceive their newborn sons and daughters very differently within the child's first 24 hours of life.[1] After comparing these newborns' weight, length, strength and alertness, the researchers concluded that there actually were no significant differences between males and females. Nonetheless, both parents characterized baby boys as more alert, stronger, larger featured, more coordinated, and firmer. They described girl babies as less attentive, weaker, finer featured, less coordinated, softer, smaller, more fragile and prettier.

Fathers sex-typed their infants more dramatically than did mothers, who were less likely to report great differences between newborn girls and boys. Students of power might interpret this paternal perception and reinforcement of greater differences between female and male children as an example of the dominant gender group's unconscious tendency to maintain the power differential between males and females. Rubin et al. speculate that parents' sex-typed judgments, based on limited information about their newborn children, contain the seeds of sex stereotyping. These sex-stereotyped expectations influence the parents' behavior toward their children, which subsequently shapes the children's self-concept and gender role expectations.

A small observational study of toy selections made by mothers playing with a six-month-old child reveals the impact of sex stereotyping.[2] The mothers, half of whom were told the child was female and half of whom were told it was male, were asked to select one of three toys (a fish, a train, or a doll) to offer the child. Those mothers who believed the child was male were more likely to present "him" with the train; those who thought the child was a girl more often offered "her" the doll. Interestingly enough, all the mothers reported they would not treat boys and girls of that age differently—evidence indeed that cultural sex stereotypes wield a subtle but strong influence from one generation to the next.

TWO DIFFERENT SOCIALIZATION EXPERIENCES

The expectations of parents, and later of teachers and peers, prepare little girls and boys for realities that diverge not only from the previous generation's, but even more from one another's. These socialization experiences groom females and males to live in two very different worlds.

Training for Masculinity

Independence and Aggression. Even as small boys, males are trained for a world of independent, aggressive action. In this "blue world," males are groomed to take the universe by storm, to confront the environment directly. Males learn that society's goals are best met by aggression, by actively wresting their accomplishments from the environment. Force, power, competition, and aggression are the means. Achievement, males are taught, is measured in productivity, resources, and control—all the result of direct action. In the Western world, the importance of self-reliant, individual action is systematically inculcated in males. To be masculine requires not only self-reliance and self-control, but control over other people and resources. Thus, dominion over weaker men and over all women is an important goal whose accomplishment is practiced early, even in the dominance hierarchies of very young children, according to psychologist Carol Jacklin.[3]

Early on, boys are encouraged to explore and investigate fearlessly. Although males and females do not differ in their "exploratory" behavior before age 3, between the ages of 3 and 6 boys begin to outdistance girls in their "willingness to explore new environments," according to Maccoby and Jacklin.[4] Unlike girls, who are more protected from physical danger, little boys are allowed to wander farther from home.[5] Not surprisingly, by the time they enter school, boys are more likely than girls to play far away from the teacher.[6] As part of this training, boys are encouraged to be daring, to suppress fear. The classic work on sex differences in children's fears by Jersild and Holmes reported no differences in the proportion of each gender actually manifesting fear in a wide range of experimental situations; however, the study cited more intensity of fear among girls, perhaps a reflection of the greater emotional intensity permitted and encouraged among females throughout life.[7]

More recent work on actual fearfulness has not produced particularly convincing evidence that young boys actually are less fearful than girls.[8] However, other studies have revealed that females as young as 8 years old report self-appraisals of fearfulness more often than their male age-mates. Thus, despite no objective differences in fear-related behavior, females somehow begin to believe they are more fearful than males.[9]

Studies of adult females found that some women who reported themselves afraid of snakes were no less able to approach and touch snakes than other adults who did not describe themselves as fearful.[10] We might interpret women's self-described fearfulness as "recognition" of their weakness, which opens the way for a stronger, dominant, less fearful male protector.

Even though no firm evidence of early sex differences in fearfulness exists, somehow, over time, gender-role socialization teaches women, and insulates men from, the expression of fear. Through the many byways of gender-role socialization, females and males learn to define themselves and subsequently to behave and think in accordance not simply with their actual tendencies, but with cultural stereotypes of feminine and masculine behavior. The research data on gender differences in fearfulness offer one clear example of control myths as powerful socialization mechanisms, which we shall explore in a later chapter.

Games and Play. Psychologists who study children's play interpret their games as preparation for adult life.[11] In their earliest efforts at play, small children exhibit few gender differences. In fact, studies of children below 2 years of age show no consistent gender differences in toy preferences. By preschool age, however, gender differences appear that seem linked to adult gender-typed behavior: boys prefer trucks, guns, and carpentry; girls choose beadstringing, sewing, and housekeeping play.[12] Once evident, these differences receive encouragement from many quarters.

Psychologists tell us that boys engage in large-muscle activity—that is, running, leaping, pushing, and fighting. In childhood games, boys explore their strength and agility without fear. This pattern is consistent across many cultures. For example, in four out of six societies studied by a team of anthropologists, boys 3 to 6 years old exhibited more "rough-and-tumble" play than did their female age-mates. This was also true for children 7 to 11 years old in five out of the six societies studied.[13]

Developing and testing one's physical and psychological strength, as well as one's "combat readiness" for life, are simply not encouraged in little girls. And although some "tomboys" do participate in these activities in their preadolescent years, strong sanctions are used to force them back into line by the time they reach puberty. Sociologist Mirra Komarovsky's classical research on gender role socialization offers poignant firsthand recollections of such experiences by her female subjects:

> I started life as a little tomboy but as I grew older, Mother got worried about my unladylike ways. She removed my tops, marbles, football, and skates and tried to replace these with dolls, tea sets and sewing games. . . . When despite her efforts she caught me one day trying to climb a tree in the park she became thoroughly exasperated and called me a little "freak."[14]

At an early age, boys learn to play team sports. Through this and other experiences, they grasp the complexities of cooperation with teammates and competition against the opposition (or "outsiders") in the sandlot ball games. Many observers believe such early training serves men well in adult organizational life, where being a good team player is highly valued.

Team games socialize males to still other important social processes. For example, young boys learn to play cooperatively with teammates whom they personally do not like but who are competent for the team task. Through team sports, boys develop skills that later enable them to work effectively with colleagues whom they might not choose as friends. Team play teaches boys the importance of leadership and winning. The team captain controls players by creating strategies, issuing orders, calling plays; team members learn to work together to follow the captain's directives. This provides important training for playing the captain's role with subtlety and skill when their turns come.

Winning in competitive sports provides practice in planning, coordinating, and implementing a plan for successful goal attainment. Such processes are essential components in the control and management of social institutions. The dedication to the goal of winning that boys learn on football and soccer fields is useful practice for serious adult games, where tenacity and purpose are prerequisites for success. Little boys and young men groomed to lead and win through competitive team sports more easily climb the ladder of adult success. Little girls, taught to value relationships above winning, often forego the winner's crown in the name of friendship or love.

Team sports teach young males another important lesson: how to transform earlier defeats or limitations into ammunition for renewed efforts to win. Research on persistence in the face of failure and frustration suggests that young boys are more likely than their female age-mates to "hang in there" longer on initially defeating tasks. This painful lesson is repeatedly absorbed on the basketball court and the football field; later this instruction is translated into successful performances in courtrooms, emergency rooms, and congressional offices.

Emotions. Dealing with emotions is another major domain of gender-role socialization. The emotional spectrum allowed males varies from one culture to another, as well as from one social class to the next, but it is always narrower than the emotional range allowed females. In many Western societies, stoicism is a highly valued masculine pattern, although here too there is variation. Sociologist Lillian Rubin reports that American working-class families set stricter emotional standards for sons than daughters and certainly more severe norms than those characterizing professional middle-class families.[15]

In Western culture, crying is considered unmanly, except in bereavement. Research suggests that little boys initially cry as much as or more than little girls; eventually, however, young boys are trained to suppress their tears. Several experimental studies report that boys 2 years and younger are more likely than girls to cry when a parent leaves the room. Still other observational studies of 3- to 5-year-old children in home and nursery school settings indicate: (1) boys cried more at home; (2) boys and girls cried about the same amount in nursery school; but (3) boys cried in frustration and conflict situations, whereas girls cried mostly when injured.[16] Other experimental work reveals that boys left alone by their mothers in an unfamiliar room are more apt than girls to cry loudly, as well as to kick and hit the door through which the mother left.[17]

Despite evidence that boys are not necessarily less likely than girls to cry, crying is not included in the accepted repertoire of masculine emotions. Little boys are admonished not to weep, lest they be labeled "sissies." Grown men are subject to this same prohibition. The severe penalty linked to adult male crying was demonstrated not too long ago when an American presidential candidate was eliminated from the political fray after he wept publicly over unfair media attacks on his wife. Socialized to their gender roles, males bear the burden of suppressing tender emotions throughout adulthood. Only strong, angry feelings may be given vent. The "strong silent male," a familiar character in literature and film, is the quintessential American Western hero—who, incidentally, is allowed to kill opponents in a High Noon shootout. He sheds no tears, a clear intimation that only certain emotions—like anger and hostility—may be expressed.

Research studies confirm these patterns. Observational research on children after the age of 28 months describes boys as more likely than girls to give vent to negative feelings in angry outbursts.[18] Although males are trained to deal internally with fear and sadness, they are socialized that it is acceptable to react openly with anger and hostility, both expressions of power. Anger is an expected, often rewarded, mode of male expression. The television and motion picture industries create daily models of male anger erupting into violence, dramatic evidence of unbridled power. Male violence and anger may be justified as a means of restoring law and order, or meting out deserved punishment. At a minimum, it inspires fear, even awe, in the less powerful.

Aggression, the intent to hurt another, is reportedly more characteristic of males than females.[19] In fact, aggression is one of the few characteristics that systematically differentiates the sexes, leading many researchers to focus on a hormonal basis for this difference in aggression.[20] Across many experimental conditions and by a vast array of behavioral measures, male subjects are consistently more aggressive than females.[21] These findings recur in several cross-cultural studies.[22] In fact, greater male aggression seems to be the only consistent finding in male-female differences across most societies.

Maccoby and Jacklin,[23] focusing more on aggression's objectives than its origins, suggest that "attempts to hurt may reflect either the desire to hurt for its own sake or the desire to control another person (for other ends) through arousing fear." Anger and violence used in the service of power offer serious warnings to the less powerful to keep their place. The powerless recognize the unpredictable quality of the powerful's anger: as protection, punishment, or control of the powerless.

Independence, aggression, fearlessness, leadership, tenacity, anger, stoicism, and triumph over defeat are the psychological bricks and mortar of male gender roles, geared for powerful, controlling adult positions. This socialization creates a tongue-and-groove fit with female gender roles.

Training for Femininity

The Gentle Pink World. Female socialization is in sharp contrast to the male socialization we have just described. Girls enter the "pink world" at the moment of birth.[24] From the outset, female infants are handled more gently than males, without any substantial evidence of greater fragility. In fact, according to infant mortality figures, female neonates (children under one month of age) are more likely to survive the hazards of the neonatal period than are male infants. This differential gentleness toward the sexes continues to be evident from toddler to teenager in the rougher play between parents—particularly fathers—and sons.[25]

Little girls are more likely to be protected from physical harm, and parents are more apt to worry about the physical well-being of daughters, even as young as 9 months old.[26] This concern leads to greater restrictions on the physical activity of girls. Little girls are kept closer to home than their brothers, a pattern anthropologists have observed in preliterate as well as postindustrial societies.[27] This pattern of keeping little girls nearer home is also associated with assigning them household and childcare tasks at relatively early ages. The rough-and-tumble play studies described previously show girls less likely to engage in such behavior; however, it is not entirely clear how much this difference is related to different body structure and how much to different messages ("be a little lady") they receive from their caretakers.

The delicate clothes in which small girls customarily have been dressed created further limitations on their physical activities. In earlier historical periods, upper-class females required a maid's help to lace their petticoats and fasten their back-closing dresses. Social historians remind us that women's clothes buttoning to the left are vestigial evidence of that earlier time when buttons were placed to enable another person, usually a maid, to dress well-born females. These delicate and complicated clothes were meant to be handled carefully and to be kept clean, providing further restraints on females' physical activity and independence.

The recent trend toward dressing little girls in overalls or pants rather than dresses inevitably influences girls' physical activity. Graduating into blue jeans rather than skirts has already enabled teenage girls to shed certain physical limitations tied solely to restrictive clothing. Clothes that allow females to dress themselves and to move easily ultimately influence their self-confidence and independence. But the initial social resistance to unisex clothes and hairstyles might well be interpreted as reluctance to allow females to share in more unrestricted, and therefore particularly powerful, styles and symbols.

Toys and Games. Toys are the visible tools of early socialization, preparing children for adult roles.[28] The typical toys offered little girls are soft and unmechanical; boys are given mechanical toys, such as cars and tool kits to repair them. The closest thing to tools that girls receive are sewing kits. Dolls are the primary toys offered girls, and some researchers believe that through the play activity of talking to and caring for dolls, girls train themselves to be ideal recipients of gender-role socialization.[29]

As they grow older, girls are assigned small household and childcare responsibilities, part of the tasks they watch their mothers perform. Girls learn to wait on fathers and brothers, a lesson they will carry over into adult relationships with men. These early lessons in "servicing," "mothering," and "helping" are played out in the classroom, where third-grade girls often assist their male classmates in finding the correct page and following the teachers' instructions. Girls are more likely to be selected as teachers' helpers, except for the "heavy" tasks of cleaning erasers and moving classroom furniture.[30]

Unlike boys, little girls rarely play in large groups or teams.[31] Typically, they play in small two- or three-person groups, a pattern carried over into the teenage years. Not too long ago, competitive team sports were the exception rather than the rule for girls. Until the resurgent women's movement emphasized the importance of these games for adult skills, overt physical competition was still actively discouraged among females.

Not surprisingly, competition to win at games is less evident among girls. Little girls are taught that overt competition in general, much less against friends, is unfeminine. In the female world, friendship and relationships are more important than winning. Girls learn to select valued friends as playmates, even if the friend is less competent at the game than a nonfriend. One anthropological study of third-grade children observed little girls deliberately allowing their friends to win the race in the name of friendship.[32] This stands in direct contrast to the male pattern described earlier, in which boys are socialized to compete overtly, even against friends, to play to win, and to tolerate unliked teammates for the sake of the game. One result is that women are less prepared for the realities of Western organizational and political life, which require competition, team play, and a winning orientation.

Individual success is not the point in female socialization. Recent studies of female play strategies indicate that females are more likely to collaborate that compete with one another, particularly when the welfare of the group is at stake.[33] With friendship and relationships so highly valued in female socialization, it is not surprising that female achievement is cast within the context of relationships. Studies of gender differences in achieving styles by Lipman-Blumen, Leavitt, and their colleagues reveal that female groups, regardless of age, education or occupation, are less likely than matched male groups to select competitive means for accomplishing goals.[34] Rather than competing to win, females are far more apt to contribute to other people's success or take pleasure vicariously from the success of others. Trained that achievement comes through relationships, females develop a different view of life's goals and the strategies for accomplishing them.

Vicarious Achievement. Taught that overt competition is unfeminine, most girls learn to avoid it. They compete indirectly, by associating with males who are active competitors. Girls are taught the intricacies of vicarious achievement, learning to value roles such as the football hero's girlfriend, the president's wife, the vice-president's Girl Friday.[35] As we have seen, lists of most admired women are frequently dominated by the wives of famous men, with only a sprinkling of women whose own accomplishments have brought them public acclaim.

Since men's early and persistent control of societal and institutional resources made it difficult for women to compete against men, it is hardly surprising that women's competitive inclinations were channeled toward other women. Often women competed indirectly against other women through their links to highly competitive and successful men. Because association with powerful and resource-controlling men often was women's major, and sometimes only, route to success and power, females were socialized to compete with one another for marriage partners or other long-term liaisons. Before women could support themselves economically, and before divorce and remarriage became more possible, the stakes in such competition were exceedingly high. This was a woman's one and only chance. The outcome: Men became even more prized by women.

Schooled to compete subtly with one another for men, women rarely learned to work together for their own mutual interests—only, as we shall see, for the sake of others. While boys were trained to compete, to act directly in their own behalf, to gain power and resources, girls were socialized to view such overt competition and jockeying for success as unfeminine. Again, definitions of masculinity and femininity set limits on what women and men could or should do. And the misogyny (hatred of women) that males felt, females often accepted as an appropriate evaluation of themselves. Anna Freud has suggested that oppressed groups often internalize the negative stereotypes their oppressors use to describe them. So it was with women, who accepted the powerless, dependent, vicarious caricature the male culture painted of them. These negative images of women abound in the media, the arts, myths, and religion, as we shall see.

Defined Dependency and Timidity. Boys are socialized to be the stronger sex—to protect, sometimes to punish, weaker females. Girls are taught to accept the definition of their dependency. How, we might ask, do girls learn to see themselves, and therefore to act, as weaker and dependent?

Although on the average boys are indeed physically stronger than girls, it is clear that many girls are stronger than many boys, an often overlooked fact. Most seriously, this female dependence is accepted by girls as well, who are conditioned from birth to believe in their own helplessness and dependency.

Earlier we noted the studies of new parents who believed their newborn daughters were weaker and more delicate than male children, despite no measurable differences[36] Fathers, more than mothers, believe daughters are very fragile and therefore need protection. Daughters learn early that fathers "melt" in the face of little girls' helplessness (their first lesson in micromanipulation). As a result, female dependence is encouraged almost from the moment of birth. Fathers play less vigorously with their daughters, demonstrating their belief in girls' fragility and need for protection. And fathers, more than mothers, reward daughters for delicate, helpless, dependent behavior, and punish them more severely for competitive, aggressive, self-assertive, or "tomboy" actions. The lessons learned early in life are transferred to adult relationships with men. Tears are the expression of helplessness, and many women are conditioned to use tears as a powerful weapon. The tearful demonstration of powerlessness and dependence further convinces males and females alike that the "weaker sex" deserves this label.

Groomed to helplessness and dependence by fathers who love them and have their "best interests" at heart, girls are socialized to put their trust in their fathers, and later their boyfriends, husbands, and lovers. From there, it is a small step to entrusting their political fate to the male leaders of society. Fathers presumably act in the best interests of their offspring, so daughters learn to respect their fathers' "better judgment." Father, as the head of the house, is revered as the all-knowing and powerful parent. His help, particularly his access to resources, frequently is more critical and useful than the tender, weaker nurturance of Mother. Daughters, often the "apple of their father's eye," learn that dependence is one sure-fire trigger for father's help. Thus, females learn the subtle lesson of controlling the powerful through demonstrated helplessness. But this "learned helplessness" simultaneously entraps women.

Learning helplessness and dependence rather than self-assertion and self-reliance becomes a primary task of female socialization. This crippling dependence on men is transferred into adult life, where women are expected to depend on men in the home, the community, and at the nation's helm to see to their best interests. Many women learn too late that even the best-intentioned men may not understand women's best interests. Many discover they have surrendered power too willingly, and their dependence is too heavy a psychological mantle to cast aside easily. Men, bearing the yoke of power, protection, and responsibility, are harnessed into their own burdensome gender roles.

Timidity and fearfulness are other attributes females are socialized to include in their repertoire of gender characteristics. As we noted earlier, females begin to perceive themselves as more fearful than others, even when their actual behavior is no more hesitant or timid than that of individuals who define themselves as fearless. Taught to control their own anger and hostility, women learn to fear men whose socialization encourages the expression of negative emotions through violence. Learning to be afraid keeps women from pursuing their own self-interest. It throws them on the mercy and reliance of others who would act for them. It clears the way to dependence on powerful man whom they expect, sometimes unrealistically, to act chivalrously on their behalf. And although many, if not all, men are able to act protectively, even lovingly, toward a particular woman, they often do not recognize when this protection serves primarily to infantilize and cripple that woman. Furthermore, men commonly act with much greater indifference and even hostility toward women as a group.

Emotionality. According to most cultural stereotypes, females are more emotional than males. Few would dispute that females are socialized to express their emotions, or at least not suppress them. Researchers find little initial difference in emotional expression between preschool girls and boys.[37] What small difference exists seems to favor male children as more emotional—more likely to cry, more prone to angry outbursts.[38] But this early expression of emotionality is soon constrained, with boys being socialized to suppress emotions that do not express strength and power. Women, raised to believe that relationships are the primary tributary of all life's rewards, find little reason to repress affection and love. Madame de Stael caught this difference when she wrote in 1796: "Love is the whole history of a woman's life, it is but an episode in a man's." Lord Byron echoed this observation in *Don Juan* (1818): "Man's love is of man's life a thing apart, 'Tis women's whole existence."

Although somewhat overstated, such a tendency in Western culture is hardly surprising when we consider that girls are raised on love and affection, boys on challenge and demand. Withdrawal of love is the major disciplinary tool for girls, while physical punishment is more often used with boys. Withdrawing love trains the female child to depend on others' good will and affection. Physical punishment socializes young boys to a life of autonomy and self-reliance, unfettered by strong needs for the approval and affection of others. The love-and-affection-oriented upbringing of girls seems appropriately linked to the maternal role girls have been trained to expect and seek in adulthood. For many centuries, the wife and mother role has been the central, if not the only, role valued by parents for their daughters and, in turn, by daughters for themselves. Teaching daughters to expect and give love was ideal preparation for the maternal role. "Love and/or duty" was the motto of the female world.[39] Here girls learned to set aside their own embryonic longings for worldly accomplishments, leadership, and resources to tend to the needs of others, particularly male family members.

Nurturance, which Webster defines as affectionate care and attention, is another quality highly valued in females. Nurturance is a key ingredient in the traditional roles assigned to females: mother, wife, teacher, nurse, babysitter, secretary, social worker. Here too, research on very young children fails to demonstrate any marked tendency on the part of girls to outdistance their male age-mates in nurturance. A six-culture study conducted during the 1950s that observed children in naturalistic settings concluded that among children aged 3 to 6 no differences in nurturance were observable. There was slight evidence that at 7 to 11 years old girls were somewhat more likely to be supportive or offer help to others. These data suggest that in-born nurturance differences between the genders are not evident, and what slight differences do occur among children appear only among somewhat older children, well into gender-linked socialization.[40] In fact, even when differences do appear, they do not always occur in the direction gender stereotypes would lead us to expect. For example, in Okinawa, anthropologists report, boys are more nurturant than girls.

Some hint of how females' nurturant behavior and attitudes flow from societal expectations and training comes from a study in which male and female college students were asked to record their responses to infant monkeys and apes (and so, presumably, to human infants). Certain groups responded publicly, others privately. Those groups that recorded their reactions privately showed no differences between male and female responses. Among the groups responding publicly, however, clear gender differences emerged. Women obliged to respond in the presence of others gave more positive average scores than women answering privately. Men gave more negative answers in public.[41] This and other research suggest that response to social expectations makes women and men conform more closely to the gender-role attitudes and behavior they perceive are expected of them.

If women learn through socialization that emotional support, affection, and tenderness are important components of the female gender role, they also discern that anger, at least interpersonal anger, is not an acceptable part of the female emotional vocabulary. Only anger at social injustices to others has been allowed women, an emotional loophole that has enabled them to move beyond homebound roles into political movements. How to deal with their anger at injustice to women, however, still remains a problem for many women.

Soothing the anger of others, playing the peacemaker role, at least at the interpersonal (if not the international) level, are important components of the female stereotype. Trained to calm the troubled emotional waters of the men and children in their lives, women fall prey to the illusion that their own temperaments are far removed from such anger and competitiveness. This idealization and limitation of women's emotional spectrum have entrapped women, hampering their advance toward worldly goals reserved for those more willing to battle for position and power. Men, themselves caught in the emotional cage of anger, aggression, and stoicism, are often prevented from seeking more comforting experiences as well.

POWERLESSNESS: A SELF-FULFILLING PROPHECY

Groomed from early childhood to bridle their anger and ambition, females soon learn that their psyches and intellects are bent into a position of powerlessness. Much as the ancient Chinese custom of binding young girls' feet to symbolize femininity and social class left women crippled as adults, so Western culture has bound the minds and emotions of females, with comparable results. Raised to please their fathers by acting dependent, even helpless, young women learn that independence, autonomy, and aggressive striving for the nonmaternal rewards of society may mark them as deviant and unfeminine.

The weak, as Elizabeth Janeway notes, develop their own powers.[42] They learn to read the faces and minds of the powerful, to anticipate their needs, to avoid their anger. Learning to monitor and understand the feelings and expectations of the powerful (in this case men), women develop skills at interpreting nonverbal behavior—a talent society labels "feminine intuition" and "empathy."

Researchers have studied the special skill women display in understanding nonverbal behavior.[43] Small children are also adept at interpreting and anticipating their parents' moods and reactions. By adulthood, males who command the resources of the society are less dependent on the good will of those whose compliance they can force. As a result, their ability to interpret others' nonverbal behavior falls into disuse. Adult females, however, must continue to anticipate the wishes of the powerful in order to maintain their own tenuous position. If such necessity provokes behavior that is then labeled "intuitive," "nurturant," "empathetic," or "people-oriented," it surely provides a euphemistic view of dependence and powerlessness.

This self-concept of helplessness and dependence, coupled with nurturance, intuition, and people orientation, leads women to fashion adult lives consistent with this definition. Until quite recently, many women evolved self-images that denied their ability to handle "powerful" decision-making roles in organizations, but saw no contradiction with the maternal role and its control over children, other family members, and household decisions. Some observers believe this negative self-picture has been one component in women's acceptance of the social barriers that keeps females from entering the professions and other high-level occupational and societal roles. Socialization for dependence and helplessness, linked with nurturance and affection, inevitably became a self-fulfilling prophecy. Other analysts warn us against blaming the victim. Society's structural barriers, including laws and informal institutional practices, create additional insurmountable obstacles to individuals with limited societal resources, not to mention dependent self-images.

Since the women's movement undertook to raise not only the consciousness but the self-image of women, psychological and emotional barriers, as well as legal and structural obstacles, have begun to crumble. The new wave of feminine self-reliance, assertion, and independence is evident in the growing numbers of women of all ages in the labor force in what were once nontraditional jobs. This new self-assertion by women is a monumental feat, in light of the gender-linked training females receive from parents, teachers, and other impersonal agents of socialization. It is all the more remarkable in light of the pervasive gender-coded socialization messages that emanate from earlier civilizations and form the core of control myths.

SUMMARY

Socialization is a complex set of processes, covert and explicit, that train individuals to take their places as responsible members of society. Sex and gender role socialization occurs over the entire life span, instilling females and males with behaviors and attitudes deemed "appropriate" for each gender.

Through games, team sports, family and school activities, little boys enter the "blue world" of masculinity. Stoicism, aggression, fearlessness, leadership, and power are the building blocks of masculinity. Media reinforce the message. Despite no proven innate predisposition to such modes of behavior, by school age young boys are well on their way toward mastering these basics of masculinity.

Girls too learn through play, school, and family life that they are being groomed for adult lives marked by emotionality, passivity or dependence, fearfulness, and obedience. Until recently, girls' play activities and dress were geared to physically more restrictive conditions. Trained to achieve vicariously through successful males, young girls have been conditioned to set their individual needs aside to assist and nurture others. Bridling their aggression and anger, females have been schooled to make powerlessness and dependence a self-fulfilling prophecy. Rewarded for helplessness by fathers who set stricter gender-linked standards for both sons and daughters, girls learn that male power and protection are the "natural" accompaniment to female powerlessness and dependence. Only recently has attention to the negative effects of such highly differentiated gender roles created a milieu for reevaluating socialization processes.

NOTES

1. Jeffrey Z. Rubin, Frank J. Provenzano, and Zella Luria, "The Eye of the Beholder: Parents' Views on Sex of Newborns," *American Journal of Orthopsychiatry*, 44, 4 (1974), 512–19.

2. Jerrie Will, Patricia Self, and Nancy Datan (unpublished paper presented at 82nd annual meeting of the American Psychological Association, 1974), described in Carol Tavris and Carole Offir, *The Longest War: Sex Differences in Perspective* (New York: Harcourt Brace Jovanovich, 1977).

3. Carol N. Jacklin, "Sex Differences and their Relationship to Sex Equity in Learning and Teaching" (paper prepared for the National Institute of Education, Washington, D.C., Sept., 1977).

4. Eleanor E. Maccoby and Carol N. Jacklin, *The Psychology of Sex Differences* (Stanford, Cal.: Stanford University Press, 1974).

5. R. L. Munroe and R. H. Munroe, "Effect of Environmental Experience on Spatial Ability in East African Society," *Journal of Social Psychology, 83 (1971), 15–22; S. B. Nerlove, R. H. Munroe, and R. L. Munroe, "Effects of Environmental Experience on Spatial Ability: A Replication," Journal of Social Psychology* 84 (1971), 3–10.

6. L. A. Serbin, K. D. O'Leary, R. N. Kent, and I. J. Tonick, "A Comparison of Teacher Response to the Pre-academic and Problem Behavior of Boys and Girls," *Child Development,* 44 (1973), 796–804.

7. A. T. Jersild and F. B. Holmes, "Children's Fears," *Child Development Monographs* (1935), p. 20.

8. G. W. Bronson, "Infants' Reactions to Unfamiliar Persons and Novel Objects,"

Monographs of the Society for Research in Child Development (1972), p. 37; H. R. Schaffer and M. H. Parry, "Effects of Stimulus Movement on Infants' Wariness of Unfamiliar Objects," *Developmental Psychology* 7 (1972), 87; D. Baumrind and A. E. Black, "Socialization Practices Associated with Dimensions of Competence in Preschool Boys and Girls," *Child Development* 38 (1967), 291–327.

9.   A. Bandura, E. B. Blanchard, and B. Ritter, "Relative Efficacy of Desensitization and Modeling Approaches for Inducing Behavioral, Affective, and Attitudinal Changes," *Journal of Personality and Social Psychology* 13, 3 (1969), 173–99.

10.   Ibid.

11.   Erik H. Erikson, 1971, personal communication.

12.   Eleanor E. Maccoby and Carol N. Jacklin, *The Psychology of Sex Differences* (Stanford, Cal.: Stanford University Press, 1974).

13.   Beatrice Whiting and Carolyn Pope, "A Cross-cultural Analysis of Sex Differences in the Behavior of Children Aged Three to Eleven," *Journal of Social Psychology* 92 (1974).

14.   Mirra Komarovsky, *Women in the Modern World: Their Education and their Dilemmas,* (Boston: Little, Brown, 1953), p. 51.

15.   Lillian Rubin, *Worlds of Pain* (New York: Basic Books, 1976).

16.   S. S. Feldman, "Some Possible Antecedents of Attachment Behavior in Two-Year-Old Children" (unpublished manuscript, Stanford University, 1974); R. S. Marvin, "Attachment and Communicative Behavior in Two-, Three-, and Four-Year-Old Children" (unpublished doctoral dissertation, University of Chicago, 1971); M. Shirley and L. Poyntz, "The Influence of Separation from the Mother on Children's Emotional Responses," *Journal of Psychology,* 12 (1941), 251–82.

17.   E. E. Maccoby and S. S. Feldman, "Mother-Attachment and Stranger-Reactions in the Third Year of Life," *Monographs of the Society for Research in Child Development* (1972), p. 37.

18.   F. L. Goodenough, *Anger in Young Children* (Minneapolis: University of Minnesota Press, 1931); C. Landreth, "Factors Associated with Crying in Young Children in the Nursery School and the Home," *Child Development* 12 (1941), 81–97; Maccoby and Feldman, "Mother Attachment," p. 37. O. F. M. Van Lieshout, "Reactions of Young Children to Barriers Placed by their Mothers" (unpublished manuscript, Stanford University, 1974.)

19.   Maccoby and Jacklin, *Sex Differences* 1974.

20.   C. Hutt, *Males and Females* (Middlesex, England: Penguin Books, 1972); D. A. Hamburg and J. Van Lawick-Goodall, "Factors Facilitating Development of Aggressive Behavior in Chimpanzees and Humans" (unpublished manuscript, Stanford University, 1973); S. Levine, "Sexual Differentiation: The Development of Maleness and Femaleness," *California Medicine* 114 (1971), 12–17; D. T. Lunde, "Sex Hormones, Mood and Behavior" (paper presented at the Sixth Annual Symposium, Society of Medical Psychoanalysis, New York, 1973); J. Money and A. A. Ehrhardt, *Man and Woman, Boy and Girl* (Baltimore: Johns Hopkins University Press, 1972); Maccoby and Jacklin, *Sex Differences,* 1974.

21.   For reviews of the 1930s and 1940s literature, see L. M. Terman and L. E. Tyler, "Psychological Sex Differences," ed. L. Carmichael, *Manual of Child Psychology,* 2nd ed. (New York: Wiley, 1954); for the 1950s and 1960s research, see R. M. Oetzel, "Annotated Bibliography and Classified Summary of Research in Sex Differences," ed. E. E. Maccoby, *The Development of Sex Differences* (Stanford, Cal.: Stanford University Press, 1966; and for still later research reviews, see Maccoby and Jacklin, "Sex Differences," 1974.

22.   D. R. Omark, M. Omark, and M. Edelman, "Dominance Hierarchies in Young Children" (paper presented at International Congress of Anthropological and Ethnological Sciences, Chicago, 1973); Whiting and Pope, "Cross-cultural Analysis of Sex Differences," 1974.

23.   *Maccoby and Jacklin, Sex Differences,* p. 227.

24.   Jessie Bernard, *The Female World* (New York: The Free Press, 1981).

25.   H. A. Moss, "Sex, Age, and State as Determinants of Mother-Infant Interaction," *Merrill-Palmer Quarterly,* 13 (1967), 19–36; L. F. Yarrow, J. L. Rubenstein, and F. A. Pedersen, "Dimensions of Early Stimulation: Differential Effects on Infant Development" (paper presented at the meeting of the Society for Research in Child Development, 1971); R. J. Tasch, "The Role of Father in the Family," *Journal of Experimental Education,* 20 (1952), 319–61.

26. F. A. Pedersen and K. S. Robson, "Father Participation in Infancy," *American Journal of Orthopsychiatry,* 39 (1969), 466–72; C. Minton, J. Kagan, and J. A. Levine, "Maternal Control and Obedience in the Two-Year-Old," *Child Development,* 42 (1971), 1873–94.

27. Beatrice Whiting (informal seminar on Sex Roles at the Center for Advanced Study in the Behavioral Sciences, Palo Alto, California, 1978).

28. Erikson, personal communication, 1971.

29. Lenore J. Weitzman, *Sex Role Socialization: A Focus on Women* (Palo Alto, Cal.: Mayfield Publishing Co., 1979).

30. Raphaela Best, *We've All Got Scars: What Boys and Girls Learn in Elementary School* (Bloomington: University of Indiana Press, 1983).

31. Maccoby and Jacklin, *Sex Differences,* 1974.

32. Best, *We've All Got Scars,* 1983.

33. Jean Lipman-Blumen, Harold J. Leavitt, Kerry J. Patterson, Robert J. Bies, and Alice Handley-Isaksen, "A Model of Direct and Relational Achieving Styles," in *Achievement Motivation: Recent Trends in Theory and Research,* Leslie J. Fyans, Jr., ed. (New York: Plenum Press, 1980), pp. 135–168.

34. Jean Lipman-Blumen, Alice Handley-Isaksen, Harold J. Leavitt, "Achieving Styles in Men and Women: A Model, an Instrument, and Some Findings," in *Achievement and Achievement Motives,* Janet Spence, ed. (San Francisco, Cal.: W. H. Freeman, 1983), pp. 151–204.

35. Jean Lipman-Blumen, "The Vicarious Achievement Ethic and Nontraditional Roles for Women" (paper presented at the forty-third annual meeting of the Eastern Sociological Society, New York, 1973).

36. Rubin, Provenzano, and Luria, "The Eye of the Beholder," pp. 512–19.

37. Maccoby and Jacklin, *Sex Differences,* 1974.

38. Feldman, "Some Possible Antecedents of Attachment Behavior," 1974; Marvin, "Attachment," 1971.

39. Bernard, *Female World,* 1981.

40. Beatrice Whiting and Carolyn Pope Edwards, "A Cross-cultural Analysis of Sex Differences in the Behavior of Children Aged Three Through Eleven," *Journal of Social Psychology,* 91 (1973), 171–188; also second half, vol. 92, (1974).

41. Phyllis W. Berman, "Attraction to Infants: Are Sex Differences Innate and Invariant?" (paper presented at the eighty-third annual meeting of the American Psychological Association, Chicago, Illinois, 1975).

42. Elizabeth Janeway, *Powers of the Weak* (New York: Alfred A. Knopf, Inc., 1980).

43. Robert Rosenthal, Judith A. Hall, M. Robin, D. Matteo, Peter L. Rogers, Dane Archer, *Sensitivity to Nonverbal Communication* (Baltimore: Johns Hopkins University Press, 1979).

CHAPTER 7
THE PENTIMENTO OF ANCIENT GENDER IMAGES AND CONTEMPORARY CONTROL MYTHS

Socialization occurs not only through individual "agents of socialization," but also through the more pervasive social context. This social milieu—melding art, literature, and mass media—is enriched by images handed down from earlier civilizations. In pentimento fashion, each succeeding civilization paints over the canvas of previous cultures, yet the earlier images of masculinity and femininity bleed through even the most contemporary gender role portraits. These ancient images form the nucleus of full-blown control myths that shape behavior, values, and attitudes.

THE LEGACY OF ANCIENT CIVILIZATIONS

A thorough search into the treasure trove of ancient civilizations would exceed the scope of this book, but the importance of prehistoric and biblical gender role images demands that we attempt to trace their expressions in contemporary control myths. Archetypal depictions of women and men are the legacy of civilizations predating biblical times. Mythologists, poets, and feminist theorists, working from different vantage points, look to civilizations as early as 25,000 B.C. as the original wellsprings of powerful feminine images. Primitive myths and archeological findings are offered to support their claims regarding early goddess-worshipping religions, which later scholars trivialized as fertility cults.

Complex and conflicting speculations about gender roles in ancient civilizations abound. One group of noted poets and mythologists, including Robert Graves, Joseph Campbell, and others, argues that until the Late Bronze Age, worship of female creative power was a natural complement to primitive awe of other natural forces. The feminine life force was seen as part of nature, from the natural sequence of the seasons, to the extraordinary, awe-inspiring occurrences of thunder, lightning, floods, earthquakes, and eclipses. Birth, life, and death, which seemed to emanate from women's bodies, were perceived as the guiding rhythms of nature. Harmony with nature, even submission to the rhythms of nature (the feminine principle), guided every aspect of life. Not until many millennia had passed would the masculine principle of domination over nature through technology emerge.

Linked in this way to all other natural forces, women's seemingly magical powers were visible in at least four phenomena: (1) women's menstrual cycle enabled them to bleed for seemingly superhuman lengths of time without succumbing from blood loss; (2) women brought forth other smaller bodies, male as well as female, from deep within their own, without any apparent male contribution; (3) women transformed their bodies into sources of life-sustaining milk for the infants they so magically created; and (4) women exhibited a sexuality that seemed inexhaustible, powerful, and profound. These were truly supernatural and awe-inspiring wonders to the primitive mind.

That such inordinate powers could inspire hostility as well as awe, two sides of the same coin, is an obvious psychological phenomenon in the post-Freudian era. And ancient myths provide evidence of both feelings toward women. These residues of ancient civilizations depict women not only as life-bearers and goddesses, but also as witches, spell casters, contamination breeders, and death carriers. Women's alleged power to control both men and weaker women prompted fear and hostility. Modern-day analysts see these reactions transmuted into deep-seated responses toward the maternal figure, as well as into collective misogyny.

Not until the period of the Paleolithic hunt, which demanded a more nomadic life style, did the ascendance of the feminine principle weaken. The nomadic life, focusing on the hunt for bison, demanded the long-muscle running ability of males. A budding awareness of the male contribution to conception began to diminish the awe-inspiring image of females. Magic worship, which previously centered on female genitalia, now concentrated instead on the male phallus. Animals hunted by males, rather than plants cultivated by females, characterized the Paleolithic mythology. During this era, male shamans (priests or medicine men) assumed an importance that offset the power of female deities. Pictorial evidence of this crucial sociological shift is found in the deep temple caves in the south of France and Spain, where paintings of bulls, bison, and male shamans cover the walls.

Female metaphysical supremacy continued in most regions as long as the male role in procreation was not fully recognized—that is, at least until the end of the Bronze Age. Archeologists report that the Great Goddess, the center of numerous belief systems, continued to reign in Minoan Crete and Mycenae between Sumer and post-Homeric Greece, and that the transformation from female to male metaphysical dominance took place over several millennia. The transition occurred in different places at different times. According to numerous authorities, recognition of the male contribution to conception developed somewhere between the fifth and third or second millennia B.C., the period of the Late Bronze Age.

The Neolithic revolution, with its emerging technology, forged a new relationship between humans and nature. People began to harness, not worship, nature. Cremation, an attempt to escape the decay destined by nature (the female principle), began in the Neolithic era. Cremation offered a revolt against returning in death to "Mother Earth" and contrasted sharply with the careful burial customs of Great Mother-worshipping societies, which curled the dead in the fetal position, prepared to reenter the womb (the earth). The growing understanding of the male's participation in human conception thus contributed to the overturn of matriarchal mythologies. Patriarchal interpretation of mythology created a new pantheon, and the entire symbolism, previously oriented toward the moon (female principle), shifted toward sun worship, representing the male principle.

Pre-Hellenic and Classical Greek Mythology

Before the transformation from Minoan-Mycenaen culture (1500 to 1100 B.C.) to the post-Homeric classical Greek period, the female-oriented world continued to exist. The cosmology of pre-Hellenic Greece centered on a pantheon of goddesses. The Earth Mother appeared in various aspects under different names: Gaia, Pandora, Themis, Aphrodite, Leto, Rhea, Britomaris, Diktynna, Artemis, Selene, Hecate, Hera, Athena, Demeter, Persephone. In the oral tradition that predated the written classical myths of Hesiod and Homer, the universal Earth Mother, Gaia, created the world, bringing forth human life from "the gaping void, Chaos."[1] Pandora, the maiden form of the Earth Goddess, was the "giver of all gifts."[2] Themis embodied the social order, community, justice, and law.[3] Athena was the guardian of the home, and Aphrodite the goddess of fertility.

The deities of the Dorian invaders soon supplanted the benevolent pre-Hellenic female pantheon. Classical Greek mythology, written and therefore more readily preserved as "authoritative," presented remote, judgmental, angry, belligerent male gods in whom the goddesses' benevolent characterizations were inverted and distorted. The myths of the classical period transformed the pre-Hellenic sacred tales, changing the descriptions of harmony between humans and nature to a vision of celestially imposed patriarchal authority.

Changes in mythology and cosmology reflected the different religious and political structure imposed by the conquering invaders. The new political order, symbolized by a change in the power structure and predominating gender of the pantheon, suggests the archetypal meaning of gender roles for all power relationships. Goddesses representing life, nourishment, regeneration, and forgiveness were transformed into sources of treachery, human misery, sexual promiscuity, and male destruction. No longer awestruck by the "magic" of female procreative and sexual prowess, classical Greek mythology emphasized the danger of female sexuality, with its power to seduce men and destroy their self-control and physical prowess, as well as their social and political power.

This new patriarchal order, with Zeus at its apex, appeared in approximately 2500 B.C. Abraham, the original Old Testament patriarch, was described much later, around 1800 B.C. according to biblical scholars. The goddess religion, dating as far back as 25,000 B.C., had become transmuted and inverted. By the biblical period, followers of matriarchal religions were regarded as dangerous pagans.

The Old Testament

Drawing on Babylonian mythology, the Hebrews developed their own view of the universe. Their patriarchal view of the relationship between women and men, modeled on the covenant between humans and God, symbolized all power relationships in society. The Old Testament myths, some inverting Sumerian mythological poetry, cast the gender relationship in a new, more negative light.

A prime example of the Hebrew transformation to a patriarchal order is the Garden of Eden myth, adapted from the Sumerian poem "Enki and Ninhursag," in which the great goddess Ninhursag punishes, but later forgives, two jealous, treacherous male gods for picking and devouring the plants she raises to nourish the world. In the Old Testament version, the great goddess has become an unforgiving male Yahweh, who condemns the snake (from Sumerian to pre-Aryan Indian times a deity of regeneration and immortality) to eternal contempt. Eve, depicted as the temptress responsible for Adam's fall, is cursed threefold; not only is she banished forever from the Garden of Eden along with Adam, but henceforth she is to bring forth children in pain and sorrow; and finally—perhaps most important—she must submit eternally to the authority, as well as the sexual domination, of Adam. Adam's punishment is the loss of paradise; curiously, however, he becomes Eve's perpetual master.

Eve's intellectual curiosity, a trait ordinarily valued by Hebrew scholars when exhibited by males, is reduced to petty inquisitiveness. In the numerous biblical commentaries on this myth, little attention is paid to Eve's desire for knowledge as the first step toward human understanding and self-reliance. Her willingness to share this power-confirming knowledge with her mate is portrayed as an act of seduction and weakness. The message is clear. Woman's quest for knowledge leads to disaster; her efforts to share knowledge, and hence responsibility and power, are to be punished. The punishment is ingeniously designed to rob Eve of her power in two critical respects: (1) Woman's awe-inspiring capacity to bring forth life is now encumbered with toil and pain, transformed from the effortless event that bedazzled her male worshippers; and (2) her role is dramatically reduced to subservient handmaiden to her male spouse.

Numerous other Old Testament images of the gender relationship emphasize the power struggle between women and men. They clearly convey the message that the only proper relationship is one of male control and female subordination and obedience. Lot's wife turns to a pillar of salt because she disobeys her husband's command not to look back at Sodom. In these biblical tales, the power relationship between husband and wife is modeled on the relationship the Old Testament describes between God and humans and is therefore imbued with special sacred legitimacy. We see the mystification of men's and women's roles occurring within the Old Testament; man rules over woman and society in the name of God, paralleling the ultimate power relationship.

The Old Testament repeatedly underscores the importance of powerful, patriarchal men, and women's emotional and economic dependence on these men. The story of Sarah and Hagar symbolizes how women must compete for powerful males, since female power and identity are derived from these heterosexual connections. Sarah, dismayed by the pregnant Hagar's disdain for Sarah's infertility, sends away her husband's concubine—two women competing through sexuality and child-bearing capacity for the love, status, and protection of a powerful patriarch.

We also read clear messages about the danger of female sexuality, a seductive medium for subverting male power. The Delilah and Samson story encodes this message. Sexual encounters with women can be defiling. Paradoxically, women are particularly contaminating during or directly after menstruation and childbirth, two previously awe-inspiring events. The very sources of women's power in earlier civilizations are now portrayed as setting women apart, this time in a negative, repugnant manner. Inverting women's powers into sources of uncleanliness and defilement offered one clear solution to the threat they posed. The Old Testament and related scholarly commentaries meticulously document not only the procedures for isolating women during these contaminating periods, but also those for restoring feminine purity. These ancient writings offer prescriptions for male purification after contact with "unclean" women.

"Are there no admirable, strong, awe-inspiring women in the Old Testament?" we might ask. Indeed, several praiseworthy female characters are portrayed: Judith the judge, Ruth, and Queen Esther, to name a few of the better-known biblical heroines. Ruth, the most renowned minor female biblical figure, virtuously sets aside her personal needs to follow the surrogate of her deceased husband—her mother-in-law, Naomi. Her words, "Whither thou goest, I shall go," . . . "Your God shall be my God," are those of the archetypal obedient wife. That she says them to the mother of her dead husband indicates that the obedience and loyalty wives owe husbands transcend even death.

The message of a strong partiarchal social order in which the earthly reflection of the covenant between humans and God is the power relationship between woman and man rings loud and clear in the Old Testament. Male and female gender role images are unequivocally differentiated. Swift and harsh punishment is meted out to those who would challenge the gender role models and the underlying power relationship.

The New Testament

The New Testament perpetuates the patriarchal orientation of the Old Testament. The parallel between the human relationship with God and woman's union with man is a theme that threads its way through the verses of the New Testament. In Ephesians 5:22–24, for example, wives and husbands are advised:

> Wives, submit yourselves unto your own husbands, as unto the Lord.
> For the husband is the head of the wife, even as Christ is the head
> of the church; and he is the saviour of the body.

Therefore as the church is subject unto Christ, so *let* the wives *be*
to their own husbands in every thing.
Husbands, love your wives, even as Christ also loved the church,
and gave himself for it.

Paul uses the marriage metaphor to depict the closeness between God and
his people. Human marriage takes on a new meaning through this sacred
association.

The patriarchy of the New Testament is also evident in the Trinity,
which represents a male godhead. The Father, Son, and Holy Ghost are
male power figures. The central female figure, the Virgin Mary, harks back
to the parthenogenesis (reproduction by an unfertilized ovum) of the goddess religions; Mary conceives her child by Immaculate Conception. Still, the
Virgin Mother remains outside the male trinity. She is subservient to the
male principle.

Scholars now acknowledge that Mary was restored to a more important role in the Christian tradition primarily to draw converts from Medi-
terranean and Celtic cultures, more accustomed to the female figures of
earlier goddess religions. Recent scholarly work suggests that Mary's re-
trieval from oblivion by Constantine was an important turning point in the
acceptance of Christianity. Presumably, St. Patrick's recognition that the
totally male character of Christianity impeded its acceptance in areas where
goddess religions previously prevailed led to Mary's official religious
restoration.

Unlike pre-biblical deities, who created life unassisted but took male
lovers, the Virgin Mary is totally asexual. She contrasts sharply with the
other strong female role model of the New Testament: the repentant
prostitute, whose sexual defilement is purified by her acceptance of and
dedication to Christ. These two models, the asexual saint and the sexual
sinner, emerge as the two strongest feminine images in the New Testament,
images that persist over the centuries, through secular myth and contemporary media, to the present time. These biblical images—Eve, Delilah, Lot's
wife, Sarah, the Virgin Mary, and the prostitute—have left a powerful, if
sometimes contradictory, residue in Western culture. Portraits of female
weakness, petty curiosity, subordination, deceit, castration, disobedience,
defilement, contamination, jealousy, asexuality, passivity, and sexual excess
abound. Female sexuality is depicted as a dynamic weapon, sometimes the
only weapon of power left to women.

Several minor female figures are portrayed more positively in the
Bible. Their deeds are admirable, but they lack both the grandeur and
power of their male counterparts, as well as the drama and centrality of their
better-known sisters. The resounding message of the Bible—Old and New
Testaments alike—is the necessity of an unquestioning patriarchal order
between the sexes. Men rule, women obey; men exercise authority, women
follow their direction. Those women who are passive, obedient, asexual, and
accommodating, who assist men in their labors, who take men's gods and
goals for their own, resisting temptation to exercise their own power, are
worthy. The men of the Old Testament, patriarchal, authoritative, God-
fearing, acting in God's name, sexual, powerful, daring, and bellicose, know

they are born to dominate women, weaker males, and nature. The masculine images of the New Testament are more passive, less sexual. Nonetheless, even New Testament males are served and adored by women.

The gender-role message of the New Testament uses the male figure of Christ to convey female values of love, acceptance, and self-sacrifice. This message, closely akin to the contemporary female stereotype, no doubt complicates Western civilization's understanding of appropriate gender roles. Women, the most faithful churchgoers, are socialized to offer love, acceptance, and self-sacrifice to those males who exercise power, make demands and decisions, and bend all others to help meet their own defined expectations.

CONTEMPORARY CONTROL MYTHS

The significance of these ancient gender-role images lies in their power to distill a set of control myths or social stereotypes about the "true nature" of women and men. Once internalized, these myths serve as self-control mechanisms used by both genders to regulate their own behavior and attitudes. The socialization efforts of parents, teachers, and others are strengthened by these powerful myths. In this way, society completes its socialization work; males and females learn to control themselves through internalized beliefs about appropriate gender-role behavior.

Roland Barthes, the twentieth-century philosopher-linguist, argues that societies create "signs"—that is, meanings and definitions—which eventually appear inevitable, natural, indeed, the very "nature" of the social phenomena they describe. Language, Barthes contends, is simply a sign system used by the powerful to define, label, evaluate, and rank-order. This sign system creates the illusion of simply describing the innate essence of phenomena, when in reality it is deliberately chosen by the powerful to depict the world they would have. This "naturalized" language crystallizes into myths, which lie at the core of stereotypes. Barthes's concern for the sign systems used by the powerful guided his explorations of mythologies, in which he probed the ways in which a "society produces stereotypes, i.e., triumphs of artifice, which it then [accepts] as innate meanings, i.e., triumphs of Nature."[4] According to Barthes, humans deny their responsibility for creating these definitions and rank-orderings of social phenomena, including categories of people. Instead, Barthes assures us, people lay the blame on "nature"—the innate essence of things. Refusing to recognize the human role in creating these sign symbols encourages people to accept them as valid and inevitable.

Women and men alike are encumbered by control myths, those conscious and unconscious beliefs about the "intrinsic nature" of the two sexes inspired by ancient images. Both gender groups internalize beliefs about so-called appropriate, even natural, characteristics society expects them to develop. Once internalized, these myths become potent social mechanisms, used by males and females to keep themselves and one another in their "appropriate"—but vastly unequal—places. Both women and men are socialized to believe that these distinctive gender traits are designed to facilitate complementary relationships between the genders. That this complementarity, based largely on stereotypes packaged as control myths, masks an unequal power balance is only now beginning to be understood.

Control Myth # 1: Women are weak, passive, dependent, and fearful; men are strong, aggressive, independent and fearless.

Control Myth #1 depicts women as weak, passive, dependent, and fearful. It draws men as strong, aggressive, independent, and fearless. The research reviewed earlier (see Chapter 1) suggests that, from the child's first day of life, parents "perceive" such differences, even when scientists examining these infants disconfirm these impressions. Parental expectations eventually produce the characteristics originally imagined—the self-fulfilling prophecy at work. The expectations of teachers, relatives, and eventually peers move the process along.

Little girls learn that displaying "male traits"—strength, aggression, independence, and fearlessness—will only yield trouble. As youngsters, such behavior will earn girls the label "tomboy," a mark of pride in pre-adolescent childhood but a dubious and painful epithet for adolescent girls. Gender identity is an essential component of one's self-image. To attack a youngster's gender identity is to strike at the heart of his or her sense of self. Small wonder labeling girls "tomboys" and boys "sissies" is a forceful tool in controlling behavior. Boys suffer perhaps even more than girls, because being likened to the weaker, less valued group is naturally more demeaning than being compared to the stronger, superior group.

Although scientific evidence of hormonal sources of aggression continues to be debated, little girls eventually learn that dependent, weak, passive, and frightened actions—so-called "female traits"—are rewarded positively, particularly by fathers, and later by other male figures. Little girls learn at their father's knee that independence, assertiveness and strength (power) are unladylike traits that evoke punishment. In Shakespeare's *The Taming of the Shrew*, Kate's father seeks a son-in-law to tame his daughter's independence, even if by physical force. Bianca, Kate's gentler, passive sister, is the ideal picture of feminine obedience and congeniality. The Garden of Eden story, as we saw, also warns of the divine wrath women will stir by expressing strength or self-reliance through independent behavior.

In a previous chapter, we saw how little girls learn to believe they are afraid and to describe themselves as fearful, even when their behavior is no different from boys who describe themselves as unafraid. This self-description as fearful sets the stage for girls to agree with boys that they do, indeed, need male protection. It creates a "natural" setting for life-long female subordination and male liability—"tender traps" for both.

Little boys learn that they must exhibit not only fearlessness, but also strength and independence. If their hormones predispose males to aggression, socialization encourages its expression. Overcoming maternal (female) power through self-assertion, independence, and aggression is a fundamental task of male adolescence, according to psychoanalytic theory. To reach adulthood, males must demonstrate their independence and difference from, as well as their power over, women. Even under fear-provoking conditions, men learn they must act fearless; to be well-regarded, they must prove themselves stronger, more independent, and more aggressive than women.

The great warriors of myth and history have been men. Waging war, an exclusively male activity, is the archetypal demonstration of power. Few women join the ranks of warriors; instead, they and their children become the victims, often the booty of war. The well-known and recently much-criticized "macho" orientation of men is external evidence of Control Myth 1's message: men rule, women obey. Each group learns its appropriate part and acts accordingly.

This internalization of the dependent-independent, weak-strong, passive-aggressive, fearful-fearless contrast between women and men is the underpinning of a social order in which men are expected to be stronger— physically, intellectually, and politically—than women. It is an easy step from believing in one's own weakness to entrusting oneself to the protection and control of the stronger and smarter group. Women, accepting the myth, have been taught to keep themselves from acting independent and strong. Socialized to believe dependent, passive, and obedient behavior is more feminine, many women deferentially step aside to allow men to operate the levers of institutional power. Any other female behavior would be a clear violation of the norms imposed by this primary control myth.

Men, also submitting to the norms implied by this myth, accept the burden, as well as the rewards, of societal responsibility. Having internalized the expectations (if not the firm belief) of their own strength, independence, and aggression, they understand from early childhood that they are expected to undertake important and responsible tasks in adulthood. Little boys are trained to be responsible, to protect little girls, whom they perceive as weak and dependent on stronger males (even when the girls can fend for themselves). As adults, men continue to regard themselves as more powerful than women, and therefore rightfully "in charge." They eventually recognize that the protection and support of women is an inescapable male burden, one few men can abandon without guilt. Learning to take responsibility for themselves and others builds self-confidence, even the illusion that they are in control of life. This perception stifles any lingering self-doubts, teaching individuals to act despite unresolved fears. The consequent increase in self-esteem may offset the burden of assuming responsibility for others.

Women learn something very different: to feel impotent and fearful, to need protection. This "trained incapacity" or "learned helplessness" keeps women powerless. From this enfeebled position, the protection proffered by the powerful seems welcome; the control it entails becomes a necessary, perhaps initially unnoticed, tradeoff.

Built into this control myth is a belief that the power relationship between women and men is modeled on the ultimate power relationship many religions describe between humankind and a supreme being. Several implications flow from this religious analogy: First, the relationship is part of the divine or sacred order and therefore immutable; second, the powerless owe obedience and service to the powerful in exchange for protection and help; and third, just as this relationship is a microcosm of the larger power relationship between humans and God, the female-male relationship in turn serves as the model for all other power relationships in and across societies.

From biblical times to the present, Western civilization's acceptance of the patriarchal model is epitomized in the domestic relationship between women and men. The domestic relationship, in turn, creates the model for relationships between groups. Relationships between men and women as groups, between members of different social classes, between various ethnic and racial categories, between the generations, between colonial powers and their "protectorates," as well as between more developed and less developed nations, are all surprisingly similar to the domestic relationship between women and men. This is the blueprint problem described earlier.

The weaker party in each of these power relationships is childlike compared to the powerful one. The weaker group requires protection from nature, other groups, and itself. The weaker party often needs direction, correction, even punishment to improve its behavior, according to the myth. In addition, the weaker group cannot be expected to think or act for itself, having neither the intellectual, physical, nor political capacity to do so. The powerful group, like the all-knowing father, acts as a benevolent despot to help guide and control the powerless group and the society in which both live. The powerful group offers protection in exchange for subservience from the powerless, punishment for insubordination. This primary control myth sets the stage for other related myths.

Control Myth #2: Women are intuitive, holistic and contextual, but men are analytical, abstract, field-independent, and therefore smarter than women.

Control Myth #2 insists that men are more intelligent than women. According to this myth, the male mind uses abstract, analytical, cognitive strategies to grasp mathematics, economics, politics, science and technology, even philosophy, law, medicine, and engineering—fields of knowledge important to the control of social institutions. The female mind, by contrast, is intuitive, holistic, and contextual, relying on feeling rather than thinking.

If we relied solely on United States educational statistics through the 1960s, we would indeed be tempted to believe this myth, since women have been strangely absent from graduate and professional schools. Moreover, the numbers of women enrolled in mathematics, engineering, and science courses both in high school and undergraduate programs have been well below male enrollment levels.[5] Social scientists are beginning to understand how our social institutions have been structured to accommodate and perpetuate this pattern. The long history of science and letters in the Western world, dominated by men, has provided further "evidence" for this myth.

The Knowledge Game

Men have studied in the academy; they have administered and taught in the colleges and universities of the world. Even when the "knowledge" they taught was inaccurate (for example, that the earth was flat, that gravity did not exist, that the earth was at the center of the universe), men dominated the institutions that purveyed knowledge. When allowed to study at all, women were schooled at home, isolated with private tutors and governesses. Their subjects of study were carefully chosen; politics, economics, law, mathematics, and medicine should not burden the female brain. Chapter 10 will discuss some not-so-early male educators who actually went on record warning against the physiological and emotional damage the presumably smaller female brain would sustain from studying—echoes of Eve's punishment for eating from the tree of knowledge!

The twentieth-century writer Virginia Woolf, daughter of a Cambridge don, could only yearn to enter the same academic institutions so readily accessible to her father, uncles, and male friends. In *Orlando* she criticized the casual dismissal of women's intellectual power, as well as the institutional and attitudinal barriers that prevented its expression. In *A Room of One's Own*, she proposed that women need time and place away from husband and children to consider intellectual matters. Not surprisingly, the book later became a rallying point for latter-day feminists. Before Woolf, only a few women dared assault such male territory as the field of letters. (Of course, women's novels did not count!) Women who seriously sought to introduce their ideas and knowledge into the intellectual mainstream often had to assume male pseudonyms. Of these, George Elliott and George Sand are "shining examples."

According to Control Myth #2, men know how to run things and fix things, how to make things work—from faucets to foreign exchange. That this knowledge is not innate, but is structurally perpetuated by institutions designed exclusively for and by men, is an issue yet to be resolved. Myth #2 not only helps men believe in their own abilities and society's praise; it also leads women to agree that they can never undertake such important roles or understand the crucial problems in society. Many women, long convinced they were neither mathematical nor mechanical, gave up, preferring not to try than to fail and offer living proof of the myth. How did women, who as preadolescent girls displayed mathematical superiority, reach this point?

Expectations and Self-Fulfilling Prophecies

Expectations are potent shapers of behavior. Parents and teachers, as society's arbiters, expect boys to know and do more. From the start, young boys are given more space, more permission to express their energy and force. We have seen that their toys are strong and their clothes plain and sturdy, the better to withstand rough and tumble play. That boys are *expected* to study trigonometry, that young men are *expected* to learn engineering, that they are *expected* to go to medical and law schools, is only beginning to be recognized as a serious force in shaping men's destinies.

Research on the power of expectations is very revealing. The Pygmalion experiments at Harvard University investigated the influence of teachers' expectations on pupils' academic performance. In this well-known research, Rosenthal and his colleagues randomly selected pupils they then identified to the teachers as "gifted children."[5] The students labeled as "outstanding performers" did indeed outperform their unselected classmates. This research suggests that expectations—even scientifically unfounded expectations—are potent determiners of behavior, including academic behavior. Intelligence is not only in the eyes of the beholder, it is reflected back to the one thus perceived, who then struggles to live up to the expectation.

Low expectations are equally influential. Those for whom low expectations are held also participate in the self-fulfilling prophecy. Thus women—whom parents, teachers, male relatives and friends alike expect to be less bright, less able than men—limit themselves in ways that make the prophecy a reality. Until recently, few questioned the institutions based on this premise that limited women's intellectual opportunities. Men, no more intellectually endowed than women but anointed with high societal expectations, strive to meet these standards of intellectual power—a resource linked to all other power tributaries of the society.

Feminist scholars have begun to explode this control myth by reexamining research findings on gender differences in mathematics and other fields. They have begun to question the very premises on which the original research was based. Their efforts have begun to drain the force of Control Myth #2. But while the myth remained intact, individual women could hardly offset the pervasive institutional arrangements that made the myth a self-fulfilling prophecy.

Changing social conditions have forced many women to undertake roles previously reserved for men. Women, confronted by the reality of war, family illness, divorce, single parenthood, or widowhood, attempted tasks requiring intellectual and mechanical skills they had been taught they lacked. The success they encountered in these new roles both surprised and encouraged many women to develop higher self-expectations. Social change, particularly in the form of crisis, offered opportunities for new solutions to old problems. But Control Myth #2 still operates in some quarters, a rear-guard action to prevent women and men from throwing off the shackles of all the related control myths.

Intuition: Mysterious and Menacing

Women's intuition is regarded ambivalently. It is both less valued than men's alleged analytical capacities and simultaneously more mysterious, magical, even menacing. Women's highly touted "female intuition" (the antithesis of "male analytic reasoning") offers a strong counterbalance to men's assumed greater intellect. A vestige from ancient images of women's awe-inspiring magical powers, intuition casts its own mysterious aura. Freudians perhaps would argue that intuition's mystical, menacing quality stems from the child's early belief in the omniscience of the mother figure. Women's intuition is credited with correctly predicting outcomes, often in contradiction to analytical (read "male") interpretations. To the astonishment of those who depend on "facts and figures," women's intuition commonly proves to be more accurate than these more quantitative, "hard-nosed" appraisals of social situations.

Although many prefer to construe women's intuition as quasi-magical, there are simpler explanations. First, the powerless must carefully attend to the moods and inclinations of their rulers. As we have seen, the powerless learn to "read" the nonverbal communication (and hence seemingly the minds) of those who control their destiny. Children, for example, develop an uncanny ability to "psych out" their parents. Slaves too learn to sense the master's moods and gauge when to offer assistance and when to stand silently. Females, like other powerless groups, maintain these skills throughout life; males, who move into institutionally powerful roles in adulthood, often let these skills atrophy. Women who live intimately with males on whom they are dependent learn to read the subtlest messages. Their understanding of nonverbal behavior and other situational cues is interpreted, not so surprisingly, as women's intuition.

A second aspect of women's lives sustains their ability to understand nonverbal cues: their maternal role. Learning to interpret the needs and meanings of a baby's cries, muscle tension, and fleeting facial expressions teaches women to comprehend the nonverbal behavior of others. Many children—even adolescent and adult children—marvel that their mothers often seem able to read their minds. But it is not so surprising, considering the many years a mother has spent trying to understand her child's needs, even before the child knew words to express them.

This ability to understand the subtle cues that others project provides women with what appear to be prescient abilities. (It is interesting to note here the relationship between the word *prescience*, which Webster defines as "human foreknowledge of the course of events," and *prescientific*, defined as "prior to the application of the scientific method." Science, after all, has historically been a male endeavor). Undoubtedly, the ability to foresee events is partially grounded in the capacity to understand or "read" people and, based on such reading, to predict their future behavior.

A third source of women's intuition is the well-documented female propensity for contextual, holistic, or *field dependent* analysis, which, psychologists tell us, simply means taking all aspects of a situation into account. Contextual or holistic analysis allows individuals to view things and events within their total context, to examine the relationships among all the parts. The male propensity for *field independence* and abstract analysis involves the opposite ability to separate an element from its context, to eliminate the "distraction" of related factors. The female capacity for holistic analysis presumably contributes to women's sense of likely outcomes (female intuition). And, let us hasten to add, there is no research that documents either approach as an innate gender-linked characteristic.

We might speculate on at least one possible source of the differences psychologists have reported between women and men regarding field dependent/field independent behavior. More likely than not, these differences flow from the training males and females are "tracked" into early in educational systems, as we shall see in Chapter 10. For example, males are more likely to be urged to concentrate on a given field of study at an earlier period than females. Being forced to narrow their focus to mathematics, science, or other mechanical fields from which many traditional male disciplines and vocations are derived early in their educational careers probably predisposes males to think in a less holistic, more compartmentalized, field-independent, and "analytic" way. Women's freedom to explore different educational avenues for a longer period of time probably offers women the opportunity to develop a more holistic, contextual, intuitive approach to people and events.

These are only a few possible sources of the mystique surrounding "women's intuition." Few women would choose to dispel this mystique, considering its value in offsetting male certainty based on presumably "more scientific" evidence and analysis. Given that women's intuition is harder to document, and therefore also harder to discredit, the mystery or awe surrounding that ability projects power. Small wonder that many men seek their wife's or other women's opinions on matters relating to future events, particularly those involving human behavior. Newspaper accounts of politicians consulting female psychics before making important decisions is a variation on this same theme.

If women's intuition is such a powerful weapon in the power struggle between women and men, why don't women use it more often? Why don't they capitalize upon it in their efforts to establish equality with men? Many women do, in fact, recognize the importance of their subtle understanding of people and situations and use such knowledge to establish influence, if not power, in their relationships with men. But the Western values of rational thought and systematic, scientific analysis have convinced most women that female intuition is, at best, a secondary source of knowledge. Students of power relationships note that the less powerful group often accepts the values considered important by the powerful. Women's acceptance of male-valued detached, scientific, abstract, field-independent analysis as more important than people-oriented, holistic, contextual or field-dependent approaches is consistent with their powerless role—an example of Roland Barthes's claim that language is a sign system created and used by the powerful.

The situation may be changing, however, as recent criticisms of overly "rational" and "analytical" approaches to human events continue to grow. David Halberstam's account of Defense Secretary Robert MacNamara's super-rational strategic analysis during the Vietnam War (in *The Best and The Brightest*) is a serious condemnation of this approach. Large-scale organizations, usually run according to quantitative and rational analyses, are facing "people" problems that have caused organizational psychologist Harold J. Leavitt to call for a mode of understanding organizations, events, and people that goes beyond the analytical manager.[7] This new concern with more intuitive approaches to understanding problems eventually may result in efforts to "teach" such subtle, complex skills. The recent interest in understanding body language is just one step in that direction. As more intuitive approaches to understanding people and events are accepted within corporate and governmental decision-making groups, female intuition may become a more valued asset for women in adjusting their power relationships with men.

Control Myth #3: Women are more altruistic, more nurturant, and thus more moral than men.

Control Myth #3 tells us that women are more altruistic, nurturant, and moral than men: Self-sacrifice, self-denial, and immersion in the lives and accomplishments of others are values central to the female socialization process. Young girls learn that helping others win, rather than competing to win oneself, is both "naturally" feminine and at the same time morally superior.

Caring for others is a cardinal virtue in women. First through doll play, and thereafter in the real-life care of younger siblings, girls are carefully schooled to nurture others, even to their own detriment. Inkeles and Smith's work on modernity and personality examines how the work one does shapes personality.[8] So it is with young girls, who, beginning at a tender age, are assigned progressively more responsible domestic chores; this early work as "mother's helper" trains little girls to put the care and safety of others above their own. Long before adulthood, girls incorporate nurturance, altruism, and self-sacrifice into their self-concept—indeed, into their very personalities. Not so little boys, who learn they are *not* expected to put others ahead of themselves; in fact, others will step aside to put *them* first. Boys, and later men, learn to expect others (women) to sacrifice themselves to assist masculine success.

What is the rationale that breeds satisfaction and contentment from self-sacrifice? For one, several major religions preach that self-sacrifice represents a higher level of morality. Such morality sets a standard for human behavior to which others (in this case, males) can only aspire. For those who accept the religious value of selflessness, it is no sacrifice. Its rewards, for some believers, come in another life. For the less religious, selflessness is nonetheless a moral value and an important source of self-esteem.

Learning to put oneself second (or third, or even last) is the proper feminine way to play the gender power game, where being weaker, having less, is somehow construed as better. By making one's own needs secondary, one becomes first in goodness and morality. Competing to be first disqualifies one from receiving the moral gold star. Only men—with their brute strength and aggression (remember Control Myth #1)—should compete; women should selflessly contribute to others' well-being. And the social group does, in truth, reap tangible benefits from women's selflessness. That females sacrifice their individual gain for the good of the group is not merely an abstract description of female behavior; nor is it limited to their family roles. Hospitals, schools, museums, and other community services are but a few of the beneficiaries of women's nurturant, altruistic contributions. And, as we noted earlier, women's propensity to put the welfare of others above their individual gain has been demonstrated in laboratory experiments.

Although little girls learn early in life that self-sacrifice, helping others, and not competing are important parts of the ideal feminine profile, this lesson takes tenacious hold when females become wives and mothers. These traditional female domestic roles offer structured self-sacrifice and self-immersion in others. A "good" wife finds satisfaction not in her own career, but in assisting her husband and children in theirs. Lipman-Blumen, Handley-Isaksen, and Leavitt have documented women's greater propensity to use vicarious, contributory, and collaborative achieving styles.[9] Hanah Papanek's research on two-person careers, which pay one person but demand the work of two, easily illustrates this point.[10] In this same vein, a "good" mother experiences complete happiness when her children succeed.

This notion that women meet their own achievement needs through the success of others (particularly men) is strong. So strong, researchers report, that even when the female is only distantly related to the successful male (a classmate), observers still feel she has met her own achievement needs through his success.[11] As the relationship between the male and female becomes closer (fiancé, parent), observers think the female's vicarious achievement satisfaction grows greater. Not surprisingly, male subjects attribute higher levels of satisfaction to the vicariously achieving female character than do female observers.

Being altruistic, particularly sacrificing oneself for others, sets a high moral standard for one's own and others' behavior. Such behavior is often perceived by both men and women as morally superior to expressing individual self-interest. And this moral superiority becomes a characteristic whose mantle spreads over all realms of behavior—social, sexual, economic, and political. Again and again, we hear that if women led nations, we would have fewer wars (despite the leadership records of Indira Gandhi, Golda Meir, and Margaret Thatcher). We know that women have been in the forefront of movements to end slavery, war and other social injustices, as we shall discuss later. In a very clear way, the cloak of moral superiority is a resource, a weapon against the power of the mighty. Women can, and indeed have, influenced the behavior of powerful men; for example Mary Wollstonecraft often controlled her philosopher-soldier husband's sexual dalliance by expressing her moral contempt for his self-reported weakness.

The female as self-sacrificial supporter of others takes her quintessential form in the Lady Bountiful, the volunteer par excellence. Until this century, the bulk of women's work outside the home was performed on a "volunteer" basis in hospitals, churches, and schools. In fact, the only type of activity outside the home deemed appropriate for respectable females of an earlier era was so-called "charitable" work.[12] Even in twentieth-century America, with 52 percent of all adult women in the paid labor force by 1981, legions of their sisters continue to work as volunteers. They contribute to the gross national product in ways that economists are just beginning to measure. But for women, working either for pay or for personal or professional benefit is perceived as selfish; for men, this behavior is expected, even commended. Historians and labor economists have recorded how women's belief in Control Myth #3 was adroitly manipulated during World War II to draw women into defense plants and in the demobilization period, later, to make women yield their jobs to returning veterans.

In the wake of feminist protest that women should be paid for their valuable voluntary contributions to the community—not to mention their unpaid domestic labor—women began to reconsider Control Myth #3. During the rising social consciousness of the 1970s, many women tried to translate their volunteer experience into paid employment. Potential employers frequently met these efforts with little enthusiasm, if not outright confusion and resistance. Men, also victimized by Control Myth #3, have been carefully taught that women's work should not be recompensed by wages. For husbands, accepting this myth means men alone should bear the economic burden of supporting the entire family. The historical belief that females should altruistically donate their services deprived many women of the experience necessary to compete in the marketplace. Further evidence of middle-class women's self-consciousness, if not outright guilt, at working for pay is found in research studies in which upper-middle-class women cited "economic necessity" as their major reason for seeking paid employment.[13]

For working-class women, the self-sacrifice myth operated slightly differently. Working-class women sacrificed themselves to work at low-paid, low-status jobs to help keep their families in food, clothing, and shelter. Black women, particularly, paid a double price. Because many black women found it easier than black men to secure paid employment, they frequently became the primary, if not the sole, family breadwinner. Working long hours for little pay, black women faced the paradoxical accusation of creating a male-castrating matriarchy. The resurgent women's movement, which called for women's professional advancement, caught black women in a serious bind. How could they seek professional advancement while still being ambivalent about their primary breadwinner role even in nonprofessional occupations? For many black women, this handicapping ambivalence persisted despite the recognition that discriminatory social and economic circumstances, not choice or overriding ambition, dictated their breadwinner role.

Control Myth #3 has worked effectively to limit women's innate abilities through guilt and self-doubt, depriving women of experiences through which men learn to act in their own self-interest. Second, it guaranteed that employers would offer women low pay. Third, it taught husbands that they must bear the economic burdens of supporting "volunteer-worker" wives or accept the notion that their wives would not earn much for their labors. As Thorstein Veblen observed, an unemployed wife was the conspicuous symbol of a husband's solid economic state, thereby strengthening the myth's hold.[14] Fourth, justified as moral superiority, Control Myth #3 proved highly seductive. By instilling women with morally valued but self-enfeebling attitudes and behavior, and men with expectations that women should assist others and work for little or no pay, the society ensures business as usual. Men will remain in control of resources and power. Women will willingly assist men in their efforts to achieve. In this way, Control Myth #3 keeps women from acquiring valuable economic, occupational, and psychological resources that could help them reset the balance of the age-old power relationship. This same myth traps men into hanging onto inordinate burdens of support and protection for others who could make their own way in the world. Males, seduced by the false flattery of responsibility and the guilt associated with relinquishing the supporter-protector role, often spend their lives in the relentless yoke of responsibility and power.

Control Myth #4: Women's sexuality is inexhaustible, uncontrollable, and even dangerous to men. Male sexuality is more limited and delicate, requiring greater stimulation for arousal and more protection from injury.

Several differences between women's and men's sexual capacity coalesce into a potential power issue. On the female side, women can engage in coitus with only minimal arousal. Thus, women seem able to engage in sexual intercourse at will, whereas men are dependent on arousal to erection before they can participate fully. Second, women, or at least some women, can achieve multiple orgasms without the recovery period men require between ejaculations. Third, men's external genitalia are more exposed to injury than are women's internal genitalia.

These differences lead to perceptions of women's sexuality as inexhaustible, uncontrollable, potentially draining, and even harmful to men. Women's seemingly boundless sexuality is a major threat, one that must be controlled, as we see from the disproportionate number of female "sex offenders" in our penal institutions.

The mystique of women's sexuality, tied to their capacity to bear children, is fostered by images from ancient profane and sacred writings. Female sexuality is a source of mystery, awe, fascination, and fear. Women's ability to overpower and even destroy men through sexuality is a recurrent theme in ancient myths of vaginal teeth (that also appear in Freudian dream interpretations), in biblical tales (such as Delilah's seduction and destruction of the powerful Samson), and in some psychiatrists' interpretations of the relationship between male impotence and the feminist movement.

Although Control Myth #4 warns men to beware of women's potentially uncontrollable sexuality, it also sets the stage for strategies to control this awesome power. Men's macho sexuality, the phallus as the sword, the potential for turning masculine strength into an instrument for rape, all represent possible ways for controlling women's infinite, seductive sexuality.

Control Myth #5: Women are contaminated and contaminating.

To ensure that both groups keep their "places," the chasm between their respective domains must be wide. This is accomplished by harking back to other ancient myths and sacred writings that depict women as contaminating. Control Myth #5 focuses on women's power to contaminate both physically and socially. As we have noted before, for a male to be perceived as feminine (a sissy or gay) is a form of contamination. For men to enter those occupations designated as feminine is to suffer a form of contamination. Sociologist Alex Inkeles' worldwide survey of family patterns assures us: "In that part of life that involves intimate relationships, men and women do not do the same work"—data understandable within the context of Control Myth #5.[15]

The belief in the inherent contamination of women and their ability to contaminate men can be traced back to the Hellenic myths and biblical images discussed earlier. These ancient images, preserved through the ages in sacred writings, poetry, literature, and more recently the mass media, locate women's contamination in what ancients perceived to be women's very sources of power: menstruation, childbirth, lactation, and sexuality. This is, indeed, an ironic method for invalidating women's unique powers, the very powers that left ancient man awestruck.

Until girls reach puberty, they are perceived as weak but clean. Only with the onset of menarche (menstruation) in puberty does it become important to control women by labeling them dirty, foul-smelling, and contaminating. The potent body odors of adult men receive much less social attention. Before puberty, girls offer a minimal threat to society generally or men's power to control it. Little girls are readily controlled by parents who limit their geographic distance from home, the physical rigor of their play, and the nature of the activities they are allowed to undertake. With the onset of adolescence—the gateway to young adulthood—females begin to emerge as a serious force with which to be reckoned.

Adolescent women begin to sense their own power, if only reflected in the intensity and complexity of the efforts society exerts to control them. Fathers, particularly, worry about protecting their daughters' sexuality, their capacity to produce new life, their emerging power. The need to control the sexuality of young girls is reflected in the American jurisprudence system, which imprisons girls, but not boys, for sexual activity. Girls receive indeterminate prison sentences for "incorrigible" behavior (read "running away from home or staying out all night, presumably with boys"). When young women reach puberty, when they become sexually active, when their mystical capacity to bleed cyclically without dying first occurs, when they are capable of bringing forth new life, the social institutions controlled by men begin to exert vigorous restraints on them.

Myth #5 teaches women to believe they are wellsprings of contamination. For women, the first bodily changes signaling adulthood are shrouded in mystery as well as embarrassment. In preliterate societies, menstruating females are isolated in special huts far from the active society, lest they contaminate others. Plants presumably die at the touch of a menstruating woman. Biblical proscriptions warn against socializing, much less having any intimate contact, with menstruating women. Rituals for purifying women after menstruation, childbirth, and lactation are described in biblical commentaries as well as in anthropological accounts. Television commercials for feminine deodorants perpetuate the belief in women's contamination and offer contemporary purification rituals.

Women, thus, begin to believe that their very physiological differences from men are a source of contamination. They become the "untouchables" of the society; their cyclical bleeding bears testament every month to women's biological and sociological destiny as the profane gender group. Stereotypically, emotional instability is tied to menstruation. If women are so profane, contaminated, and contaminating, how can they be anything but the untouchable, the weak, and the powerless in the dominance relationship between the genders? How can they ever hope to be social equals? Internalizing this belief, women often acknowledge their own subordinate status.

The perception of menstruating, pregnant, and lactating women as individuals with a "delicate" condition, even an illness, is a variation on the same theme. But several ironies are worth noting. First, these same conditions arouse anger and hostility in others, indirect evidence of the power sensed in these physiological states. Witness the recent reports of physical abuse of pregnant women, social dismay at mothers nursing their infants in social situations, and the great numbers of hostile jokes directed at menstruating women. It is not difficult to interpret these phenomena as social mechanisms for heightening women's awareness of their "contaminated" condition and destroying women's power.

Second, while society depicts pregnant women as most vulnerable, delicate, and in need of medical care, legislators and employers have remained unconvinced that pregnancy should be treated as a standard medical disability like other medical conditions. Maternity leave, a method for preserving the new mother's job until her return to the labor force (modeled on the protection afforded disabled workers through sick leave), continues to spark heated debate, particularly in the United States. To intensify this irony, paternity leave (official time off for fathers to care for their newborn offspring) is a relatively recent worker demand admittedly more often requested by women for their husbands than by the new fathers themselves.

In the era before maternity leaves, pregnant women were both applauded and blamed for permanent retirement from the labor force, which simultaneously deprived them of paid wages and of any significant control over key social and economic resources. Such retirement evoked applause for women acting "appropriately feminine" and for performing "the most important (if unpaid) job in the world"—raising children. At the same time, women's subsequent lack of progress in the labor force was blamed on their inadequate labor force "attachment"—that is, their tendency to leave paid jobs for varying time periods, usually for family reasons. Women stood accused of refusing to invest in "human capital," the process of increasing one's education and training with an eye to expanding employment options.

Women's alleged weak labor force attachment, their disinterest in human capital, and their physical weaknesses are marshaled as explanations for their segregation within narrowly defined segments of the occupational structure. Women's presumed absenteeism (discounted by labor statisticians), their sexual distraction of male co-workers, and the objections their presence generates among their male colleagues' wives provide still other ready rationales for their occupational segregation. Control Myth #5 urges us to consider these factors as euphemisms for an underlying belief in women's contaminating qualities, contamination that requires women's confinement within either limited occupational roles or the isolated domestic world. This belief in women's contamination, which easily confers legitimacy on occupational segregation and misogyny, permits their structured insulation from the institutional sources of power.

Control Myth #6: Beauty and sexuality are women's most valuable assets.

Control Myth #6 can just as easily be called "the Big Beauty and Sexuality Buy Off." Beauty, inherently pleasurable and often combined with sexuality, is a key attraction women hold for men—a paradox in light of previous control myths. Even their maternal potential is less directly appealing.

Pre-Hellenic, as well as classical Greek goddesses were renowned for their beauty. Eve's comeliness flamed Adam's desire. Delilah and Bathsheba were seductive biblical beauties. Beauty entwined with the promise of sexuality was woman's most powerful asset, the means to seduce men, and hence ensure her position in society. Heroines, from Shakespeare's Juliet to Tolstoy's Anna Karenina to Scarlett O'Hara, Cinderella, and Snow White, are always wondrously beautiful. Modern-day movie stars, not coincidentally referred to as movie "queens," share the same worship-evoking beauty. Women and men alike are taught that beauty and sexuality are what really count for females.

Little girls are "sugar and spice and everything nice," and too much knowledge defeminizes them, endangers their beauty, makes them boyish. Beauty is fragile; it requires protection, much like museum art. Beautiful women are priceless treasures, enhancing the power of those who control them, but powerless themselves. Little girls who play boys' games are in danger of letting their physical and intellectual strength develop, while their beauty and sexuality evaporate. Delicate clothes and careful play activities help to protect female fragility and define little girls' gentler hold on society.

Physical beauty is eventually likened to moral beauty, as we saw in Control Myth #3, and the beauty-sexuality "buy off" is complete. Women, they are told, are more beautiful, more delicate, more moral, more understanding and humane than men. They should be happy that they do not have to get dirty, wear plain clothes, fight, and compete for wages. This message induces both women and men to overemphasize and overvalue female beauty. We have seen how, until recently, little girls' clothes made a statement about the delicacy of their physical movements. Even their play clothes were restricting, until overalls became acceptable for little girls. The recent worldwide craze for jeans has helped to weaken the restrictive clothes barrier for women and the gender inequality it symbolizes.

Nonetheless, the attention to female self-adornment through clothes and cosmetics remains a stubborn residue of the beauty-sexuality buy off." Thousands of cosmetics are manufactured to keep or make women beautiful and sexually desirable. Clothes and hairstyles are redesigned every season to maintain women's allure. Magazines advise young girls on how to be more attractive to men. The media teach women to decorate their homes as beautiful reflections of themselves. A recent best-seller instructs women how to color themselves "beautiful."

And where does all this beauty and promised sexuality lead, according to Control Myth #5? To success, female style, defined as a relationship with a man, preferably a powerful man. The beauty-sexuality buy off is the traditional road to achievement for women. As Lipman-Blumen and Leavitt's work suggests, women's achievement traditionally has been experienced vicariously through relationships with successful men, who were enticed by their beauty, sexuality, and charm.[16] Princess Diana, Jacqueline Kennedy Onassis, and the late Princess Grace of Monaco are relatively recent additions to the list of women whose beauty brought them wealth and power through marriage.

Men too are caught up in the definition that weds female beauty and implied sexuality to male success. A beautiful and sexy woman is considered an enviable prize for the successful man. The older, not particularly attractive, powerful and wealthy man with the much younger, glamorous, and sensuous woman are a common pair. The reverse is only occasionally true, but may become more common as successful women follow men's lead in trading their power, success, and wealth for men's youth, beauty, and sexuality.[17]

Despite the 1970s "peacock revolution" in men's fashions, more effort is still spent on women's physical appearance. Cosmetics are a billion-dollar industry. This emphasis on female style simultaneously underscores how different men and women really are. How delicate and beautiful are women, how strong and knowledgeable are men. Power and strength—not beauty—count for men. Since the institutions and definitions of Western society strongly encourage the general belief that men know more and can do better, why not let them do the difficult, hard, oppressive work of running society? Why *not* let women, with their fragile, treasured beauty, spend endless hours selecting cosmetics, clothes, and interior decoration to preserve and complement their appearance? As long as female beauty and sexuality can be traded for male wealth, power, and status, only the most stubborn, ugly, sexless, or idealistic women will persist in trying to demonstrate that they are as intelligent and able as the men. The sixth control myth convinces women that female beauty and sexuality are the direct avenue to vicarious success and status. For men, such attributes in their women are important symbols of masculine success. Once this myth, like all the others, is internalized, both men and women unwittingly behave to perpetuate its truth.

Control Myth #7: Women talk too much.

The seventh control myth concerns women's so-called tendency to talk too much. Women are portrayed in the arts and media as talking more than men. Even when women talk no more than men, their verbal behavior is viewed negatively. This is hardly a new phenomenon. Aristotle reminds us: ". . . a woman would be thought loquacious if she imposed no more restraint on her conversation than a good man."

Control Myth #7 warns women that they talk too much. In an effort to offset this negative stereotype of themselves, women control their own verbal behavior in the presence of men and thus also keep themselves from being perceived as knowledgeable. Talking or communicating is an important aspect of leadership, as Chester Barnard and other students of organizational leadership have observed.[18] Yet women, because of the negative stereotype associated with their verbal ability, limit their own communication in groups. The resource of female verbal ability becomes transformed into a deficit.

An important and surprising generalization about verbal behavior emerges from a review of the literature on differences between female and male behavior in small, mixed-gender groups, namely that men talk more than women.[19] Not only do they talk more, males "initiate more verbal acts."[20] They also interrupt others' speech more often—evidence that Control Myth #7 teaches women to limit their talking to escape this negative appraisal.

Verbal communication—that is, just plain talking—is an important aspect of leadership behavior. Leadership research suggests that the most active members—and that means verbally active, specifically—are most likely to be perceived as leaders by other group members.[21] The consequence: If women limit how much they talk in small groups, particularly work groups, they are less likely to be cast in leadership roles. The "Catch-22" dilemma women confront in their efforts to balance group behavior, verbal activity, and leadership is classic. As Control Myth #7 operates to limit women's verbal activity—despite their well-documented edge on tests of verbal ability—women lose control over one of their most significant resources in the power struggle between the sexes. Once more a control myth operates to transform a female power into a liability.

Control Myth #8: Women are manipulative; men are straightforward.

In an earlier chapter we examined the way in which women are forced into micromanipulation—that is, interpersonal, intimate influence—to offset men's macromanipulation of the institutional structures and resources of society. If women are cautioned to control their tongues, to leash their leadership, to remain within the domestic sphere, manipulation and indirection are their only alternatives. If macromanipulation and social policy are the legitimate domain of men, then micromanipulation and personal policy are clearly women's terrain. Warned to be silent, women are then accused, in classical "blame the victim" tradition, of working by indirection.

According to Control Myth #8, men are nonmanipulative, clearly direct and straightforward in their behavior. Purposive, direct behavior is necessary for leadership and institutional control. Since Control Myth #7 does not prohibit men from talking, there is relatively little motivation for men to mask their desires and intentions. Although, as Machiavelli would remind us, those men who combine the strength of straightforwardness with the subtlety of micromanipulation—that is, the lion and the fox—are the most successful leaders. They reap a handsome reward—permission to exercise open macromanipulation over the major resource-bearing institutions of society.

Control Myth #9: Men have women's best interests at heart; women can trust men to protect their welfare.

Control Myth #9 is the capstone to all previous control myths. If women are weak, passive, fearful, and dependent, while men are strong, aggressive, fearless, and independent; if women are intuitive and contextual, while men are analytical and abstract, and therefore more intelligent than women; if women are more selfless, nurturant, and moral; if women's sexuality is infinite, uncontrollable, and dangerous, as well as contaminating to men; if women use their sexuality and beauty to seduce and manipulate men, while men are intelligent, brave, strong, and straightforward, then the solution is clear. Men should—for women's and men's sakes alike—rule the social, economic, and political institutions, and women should control the less important domain of hearth and home. In the major institutions of society which amass power-sustaining resources, men rightfully should govern; women's governance within the family is legitimate only over other younger and lower-status women and less powerful males—daughters, daughters-in-law, maids, and young boys.

This is a powerful myth indeed, one that assures both women and men that males are the more competent group. The more intelligent male group understands everything from economics to physics and politics. Like Plato's philosopher-king, members of this group are the appropriate rulers. The divinely ordained and thus unchallenged relationship between men and women, modeled on the sacred relationship between God and humans, suggests that men have the best interests of the "weaker" gender at heart. If the smarter, stronger group has the weaker group's interests at heart, then everything falls into place. Men rightly should rule, and women should be grateful for their generous, protective supremacy.

Modern tales of love and romance sustain the myths of the knight's chivalry toward the beautiful maiden. Modern feminists, understanding its enfeebling power, reject chivalrous male attentions such as door-holding, much to the natural perplexity of those less sensitive to chivalry's subtle effects. The belief in men's concern for women's welfare is easier to accept when the basic social unit is the heterosexual pair. Each woman, attached to a specific man, sees the world through the prism of that specific power relationship. If affection, love, and/or concern are strands interwoven in that individual relationship, then the belief that he has her best interests at heart is easy to sustain.

The strength of this belief has its roots in early childhood, when the small girl is treated as her father's darling, as we have noted. There she discovers the power she has, through her helplessness, dependence, and feminine charms, to make him accede to her pleas. This becomes a clearly defined game. The rules are evident: The daughter acts helpless and cute; she pleads and begs; the father acts strong and loving; he is charmed into giving her whatever she wants.

All of us initially learn what to expect from adults of both sexes by the experiences we have with our parents. What little girls learn to expect from their loving fathers they similarly expect from their boyfriends, their husbands, their professors, their employers, their senators and their presidents. Women believe they are loved and/or admired by the individual men with whom they establish relationships. Trusting the individual men who love and protect them, women transfer this trust of individual men to males as a gender category.

Unlike other minority groups, women are *not* segregated from those who exert power over them. Very often, they live in the most intimate relationships with those who dominate them. To live intimately, without constant conflict and struggle, requires trust, or at least the suspension of distrust. As a result, women's intimate, often loving relationships with individual men lead them to feel safe in handing over their destinies to men in public life. Women who have experienced relationships characterized by power without love, concern, and respect undoubtedly are more cynical, and their publicly expressed cynicism "endangers" all other women's delicate sense of safety. Many women who oppose the Equal Rights Amendment stoutly defend their men's willingness to protect them. Paradoxically, others resist the ERA because they fear it will eliminate the legal protection they believe men would not voluntarily provide.

Women who as children were abused by male relatives threaten the myth that men have women's best interests at heart. Daughters who have been victims of incest have a dangerous tale to tell. The true meaning of the incest taboo has been the taboo against *revealing* the prevalence of fathers' incestuous behavior toward daughters. Mother-son incest, while a recognized phenomenon, is reportedly much less frequent. Mounting worldwide statistics on father-daughter incest provide a serious picture of the ultimate abuse taboo, off limits even to researchers.

Not all fathers demonstrate such flagrant disregard for their daughters. But even those fathers who scrupulously attempt to guard their daughters' welfare do not necessarily know what actually constitutes their best interest. Many fathers offer paternal "protection" that results in infantilization. They "protect" their daughters from learning skills, developing talents, and taking risks that would enlarge the daughters' repertoire of abilities and sense of self-esteem. In short, they "protect" them from becoming independent adults.

The structured female ignorance of financial matters may be consistent with other control myths that men are more intelligent than women, and that physical beauty is women's most important asset. Women are urged "not to worry their pretty little heads" over difficult and tedious financial details. To remain baffled and discomforted by such matters fits with the feminine stereotype. In the long run, however, this effort to "protect" women is the modern analog to the ancient Chinese custom of binding young girls' feet—a ritual that ensured their desirability as females, but crippled them for life. Women's inexperience with financial matters—including negotiating economic agreements—eventually becomes a serious, long-term disability.

Women who express doubt about men's genuine concern for and understanding of their welfare are a threat to the existing gender power relationship. Such "doubting Tomasinas" are most effectively squelched by being labeled misinformed at best, and deviant at worst. Lesbians offer a clear case of the "doubting Tomasina" syndrome. They explicitly question men's abilities and intentions. Lesbians, particularly political lesbians who have chosen a life style emphasizing political opposition to men, deliberately separate themselves from heterosexual relationships. They refuse to put their trust, much less their bodies, in the hands of men; by so doing, they represent a clear and present danger to the existing power structure. The life circumstances of separatist lesbians, who live apart from men, do not require trusting males who run society. As a result, it is hardly surprising that lesbians, previously both more discreet and ignored, are perceived in the growing gender unrest as a group whose distrust of male benevolence might strain the social fabric. Nor is it so astounding that, when suburban housewives join the women's movement, opponents attempt to discredit their calls for change through insinuating they are lesbians. Separated from others who would validate their view of men as *not* having women's best interests at heart, the cynics and doubters—lesbians and non-lesbians alike—must choose between remaining silent or risking the label of deviant.

The combined effect of these control myths has led men into the burden of the "protector" and women into the subordination of the "protected" role. The history of so-called protective legislation, based on accepted medical "knowledge" developed by the scientific establishment, illustrates this point. In the late nineteenth century, the inaccurate but widely accepted opinion of Harvard Medical School professor Edward H. Clarke insisted that education impaired women's menstrual cycle, and thus their childbearing potential. Clarke argued that menstruating women required protection; all women menstruated and therefore all women needed protection. His famous treatise, *Sex in Education*, provided the "scientific" rationale for educational policy limiting women's access to higher education, particularly medical school.[22] If this were simply accepted as the delusion of one well-placed physician, little heed should be paid to Clarke's incompetence. Sadly enough, his opinion shaped American educational legislation and practice for decades. This, in turn, provided the model for protective occupational legislation that guarded women from a wide range of higher-paid, resource-generating jobs. It would not be until the next century that women would begin to question whether male "protection" was simply a cover for male power and misogyny.

Protection, Power, Misogyny

Gender-role socialization, crystallized in the control myths, traditionally trains males to use their strength to protect females. Since men are portrayed as the stronger sex, they are easily cast in the chivalrous protector role, which fades readily enough into the "good provider" role within the family.[23] As providers, men in the industrialized world have been expected to act as the major, if not the sole, family breadwinner. The burdens of this role rarely are taken seriously enough for society to design alternative measures. The power of the breadwinner role tends to eclipse its more negative, stressful aspects.

Women's entry into the paid labor force is a prominent feature of the postindustrial world that conflicts with male socialization to the good provider role. To some, women's labor-force participation is unwelcome evidence of their growing power, as we have seen. Socialization to protect and provide for women leads men to designate certain quintessential male activities, like military service, as physically and psychologically "off limits" to women. Occupational segregation, whereby women are corralled into "feminine" occupational roles, is not an unexpected outcome of such early training. As we saw, occupational segregation has burdensome effects on men and women alike, providing an important staging ground for the gender power struggle.

To become another's protector is to recognize the protected as weaker, less able, than oneself. Individuals and groups under one's protection are usually in a lower stratum of society, where they earn less resources and less respect. To label women as less or weaker or smaller than men is to point to the critical line that men must never cross, lest they become weak and powerless themselves. Many behaviors and characteristics forbidden to men, like tears, dependence, tenderness, nurturance, physical weakness, dainty movements, as well as interest in the arts and humanities, are specifically those often identified with women. For men to exhibit any tendencies that smack of femininity is to risk demasculinization. Men are taught to root out of their psyches any vestige of the natural feminine component in their makeup. They learn, in fact, to dislike and deny any qualities within themselves that point to femininity.

Taught to hate the feminine within themselves, they find it difficult to restrict that hatred of femininity to its appearance in men. Despising femininity within the self is only the first step toward projecting that hatred externally to those who embody similar characteristics—women and gay men. Male socialization to disdain the feminine within themselves spills over quite easily into *misogyny*, which Webster defines as "having or showing a hatred and distrust for women." This does not deny that individual men are capable of loving individual women. Rather, the attitude of the male world becomes antithetical—frequently hostile—to women and more feminine men, particularly as categories.

This cultural male misogyny often turns male aggression against women who violate gender role expectations. Men and women who step "out of role," who attempt to cross the male/female boundary line, arouse a deep-seated dread in men that they too might just as easily cross over into that hated and feared territory. Women who seek to equalize the female/male power relationship seem particularly menacing and, therefore, easily become the primary targets of male anger. Recent evidence of the frequency with which male aggression and power are turned against "uppity" women comes from the rash of violence and terror films that depict men unleashing their aggression against female targets. Crime statistics, revealing a real-life increase in violent crimes against women, provoke serious concern.

Questioning the "Best Interest" Myth

Only when the weaker group in a power relationship begins to doubt the powerful's "good intentions" and benevolent authority will it face the possibility of fending for itself. And so it is with women. Only when the less powerful group recognizes that its interests are best protected by its own action will it begin to think about acting in its own behalf. Only when the less powerful group understands that it can and must control its own daily life, environment, and fate can it begin to think about taking charge. Only then will the less powerful conceive of seizing control from those who would wield power over and for them. But this is a dangerous departure, this resetting of the gender power balance. Such perilous adjustments arouse widespread anxiety among rulers and ruled alike.

Warnings against upsetting the gender power balance grow louder and more alarming. Crime statistics indicate that assaults on women—both family members and strangers—are on the rise. "Briefcase rapes and murders," played up in the press, are the latest manifestations of the backlash against women who personify the new power balance. Movie and TV screens picture women as the latest, most fashionable targets of hostility and terror. And pornographic media routinely feature sadistic treatment of female stars. The message is clear: Those who would question that men have women's best interests at heart, those who would upset the delicate, the ultimate, power relationship, must be prepared to pay dearly. Rather than confront this negative picture, many still prefer to think that men simply want and love women, and that the primary source of this desire is the great beauty and sexuality that women possess. The "best interests at heart" myth cloaks all other control myths in a benign mantle, disguising their insidious power to subordinate women and to burden men.

SUMMARY

Classical Greek myths, as well as Old and New Testament stories, transformed the powerful and positive images of women and goddesses from earlier civilizations into negative, destructive figures. Subsequently, literature and art perpetuated these unattractive female portraits. Modern-day control myths preserve the residue of gender-role images emanating from mythology, religion, literature, and art. Nine control myths teach serious lessons to men and women alike:

1. Women are weak, passive, dependent, and fearful; men are strong, aggressive, independent, and fearless.

2. Women think in intuitive, holistic, and contextual terms; men use analytical, abstract, and field-independent thinking, which makes them smarter than women.

3. Women are more altruistic, nurturant, and thus more moral than men.

4. Women's sexuality is inexhaustible, uncontrollable, and even dangerous to men; male sexuality is more limited and delicate, requiring greater stimulation for arousal and more protection from injury.

5. Women are contaminated and contaminating.

6. Beauty and sexuality are women's most valuable assets.

7. Women talk too much.

8. Women are manipulative; men are straightforward.

9. Men have women's best interests at heart; women can trust men to protect their welfare.

Through these control myths, women and men learn to govern their own behavior and internalize "appropriate" gender-role attitudes. These nine control myths victimize women and men in different, but equally destructive, ways. Conformity to the outdated stereotypes that support the control myths sustains the long-standing power struggle between women and men.

NOTES

1. H. J. Rose, *A Handbook of Greek Mythology* (New York: E. P. Dutton and Co., Inc., 1950), p. 19.

2. Jane Ellen Harrison, *Prolegomena to the Study of Greek Religion* (Cambridge, England: Cambridge University Press, 1922), pp. 280–281.

3. Charlene Spretnak, *Lost Goddesses of Early Greece: A Collection of Pre-Hellenic Myths* (Boston: Beacon Press, 1981), p. 55.

4. Roland Barthes, *Mythologies* (New York: Hill and Wang, 1957).

5. Mary Lou Randour, Georgia L. Strasburg, Jean Lipman-Blumen, "Women in Higher Education: Trends in Enrollments and Degrees Earned," *Harvard Educational Review*, 52, no. 2 (1982), 189–202.

6. Robert Rosenthal, Judith A. Hall, M. Robin, D. Matteo, Peter L. Rogers, Dane Archer, *Sensitivity to Nonverbal Communication* (Baltimore: Johns Hopkins University Press, 1979).

7. Harold J. Leavitt, "Beyond the Analytical Manager," *California Management Review* (Spring, 1975), 17(3):5–12; and Summer, 1975 17(4): 11–21.

8. Alex Inkeles and David H. Smith, *Becoming Modern: Individual Change in Six Developing Countries* (Cambridge, Mass.: Harvard University Press, 1974).

9. Jean Lipman-Blumen, Alice Handley-Isaksen, and Harold J. Leavitt, "Achieving Styles in Men and Women: A Model, an Instrument, and Some Findings," in *Achievement and Achievement Motives*, ed. Janet T. Spence (San Francisco: W. H. Freeman & Co., 1983).

10. Hanna Papanek, "Men, Women and Work: Reflections on the Two-Person Career," *American Journal of Sociology*, 78, 852–70.

11. Harold J. Leavitt, Jean Lipman-Blumen, S. Schaefer, and R. Harris, "Vicarious Achievement Orientation" (paper presented at the eighty-fifth annual meeting of the American Psychological Association, San Francisco, 1977).

12. Carl Degler, *At Odds: Women and the Family in America from the Revolution to the Present* (New York: Oxford University Press, 1980).

13. Lois W. Hoffman and F. Ivan Nye, *Working Mothers: Consequences for Men, Women and Children* (San Francisco: Jossey-Bass, 1974).

14. Thorstein Veblen, *Theory of the Leisure Class* (New York: Modern Library, 1934).

15. Alex Inkeles, "Modernization and Family Patterns: A Test of Convergence Theory," in *Conspectus of History*, Vol. 1, No. 6, eds. Dwight W. Hoover and John T. Koumoulides (Muncie, Ind.: Ball State University Press, 1980), pp. 31–63.

16. Jean Lipman-Blumen and Harold J. Leavitt, "Vicarious and Direct Achievement Patterns in Adulthood," *Counseling Psychologist*, 6, no. 1 (1976), 26–32.

17. Constantina Safilios-Rothschild, "Sex Role Socialization and Sex Discrimination: A Synthesis and Critique of the Literature" (Washington, D.C.: National Institute of Education, 1979).

18. Chester A. Barnard, *The Functions of the Executive* (Cambridge, Mass.: Harvard University Press, 1964).

19. K. P. Hall, "Sex Differences in Initiation and Influence in Decision-making Among Prospective Teachers," (doctoral dissertation, Stanford University; 1972), *Dissertation Abstracts International*, 1972, 33(8), 3952-A; see also M. E. Lockheed and K. P. Hall, "Conceptualizing Sex as a Status Characteristic: Applications to Leadership Training Strategies," *Journal of Social Issues*, 32, no. 2 (1976), 111–123.

20. Lockheed and Hall, "Conceptualizing Sex."

21. R. E. Lana, W. Vaughan and E. McGinnies, "Leadership and Friendship Status as Factors in Discussion Group Interaction," *Journal of Social Psychology* 52 (1960), 127–134; G. E. Marak, "The Evolution of Leadership Structure," *Sociometry,* 27 (1964), 172–182; S. M. Zdep and W. F. Oakes, "Reinforcement of Leadership Behavior in Group Discussion," *Journal of Experimental Psychology* 3 (1967), 310–20; S. M. Zdep, "Intragroup Reinforcement and Its Effects on Leadership Behavior," *Organizational Behavior and Human Performance* 4 (1969), 284–98; C. G. Morris and J. R. Hackman, "Behavioral Correlates of Perceived Leadership," *Journal of Personality and Social Psychology,* 13 (1969), 350–361.

22. Edward H. Clarke, *Sex in Education* (Boston: J. R. Osgood & Co., 1873).

23. Jessie Bernard, *The Female World,* (New York: The Free Press, 1981).

CHAPTER 8
GENDER ROLES AND THE FAMILY

The family is the cradle of gender roles. Both genders are represented within the marital union and often among the children that marriage produces. Gender is one of the two major dimensions of family structure, the other being age. Structural-functionalists, biological determinists, sociobiologists, and feminists have argued over the relative contributions of biology and society to the structural design of families. They all agree, however, on one point: The family still provides the basic dynamic framework within which both traditional and contemporary gender roles are learned initially.

In this chapter, we shall explore various aspects of the dynamic between the family and gender roles: first, the structural-functionalist versus the feminist paradigms; then the family as context for learning gender roles, the power gender dance, and the generation power struggle; next, an historical perspective on the family as an economic unit, as well as the multiple power relationships acted out within the family setting; and finally, the changing statistical portrait of contemporary American families.

THE STRUCTURAL-FUNCTIONALIST PARADIGM

Family and kinship organizations are the basic units of society's sex and gender-role systems. Functionalist theorists have argued that the family exists because it performs certain key functions—particularly the creation and care of children. Anthropologist Bronislaw Malinowski's description of family structure among Australian aborigines demonstrated that this aboriginal society differentiated between legal unions (or marriages) and nonmarital sexuality.[1] That a society which permitted adults seemingly casual sexual unions also had an identifiable structure of parents and children was the evidence Malinowski used to claim that the family was indeed universal. Malinowski based his interpretation of aboriginal family structures on three key observations: (1) social boundaries that distinguished between family members and outsiders; (2) a physical location, sometimes movable, where family tasks were performed; and (3) emotional ties among family members.

Structural-functionalists Talcott Parsons and R. F. Bales analyzed the modern nuclear family, identifying its function as the socialization of children and the personal replenishment of other family members. In earlier work on small groups composed of male undergraduates, Bales and Slater observed the systematic emergence of two types of leaders: (1) instrumental or task leaders, and (2) expressive or socioemotional leaders.[2] Extrapolating from Bales and Slater's small-group observations, Parsons applied this functional arrangement to the family. Men, Parsons reasoned, were the family instrumental or task leaders; women, its expressive or socioemotional leaders. The division of labor within the family, he argued, was based on this "natural" difference between women and men. That women took care of the family and home and men worked in the labor force was a "functional" arrangement for eliminating competition between husbands and wives, according to Parsons.[3]

This structural-functionalist approach blended congenially with earlier biological determinism, which saw biology as destiny. In this view, women's domestic role was inevitable, given their childbearing capacity. This, of course, did not speak to the issue of those women without children who nonetheless were also relegated to the home. Recent sociobiological approaches of E. O. Wilson and David Barash derive from such an orientation.[4] These more recent sociobiologists also claim an evolutionary, and thus genetic, inevitability to women's childbearing and rearing functions and men's social and political dominance.

THE FEMINIST APPROACH TO FAMILY THEORY

Structural-functionalist interpretations colored decades of work on the family until feminist theorists began to question these shibboleths, demanding that family structure be broken down into its underlying elements of childbearing and rearing, sexuality, and production.[5] The family, feminists reasoned, is not the only structure within which these functions can be performed. Nor are genetic factors the sole basis for family roles and functions.

The family, and even gender roles, are social inventions, according to this perspective. More specifically, society magnifies biological sexual differences into artificially dichotomous gender roles, as sociologist B. Thorne reminds us.[6] These differences lead to the sexual division of labor, whose strict enforcement fosters the mutual, if unequal, dependence of men and women. The social invention of two differentiated and complementary gender roles is inevitably tied both to the social division of labor inside and beyond the family and to the social insistence on heterosexual relationships. These complex arrangements foster a lopsided interdependence between the genders.

As discussed previously, control over female sexuality begins earlier and is disproportionately greater than that exercised over males. Within marriage, feminists suggest, women's sexuality and reproductive functions are controlled by husbands as well as by the state. Social policy is a major institutional tool for controlling women's sexual activity, which the control myths warn is potentially uncontrollable. Through social policy, society attempts to restrict access to contraception and abortion; still other laws punish women's sexual activity through the criminal justice system. Women have had no comparable control over male sexual behavior, although their political efforts, on occasion, have been motivated at least partially by such considerations.

THE FAMILY AS THE CONTEXT FOR LEARNING AND RELEARNING GENDER ROLES

Even before they enter first grade, most children easily differentiate between mothers' and fathers' household and occupational tasks, according to psychologist Ruth Hartley.[7] Scholars and clinicians have long debated the intricate processes by which children learn these gender-linked behaviors. Some argue that the same-sex parent is the most important role model. Others insist that the child identifies with and imitates the parent with the most power and resources, regardless of that parent's gender.

A more Freudian approach suggests that both female and male children initially identify with the mother. This identification subsequently must be broken by boys, who transfer their identification to their fathers or to another male figure. According to the Freudian model, little girls learn and practice how to interact with boys through the benign and loving relationship with their fathers. How boys learn the appropriate gender behavior toward girls their own age is relatively less critical than how they transfer their initial identification from mother to father, if the amount of research attention given each topic is a valid measure of importance. Boys' behavior toward girls is much less an issue than girls' behavior toward boys. The very primitive knowledge of how both genders interact is learned initially in the family setting by observing the behavior of parents and of older siblings.

Both children and adults receive detailed lessons in gender-role behavior within the family. There the child learns several important lessons: (1) what being male and female mean; (2) whether one is a girl or a boy (that is, one's "gender identity"); and (3) what different kinds of social responsibilities and power resources women and men have.

Earlier, we examined the way in which parents, from day one, perceive and treat their daughters and sons differently. We noted that fathers, more than mothers, insist on strict adherence to gender-role norms. Particularly with the onset of puberty, but even long before, children develop clear expectations for appropriate gender-role behavior. To a large extent, children learn the behavior expected of them from the example of their same-sex parent or same-sex siblings, and later from teachers and peers. The traditional gender-linked behavior they learn at home is reinforced in the classroom and on the playground. At times, the discrepancy between behavioral expectations learned in the family and the "outside world" creates conflicts. The tensions between the family and the peer group, often perceived as a "generation gap," have injected despair and anguish into relationships between parents and their teenage children. Striking the younger generation's values against the flint of their parents' gender-role definitions often produces explosive tensions. The generation gap may narrow as children enter adult, particularly marital, roles, when a synthesis of new and old values creates a subtle hold on the new adult generation's behavior and attitudes.

Children learn more than simply gender-role behavior within the family context. Sex-role behavior—that is, the basis of sex education—is transmitted in both overt and covert ways. Sex education, so widely feared by many parents, occurs implicitly in the family setting without the parents' conscious awareness. Important lessons are assimilated within the long shadow cast by the parents' own sexual behaviors, attitudes, and values. By kindergarten, children are teaching each other about sex from the lessons they have learned at home. They compare notes with enthusiastic curiosity, unrestricted by adult reprimands.

Learning the Gender Power Dance: The Homosocial Worlds

In addition to sexual behavior, small children observe and imitate the power dance between males and females, again from parents and older relatives, including older siblings. Patterns of chivalry and protection are inculcated in little boys, and dependence, coyness, appreciation, and nurturance in little girls.

According to anthropologist Raphaela Best, replicas of maternal behavior learned at home are acted out by third-grade girls who helpfully find the proper page for daydreaming male classmates.[8] Fights on the playground often determine who is whose girlfriend. The great bulk of male behavior, however, is devoted to play with other boys in team sports and in secret clubs. Here we see the tender misogynous roots of the all-male adult world that has little need for women beyond reproduction of the species and domestic service. Here begin the *homosocial* (preference for the company of same-gender others) patterns of our social institutions.[9]

Little girls, on the other hand, are taught early within the family that serving others is "ladylike," "adorable," "praiseworthy," even "attractive." They learn to nurture others by playing house, cooking, cleaning, and caring for children, whether these children are younger siblings or simply dolls. Little girls also learn to live within their own world, the female world, but with a difference.[10] Even as children, females learn to pay attention to what the boys are doing, to admire, applaud, and encourage boys in their active world. They begin to value male behavior and attributes, so much so that, even before they reach adolescence, females are likely to express a desire to be boys. Boys rarely say they wish they were girls.

The homosocial worlds of boys and girls, that is, worlds in which there is a preference for the company of the same-gender individuals, are quite different. Because the things boys are and do are more highly valued not only by little boys and girls, but by the larger society from which they take their cue, boys pay attention to boys and so do girls. Boys' activities are important, and girls are the audience that approves and encourages male activity.

Sports, an arena for displaying physical prowess, provide important insights into the male/female power differential. Boys' sports are perceived as more interesting; by secondary school, they draw a paying audience. At boys' athletic events, girl cheerleaders whip the audience into adulation of male physical prowess. Only since the resurgence of the women's movement have girls' sports received much attention at all. Parents are notoriously loyal and vociferous spectators at their sons' Little League games; the newer Little League for girls draws fewer spectators. Girls and boys learn their power differences in playground and later stadium games. This lesson, reinforced by parents and teachers, sets a strict pattern for the male/female power dance.

By their teens, boys are busily engaged in all-male athletics, urged on by parents and friends. Teenage girls are encouraged to spend hours learning to make themselves more attractive to boys. Teenage girls' magazines have one major focus: boys. For teenage boys, magazines feature cars and sports. All this is preparation for adult gender roles, which probably will be played out within a family setting.

This is also preparation for the two different sets of norms, expectations, and experiences men and women will find in their marriages. Sociologists Jessie Bernard and Mirra Komarovsky insist that within every marriage there actually are two: his and hers.[11] What we have been describing in this section is the unwitting preparation young people go through, learning what is expected of them in their separate, but harnessed, marriages. The divergent realities they find within marriage require still further adjustment and preparation for later life stages.

The Generation Power Struggle

The family is the setting within which both gender and generational conflicts are acted out. The power relationship between wives and husbands crosscuts the power balance between parents and children. Age and gender differences create long-term power contests. These contests are based on different levels of dependency, as well as divergent life views and values, and they are waged with different resources.

In early childhood, the disparity between the power of parents and children seems overwhelming. The child is dependent on the parent for everything: food, clothing, shelter, nurturance, safety, learning, love. This dependence, as Sigmund Freud understood, breeds hostility and resistance. Even by age 2, children begin to pit their young wills against parental efforts at control and direction. Toilet training and eating patterns are the traditional battlegrounds of early childhood. With each succeeding year, the power struggle increases, encompassing additional conflict zones—from choice of friends and evening curfews to homework, sex, and drugs. Parents alternately encourage and restrain the child's growing autonomy and power, while gradually recognizing their mutual dependence and decreasing parental power.

Early childhood dependence on parents gives way in adolescence to a struggle for greater freedom, independence, and power. Adolescent rebellion, the nightmare of parents distraught by the emerging visible hostility of these teenage "strangers in their midst," plagues parents, teenagers, and therapists alike. The transition from childhood to adolescence is a turbulent confluence of biological, hormonal, psychological, emotional, and social changes. This difficult corridor between childhood and adulthood is darkened by the absence of any genuine and meaningful life tasks for adolescents. The limited tasks of the student role offer teenagers the closest approximation to real responsibility.

Puberty Rites

Anthropologists have documented the complicated puberty rites of preliterate cultures. In these societies, pubescent youngsters are sequestered away from the regular living quarters in "male houses" or "female houses." They enter as children; they emerge as adults. These *rites de passage* (rituals marking transitions to new life stages) ease the passage from childhood to adulthood.

Industrial societies, lacking such clear-cut markers, suffer the ambiguities characteristic of contemporary adolescence. Few officially recognized puberty rites unequivocally signify the end of childhood and the beginning of adulthood, with all its gender-linked responsibilities. Consequently, in contemporary industrial societies, adolescent behavior is marked by repeated swings between childish dependence and adult independence, swings that leave both parents and teenagers exhausted and bewildered. Some observers of modern youth interpret teenage nonmarital pregnancy, drug abuse, and juvenile delinquency as troubled adolescents' attempts to create their own *rites de passage,* declaring themselves adults in the eyes of the world.

Covert Family Lessons

Within the family context, both overt and covert gender-role learning occurs. How individuals learn the behavior expected of their own gender—that is, overt gender-role lessons—has been the subject of endless research. Only rarely have questions been raised about covert gender-role learning. Children actually do learn the behavior of the other gender, as demonstrated by females and males performing one another's roles in a crisis. Crisis situations offer us a window through which to view such gender-role (in fact, all social role) changes. If females and males can assume one another's roles in crisis situations, how did they learn, and why do they not act that way under ordinary circumstances?

The answer lies in *latent socialization,* the process whereby individuals are socialized indirectly to those roles the society does not expect them to perform on a regular basis.[12] Ordinarily, individuals are socialized directly and explicitly only for those roles the society anticipates they will occupy. The heir apparent, but not the butler's son, is formally schooled to perform the royal greeting for adoring subjects. But the butler's son observes the prince's behavior and quietly practices it before his modest bedroom mirror, where imaginary crowds joyously respond.

In a similar fashion, families explicitly train little girls for motherhood and wifehood and little boys for occupational roles that provide their major rationale within the family. Even so, both boys and girls actually do learn by observing and occasionally practicing the behaviors, attitudes, and role tasks of the other gender group. Little girls, particularly tomboys, are allowed to "try on" male behavior. By interacting with their brothers and other male age-mates, as well as their fathers, they learn just how boys act, particularly toward girls. In addition, girls observe how boys are socialized to act like boys by their parents, their teachers, their older siblings, and peers. At least until puberty, there is relatively little restriction against, even some tolerance for, girls acting like boys. Little boys, however, are actively discouraged from imitating feminine behavior. As we have seen, the early tears of childhood, shed more easily by little boys than girls, are repressed by the time boys enter primary school, lest they earn the dreaded label of "sissy."

Learning to avoid certain behaviors and attitudes paradoxically requires carefully understanding their intricate content and meanings. Only by thoroughly comprehending these forbidden, lower-status behaviors can one escape such pitfalls. Thus, indirectly and implicitly, both girls and boys learn the behaviors, attitudes, and role tasks of the other gender. This is what latent socialization is all about. Families provide the intimate daily setting in which male and female study one another's gender roles; however, on pain of punishment, they also learn to preserve this knowledge in cold storage, at least until unusual circumstances—perhaps a crisis—permit or demand its use. Then, and usually only then, are women permitted, even required, to be the sole family breadwinner and men encouraged to assume full-time childcare and domestic responsibilities. Family illness, death, economic hardship, and war all provide familiar crisis conditions under which family members exchange roles without social disapproval. The capacity to perform the "other" gender role is based on this earlier latent socialization. The process of latent socialization also teaches males and females how their gender roles should be enacted in the new family structures we shall describe later.

Adults Relearn Gender Roles

Children are not the only ones who learn about gender roles within the family. Adults too are socialized to changing gender roles as they move through successive phases of the life span. The bride learns new gender-role requirements when she becomes a mother; the mother discovers the changes wrought by the widow's role. According to psychologist Daniel Levinson, men also go through adult gender-role transitions, which have been ignored until recently.[13]

Changes in adult female gender roles are linked very closely to women's private or domestic role; by contrast, male gender-role transformations emphasize men's public, mostly their occupational, roles. This contrast between the private, domestic female sphere and the public, occupational, even political, male domain sets the stage for the power differential between women and men. To complicate matters, a clear interaction occurs between the private and public spheres: individual domestic relationships between women and men influence the public, political relationships between women and men as groups, and vice versa. This interaction was less evident in an earlier historical time, when the family was an internally independent economic unit.

AN HISTORICAL PERSPECTIVE

The Family as Economic Unit

A quick historical overview will increase our understanding of how the American family has changed in a few short centuries. During America's agrarian period, the family was the basic economic unit. Husbands, wives, and children worked together to grow crops, raise domestic animals, and produce clothes and other staples the family needed for its own subsistence. Even after the Industrial Revolution brought family members into factory work, the family continued to be an economic entity. All family members were economic contributors, even when they worked in different settings—the father in the factory, the mother and children at home (at least, after the reforms that sent children and women home from factory work).

As men entered factories, their home-bound wives continued to perform the household tasks, some of which the husbands previously had shared. Women who remained in rural homesteads shouldered agricultural chores as well. Gradually, the distinction between women's housework and men's factory and office work sharpened. This distinction was increased by the fact that men's labors produced wages, whereas women's work brought no cash earnings. Through this differentially rewarded division of work, men came to be associated with the values of the industrial world—money, production, and power. Women were linked to domestic values—love, nurturance, and self-sacrifice, echoes of the control myths discussed earlier. In this way, husbands and wives began to accumulate very different resources.

The Legal Marriage Relationship: Power of Husbands and Mothers-in-Law

In poor and in affluent families, the husband controlled all resources. Even those wives who brought generous dowries to a marriage had no access to the resources settled on them by their fathers, except through their husbands. These middle- and upper-class wives found themselves legally in their husband's power, the same as their working-class sisters. For women who did not work outside the home, the husband had simply replaced his wife's father as the individual on whom she was forced to depend for all matter of things—her own and her children's shelter, food, clothes, transportation, medical care, and entertainment. From a legal standpoint, the wife *belonged* to her husband; she was simply part of her husband's chattel. Women's legal status as their husband's chattel began with the recital of the wedding vows.

The Judeo-Christian wedding vows, like all other life-cycle rituals, express the intrinsic nature of social relations and transitions into new roles and relationships. The traditional Judeo-Christian marriage vows reflected the legal relations between husband and wife, an otherwise arbitrary relationship that probably could not be sustained, either in earlier historical times or now, without legal support. These vows outlined the distinct but complementary roles of husband and wife with their mutual obligations. The wife was to love, honor, and obey her husband. He, in turn, was to love, cherish, and protect his wife, endowing her with all his worldly goods. The dominant role of the husband and the subordinate role of the wife were clearly delineated in the traditional Judeo-Christian wedding vows, which were to seal the relationship between husband and wife "until death us do part." Sociologist Jessie Bernard describes this transition for women as the "dwindling into wives."[14]

The wedding vows and rituals of modern-day America have been subjected to revisions and personalizations by the flower children of the 1960s and their successors. In many wedding ceremonies, the wife's promise to obey has been eliminated from the vows. In others, the entire ceremony has been rewritten by the couple to reflect their own understanding and hopes for an egalitarian marriage. This need to rewrite the wedding ceremony is clear testimony to the meaning of the more traditional rituals and vows. The husband had virtually complete legal power over his wife; marriage was a clear-cut power relationship, even if softened by genuine affection.

In other contemporary societies where tradition still permeates the wedding ceremony, the wedding remains a visible but "subtle act of incorporation (of the woman) into a subordinate position, according to anthropologist Gail Kligman.[15] She reports that contemporary rural Romanian brides are expected to shed ritual tears as they are showered with advice and consolation through the recitation of traditional or spontaneous rhymed couplets known as *strigaturi*. According to Kligman, it is not uncommon to hear the following *strigaturi* at rural Romanian weddings:

> Poor girls/ If only they would die/ And let their mothers bury them/ Let them bury them among the flowers/ Rather than become daughters-in-law/ Let them bury them among the lilacs/Rather than live among strangers.[16]

This *strigaturi* reflects the power relationship the bride enters both with her husband and his entire family, particularly his mother. The rural Romanian wedding ceremony has no verses for the husband, whose role requires no consolation or warning. He is not being incorporated into a strange family, nor is he sinking into subordination. In fact, the new husband is finally entering a relationship in which he will become the dominant figure.

In societies with extended families, in which several generations of kin may live together, the domination of the young wife by her mother-in-law is not uncommon. Endless mother-in-law jokes and complaints still give vent to the hostility surrounding this power struggle. Within the domestic sphere, older women rule over younger women, and in fact delegate much of their household work to the daughters-in-law. Young women look forward to a time when they will become mothers-in-law and, through this route, escape both household labor and the domination of their husband's mother. Small wonder that in some societies the transition from extended nuclear families was warmly welcomed, particularly when domestic servants were plentiful. Only much later did wives in isolated nuclear family units look back nostalgically at the extended family, realizing a mother-in-law's domination and some childcare help had been traded for increased domination by the husband.

THE DIVISION OF LABOR WITHIN THE FAMILY

Among traditional families, women continue to work unpaid at home, while men earn money in the paid labor force to support the entire family. Within this tradition, women produce new workers by bearing children; at the end of each work day, women also nurture and restore the present workers—their husbands and sons (and since the twentieth century, their daughters). This pattern produced a severe power imbalance in the private sphere. The homebound wife earned no wages, although she contributed to the household and the larger economy in ways only now being calculated by economists and divorce courts. Many wives who remained isolated at home "failed to grow" at the same pace as their husbands, whose occupational challenges and experiences enlarged their vision and sophistication.

In this scenario, the wife became even more economically dependent on her husband the longer she stayed out of the paid labor force. Many wives eventually grew "too old" and "too inexperienced" to start even at a junior or midlevel position in the occupational world. Not only was the wife in this scene dependent on her husband for economic support; she was also forced to rely on him for bringing growth to the relationship. As she aged without "growing," the wife felt, was perceived, and often actually was, left behind. The long-term result in many cases was divorce in midlife or later, after the wife had set aside her own occupational and economic possibilities for the sake of her husband's career. As we noted earlier, recent divorce law is beginning to take this structured imbalance into account in deciding divorce settlements. But within marriages, the power imbalance may grow unabated.

LEISURE TIME AND POLITICAL PARTICIPATION

Leisure time, a valuable resource, is unequally distributed to wives and husbands, even when both are actively engaged in the labor force. According to time-budget studies in the United States and abroad, husbands have more leisure or discretionary time than wives.[17] As a result, husbands have greater opportunities to engage in political activity. Political, community, and other activity in the public sphere provides additional opportunities for developing resources and thus power. These political resources offer possibilities for occupational enhancement, which in turn increase political power.

Women's reduced discretionary time makes it less likely that they will engage in these power-generating activities. Their time-consuming domestic role within the family limits their ability to engage in public activities where they might gain access to institutional resources. This is seen clearly in East European countries, where political activity is more closely linked to occupational success than in the United States. Women's lack of resources also makes it difficult for their voice to be taken seriously in the public arena. Small wonder that their power within the domestic relationship is sharply limited. Even smaller wonder that micromanipulation is an important domestic tool. The ricocheting effects of domestic and public domains, this interpenetration of private lives and public policy, create a complex power matrix.

UNNOTICED CHANGES IN FAMILY STRUCTURE: A STATISTICAL PORTRAIT

"The family" is often referred to in hushed tones. Traditionalists describe "the family" as a social institution divinely inspired and mirroring the sacred relationship between human beings and God. As earlier chapters have suggested, this perception of the family as a microcosmic replica of the divine relationship stems from biblical and other ancient images handed down through the ages and lends an air of permanence to family structure as well. The result is that any changes the family has actually undergone escape notice. Even though the media document numerous signposts of change in the contemporary family, we continue to think that most American families include a housebound mother, a wage-earning father, and several (usually reported as "2.2") children. We do not surrender this picture, even when it is no longer accurate.

Perhaps an overview of recent demographic trends will help us set the family within a more realistic framework. By 1980, Census Bureau reports documented clear increases in "the postponement of marriage, the proportion of young adults remaining single, divorced adults, adults living alone, unmarried couples (living together), families maintained by adults with no spouse present, and children living with only one parent."[18] These changing trends in family characteristics point to the existence of many different types of families.

Postponed Marriage

The growing American trend of postponing marriage is evident from several different demographic statistics. For one, age at first marriage has risen over the years. At the present time, the *median age* (age at which half the population falls above and the other half falls below) of first marriage is 22.1 years for females and 24.4 years for males. In the early part of this century, the median age was 21 to 22 years for women, and 25 to 26 years for men. By 1956, however, the median age at which young Americans married dropped to its lowest point in the twentieth century: 20.1 years for women and 22.5 for men. It has been rising steadily since that time as more young adults, especially women, have delayed marriage to continue their educations or to work in the paid labor force.

If the current trend in postponement of marriage continues, it could easily shade into a "never married" trend by the time the current postponers, now in their twenties, reach middle age. A recent poll of attitudes toward permanent "singlehood" revealed growing numbers of men and women who are perfectly comfortable at the prospect of never marrying.

Here again, we should consider the meaning of marriage postponement in terms of the power relationship between women and men. Clearly, the ability to remain single, particularly for women, represents a growing capacity to support oneself, since many of these young women have established individual households. As more women become economically self-supporting, their power in relation to men increases. If, as most demographers tell us, postponement of marriage is coupled with increased education and paid employment for women, this resource-building activity further enhances women's power position in heterosexual relationships. Consequently, more women are entering marriage on an equal economic footing with their husbands, setting the stage for more egalitarian domestic relationships. This is not to deny that tenacious attitudes, values, and social pressures may erode this initial equality based on economic resources.

Cohabitation, or Unmarried Couples Living Together

Demographers argue that the increase in age at first marriage is attributable primarily to changing social *mores*, or customs, particularly those surrounding sexual and social relationships between unmarried adults. Not so long ago, the idea of an unmarried woman and man living together was socially unthinkable. The revolution in sexual mores, following the introduction of the Pill, gave women greater control over their own fertility. It also contributed to changing attitudes toward unmarried people *cohabiting*, or living together—so much so that by 1979, 1.3 million households consisted of unmarried male-female couples. The numbers of cohabiting couples have more than doubled since 1970, when 523,000 comprised this category. By 1979, three-quarters of the unmarried-couple households were composed of just two adults, and the remaining quarter "consisted of two adults and one or more children under 14 years old."[19] Census reports tell us even more about the marital status of these unmarried men and women living together:

> Approximately half the men and women sharing living quarters had never been married.
>
> 28 percent of the women and 32 percent of the men were divorced.
>
> 11 percent of the women and 5 percent of the men were widowed.
>
> 7 percent of the women and 10 percent of the men were separated.
>
> 2 percent of both women and men were married, but living with someone other than their spouses.
>
> The most frequent couple combinations were a never-married woman living with a never-married man (36 percent), followed by a divorced woman living with a divorced man (15 percent).

All together, 2.7 million partners are involved in this increase in living-together arrangements—an unprecedented change, but one that still affects only a small proportion of adults. Despite the very real increase in the numbers of women and men choosing this form of family structure, the greatest number of couples living together are indeed married couples. Census reports estimate that, in 1979, 96.5 million women and men were living together as married couples. Thus, the newer living arrangement of unmarried couples sharing residential quarters affected only 3.5 percent of all couples living together. Nevertheless, that an identifiable proportion of the unmarried heterosexual population lives together, without any marked social disapproval, indicates that something important has really changed. Part of that "something" is the power balance between women and men.

Households in which unmarried women and men live together are frequently marked by shared expenses and shared responsibilities. Women and men pay their individual ways, both contributing economic and labor resources. How will this arrangement affect traditional marriage, we might ask, and the power relationship between husbands and wives? Systematic studies of couples who have lived together before their eventual marriage have yet to be done; however, impressionistic data from mass media and other sources indicate that things do change once men and women assume the formal roles of husband and wife. Anecdotal evidence suggests that once the marriage vows are taken, both parties revert to rather traditional expectations. Not surprisingly, more customary power relationships often develop. Some now-divorced couples who had lived together happily before marrying blame the failure of their marriage on the fact that one or both spouses changed (reverted to conventional marital roles) once they exchanged marriage vows. Formal marital roles may carry with them more traditional expectations, even about power. Nonetheless, those couples who have lived unmarried in a more egalitarian or balanced power relationship may be less likely to create a marital relationship in which the age-old power balance exists.

Single-Parent Families

Another form of family structure, the single-parent family, has caught public attention. By 1979, 34 percent of the families headed by men and 63 percent of those headed by women were what demographers now call *single-parent families*. In fact, 19 percent of all families with children at home were maintained by one parent, up from 11 percent in 1970. In all, families other than those sustained by a married couple numbered 10.1 million by 1979, a figure that includes previously or currently married individuals living apart from their spouses, with or without children. This represents a 50 percent increase between 1970 and 1979. Eighty percent of these "other" families are headed by women, many of whom live below the poverty line. Between 1970 and 1982, the number of families maintained by women rose from 5.5 million to 9.4 million. And in the two-year period from 1980 to 1982, female-headed families increased 25.4 percent.[20]

Female-headed households, particularly those with children under 18, are mostly impoverished families. So it does not follow that if women head households, instead of living as dependent members of a male-headed family, they will fare better in any economic, real-world sense. The economic resources available to women who head households are severely limited, particularly when they bear total responsibility for childcare as well as breadwinning.

The popular impression (fostered partly by the film *Kramer vs. Kramer,* in which Dustin Hoffman battled for the custody of his small son) that the proportion of single-parent families headed by father is rising faster than those maintained by mothers has little statistical support. In fact, in 1979, 2 percent of all families with children were headed by father alone, compared to 17 percent by mothers alone. It is true, nonetheless, that the number of families headed by fathers alone rose 99.1 percent from 1970 to 1982; but the 105.3 percent increase in the number of families headed by mothers alone outdistanced this gain. Still, this signals a growing acceptance of fathers as the main caretakers for children, a factor that has important implications for definitions of gender roles and the gender power relationship.

Among female-headed families, other discernible changes have occurred in the last decade. The number of widows has declined, while divorced and never-married female family heads have increased. By 1979, approximately 38 percent of one-parent families were headed by divorced women (versus 29 percent in 1970). Clearly, unmarried women with children are not simply "going home to mother"—a sign of growing independence. Nonetheless, these family patterns do not automatically increase the resources, and hence the power, of women.

Nonfamily Households

Still other living arrangements exist. Statistics show that not everyone lives within a family setting. One out of every four households in the United States is what the Census Bureau calls a *nonfamily household*—that is, a household with no legally related or cohabiting members. Such nonfamily households have increased by 7.9 million since 1970, to a high of 19.8 million in 1979.

Most nonfamily households of this type are maintained by women, although women represent fewer of these nonfamily household heads than they did in the early 1970s. In addition, women who do maintain nonfamily households tend to be considerably older than men who do so, with a median age of 64.4 years versus 37.5 years, respectively. From 1970 to 1979, the median age of men maintaining nonfamily households sharply declined from 53.0 to 37.5 years, while women experienced only a 1.1 year drop in median age. Apparently, much younger men than before are now living in nonfamily households, while it is still older women—often widowed—who tend to live in this type of setting. This reflects a growing number of younger never-married men, as well as younger divorced men, establishing their own households. Sociologists wonder whether such living patterns will teach men to take care of their own household needs, so that in subsequent relationships with women they will place less emphasis on

female domestic skills. Will this, in turn, affect the power balance in male/
female relationships?

The Meaning of Different Living Arrangements

What does all this mean? These statistics on living arrangements and
families tell us that the family has developed many new forms (or, as
sociologists would say, *family structures*). For example, even people who have
never married do not necessarily live with their immediate family or other
relatives. The expectations for women being protected by family and kin
have diminished, as indicated by the numbers of women, young and old,
living alone or with young children. The increase in the number of never-
married women living with children (indirectly confirming the figures on
unmarried fertility rates noted earlier) suggests that never-married motherhood may be losing its "scandalous" aura.

The increasing number of men deliberately seeking to maintain their
family roles and responsibilities by heading households for themselves and
their children, without a spouse present, also tells us things are changing.
Single fatherhood is becoming somewhat less awesome to men, and probably also to family court judges deciding custody cases.

To some degree, the tightening economy in recent years has driven
many nonfamily members, young and old, to share living quarters—an
arrangement greeted with increasing nonchalance as economic conditions
legitimate what social conditions earlier promoted. The fact that men and
women—married and unmarried, with and without children—are living
together under different types of household and personal arrangements
points toward a growing flexibility in social attitudes and behavior surrounding families. That some politicians and small but vociferous groups
continue to extol a family profile that has long since ceased to be the typical
pattern of the majority of adult Americans simply delays and confuses our
acceptance of a reality that has already arrived. These new patterns in
family structure are the results, directly and indirectly, of the confluence of
marriage, divorce, and remarriage trends. The increase in divorce, particularly, has become a worldwide phenomenon that is seriously affecting definitions of gender roles within and outside the family.

Divorce Trends

Following a peak in marriage, divorce, and remarriage trends after
World War II, the first-marriage rate began a steady decline that continued
through the mid-1970s.[21] Since 1977, however, there has been a slight but
steady increase in the first-marriage rate. For example, in the twelve-
month period ending April 1979, the first-marriage rate was 10.4 per 1000
population, up 4 percent over the rate for the previous 12 months.

Divorce and remarriage rates began to rise in the early 1960s and
moved up sharply during the remainder of that decade, reaching an all-
time high in 1970. Since then, however, the picture has changed somewhat.
The divorce rate has continued to climb, while the remarriage rate seems to

have leveled off and even declined among some groups. For example, among women at high educational, occupational, and economic levels, remarriage is more often delayed and/or avoided. This trend is interpretable as evidence of (1) women's increased economic power, enabling them to avoid entering marriage simply for the sake of economic support; or (2) the difficulty for women with increased educational, occupational, and/or economic power of finding appropriate mates; or (3) some combination of these two.

Demographers monitor the rate of change in divorce over time by tracking the number of divorced persons per 1000 persons married and living with spouses. Between 1970 and 1979, "the ratio of all divorced persons per 1,000 husbands and wives in intact marriages had risen by 96 percent, from 47 per 1,000 to 92 per 1,000."[22] The divorce rate among blacks increased over this same time period from 83 per 1000 to 197 per 1000. For whites, the ratios were 44 per 1000 in 1970, and 84 per 1000 in 1979.

Following divorce, men remarry more quickly and more often than women do. This results in a relatively higher divorce rate for women. Reflecting this, census reports indicate 111 divorced women per 1000 wives versus 72 divorced men per 1000 husbands. And although there is considerable public concern about teenage marriages leading to divorce, by 1979 the age group with the highest divorce ratio was, in fact, individuals between 30 and 40 years old.

Overall, divorce is most common among low-income groups. This is particularly the case for low-income men. And in the aftermath of divorce, as noted before, women with higher income levels more often postpone or reject marriage, while lower-income women are more likely to remarry within a short time. Between 1960 and 1970, upper-income men saw their divorce rate increase more rapidly than the rate for lower-income men, even though men with higher incomes continued to be a smaller proportion of the divorced population. Furthermore, divorced men with higher incomes remarried more frequently than men with lower incomes, a reversal of the female pattern. These shifts suggest convergence in divorce patterns among all social classes, according to demographers Alfred Norton and Paul Glick.[23]

Factors affecting the divorce rate—low economic and educational levels and early marriage age—are changing rapidly. Teenage marriages have had notoriously difficult histories, with predictably high divorce rates. Norton and Glick report that people who have not completed a high school education are most likely to face divorce. As mentioned earlier, teenage couples frequently abandon their educations before earning high school diplomas, placing both young wives and husbands in immediate and long-term economic and occupational jeopardy. For teenage girls, pregnancy often brings additional—in some places, legal—barriers to high school completion, a severe handicap in any quest for economic independence.

As educational levels have risen throughout the population, divorce trends have begun to reflect that influence. Recent figures show that nearly 75 percent of today's youth complete high school, and close to 43 percent (or some 58 percent of high school graduates) enter degree-credit programs in universities; and there is a corresponding slowdown in the increase in the divorce rate. As educational levels and marriage age keep rising, the divorce rate will continue to decelerate.

NEW FAMILY GENDER ROLES

The "sacredness of the family" has begun to exhibit fault lines created by the tremors of sociological change, fault lines that follow the curves of marriage, divorce, and remarriage trends within contemporary society. In its numerous modern guises, the family teaches many traditional and some newer gender-role lessons. For one, children observe their parents' or their friends' parents' divorce. They learn the intricacies of single-parent living and sometimes become an integral part of *blended families* (families composed of a previously married couple living with children from earlier marriages, as well as offspring from the current union). Stepchildren, stepparents, stepgrandparents, half-brothers and sisters try on their new family gender roles and relationships with varying degress of comfort and success.

The increasing prevalance of divorce, single-parent families, blended families, and cohabiting couples creates a rapidly multiplying set of possible gender roles within the family. The growing longevity gap between women and men, with women generally outliving men, adds to the complex picture. Relatively young people can expect a greater likelihood of living alone or with their children; this is particularly true for women. Single parenthood offers special challenges to be "both mother and father" to the children of divorce.

Still another version of parenthood and childhood emerges from *joint custody* arrangements, where children live part of the time with each divorced parent. Single parenthood creates the likelihood of parents' boyfriends or girlfriends. Often, as the statistics in this chapter revealed, the single parent has a live-in friend, sometimes of the same gender. As a result, new norms of parental sexual behavior are portrayed to children reared within these contemporary families.

Twentieth-century parents offer different kinds of role models to their children. Not only do they marry, divorce, remarry, or live alone more often than their parents before them; they even handle family responsibilities differently. With the disappearance of domestic servants, the technological advances in homemaking and food preparation within and outside the home, and women's growing labor force participation, family roles are changing shape. Allowing for variations among socioeconomic groups, which we shall explore in Chapter 9, men and women are more likely than before to share household chores.

Even childcare, the sacrosanct feminine domain, is increasingly, if reluctantly, shared by men. Without the extra female hands provided within the extended family, married couples in the *nuclear family* (parents and their offspring) are forced to rely more on one another for domestic help. Only those affluent couples who can afford to hire scarce household help can avoid confronting the division of household tasks between themselves. As more women enter the labor force, the sharing of adult male and female family roles accelerates. In fact, a small proportion of couples practice role reversal, with the husband at home full-time and the wife the sole bread-winner. In families where both parents work outside the home, children may share in domestic chores. This participation of children in adult family responsibilities takes us full circle. It is, in a sense, the twentieth-century variation of an earlier historical pattern marked by the family as an economic unit. Perhaps the savants are right: "La plus change, la plus le même chose"—the more things change, the more they stay the same.

SUMMARY

In this chapter we described how the family offers the original context for learning and enacting gender roles. Within the family, gender roles are complicated by age differences between generations. The relationships between husband and wife, mother-in-law and daughter-in-law, parent and child create an age and gender power matrix among actors with very different resources. Gender roles, laced with power conflicts, find their most complicated expression within changing family structures, particularly the new families fostered by marriage and divorce trends in the late twentieth century. We have examined the changing shape of family structures and the gender roles males and females learn and perform within these intimate circles. That not all families teach the same gender-role curriculum will become more evident in the next chapter, where we examine gender role differences linked to variations in social class.

NOTES

1. Bronislaw Malinowski, *The Family Among the Australian Aborigines* (London: University of London Press, 1913).

2. Robert F. Bales and Philip E. Slater, "Role Differentiation in Small Decision-Making Groups," in *Family, Socialization and Interaction Process,* T. Parsons and R. F. Bales with J. Olds, M. Zeldich, Jr., and P. E. Slater (New York: The Free Press, 1955), pp. 259–306.

3. Talcott Parsons, "The American Family: Its Relations to Personality and to the Social Structure," in *Family, Socialization and Interaction Process,* T. Parsons and R. F. Bales, with I. Olds, M. Zeldich, Jr. and P. E. Slater (New York: The Free Press, 1955), pp. 3–33.

4. E. O. Wilson, *Sociobiology: The New Synthesis* (Cambridge, Mass.: Harvard University Press, 1975); David Barash, *Sociology and Behavior* (New York: Elsevier, 1977).

5. Juliet Mitchell, "The Longest Revolution," *New Left Review,* 40 (November/December, 1966), 11–37.

6. Barrie Thorne, "Feminist Rethinking of the Family: An Overview," in *Rethinking the Family: Some Feminist Questions,* ed. Barrie Thorne with Marilyn Yalom (New York: Longman Inc., 1982), pp. 1–24.

7. Ruth E. Hartley, "Sex-roles and Urban Youth: Some Developmental Perspectives," *The Bulletin on Family Development,* 2, no. 1 (1961), 1–12.

8. Raphaela Best, *We've All Got Scars: What Boys and Girls Learn in Elementary School* (Bloomington: University of Indiana Press, 1983).

9. Jean Lipman-Blumen, "Toward a Homosocial Theory of Sex Roles: An Explanation of the Sex Segregation of Social Institutions," *Signs,* 1, no. 3, part 2 (Spring 1976), 15–31.

10. Jessie Bernard, *The Female World* (New York: The Free Press, 1981).

11. Jessie Bernard, *The Future of Marriage* (New York: World Press, 1972); Mirra Komarovsky, *Women in the Modern World: Their Education and Their Dilemmas* (Boston: Little, Brown, 1962).

12. Jean Lipman-Blumen, "Role De-differentiation as a System Response to Crisis: Occupational and Political Roles of Women," *Sociological Inquiry*, 43, no. 2 (1973), 105–129.

13. Daniel J. Levinson and others, *The Seasons of a Man's Life* (New York: Knopf, 1978).

14. Jessie Bernard, *The Future of Marriage*.

15. Gail Kligman, "The Rites of Women: Oral Poetry, Ideology, and the Socialization of Peasant Women in Contemporary Romania" (paper presented at the Sino-Soviet Conference on Changes in the Status of Women in Eastern Europe, George Washington University, Washington, D.C., December 4–6, 1981), p. 9.

16. Kligman, "The Rites of Women," p. 9.

17. Jean Lipman-Blumen and Jessie Bernard, eds., *Sex Roles and Social Policy* (Beverly Hills, Cal.: Sage, 1979).

18. U.S. Department of Commerce, Bureau of the Census, *Current Population Reports*, #349 (Washington, D.C.: Government Printing Office, February 1980), p. 200.

19. Ibid.

20. U.S. Department of Commerce, Bureau of the Census, *Current Population Reports* #381 (Washington, D.C.: Government Printing Office, March 1982), pp. 2–3.

21. Jean Lipman-Blumen, "The Implications for Family Structure of Changing Sex Roles," *Social Casework*, 57, no. 2 (1976), 67–79.

22. U.S. Department of Commerce, *Current Population Reports*, p. 20.

23. Arthur J. Norton and Paul C. Glick, "Marital Instability in America: Past, Present, and Future," in *Divorce and Separation: Context, Careers, and Consequences*, eds. George Levinger and Oliver C. Moles (New York: Basic Books, 1979), pp. 6–19.

CHAPTER 9
THE SEX-GENDER SYSTEM AND SOCIAL CLASS

The nature and expression of sex and gender roles vary in families with different social-class backgrounds. Families at the two ends of the class spectrum—upper and working class—differentiate the most between female and male roles, according to sociologists; the nature of the differentiation, however, is not the same for these two groups. Not surprisingly, the middle-class family, caught between the two, shares some features with each, while the internal distinctions middle-class families draw between male and female gender roles are less sharp.

WORKING-CLASS FAMILIES

Division of Labor

Stereotypes of working-class families depict women as full-time homemakers and childrearers, and men as the sole breadwinners. Like all stereotypes, this picture of the working-class family exaggerates reality. At the very least, this working-class caricature obscures the wife's real-life labor force activity.

For many decades, working-class women have played a significant role in the paid labor force. Even in the early 1960s, sociologist Mirra Komarovsky chronicled the working-class wife's paid work role.[1] In the mid-1970s, psychologist Lillian Rubin's study of working-class families revealed that still more wives worked at paid jobs outside the home.[2] And with tightening economic conditions, an increasing number of previously homebound working-class wives are supplementing the family income as service and other "pink-collar" workers.

Unlike their middle-class sisters, however, working-class women rarely perceive their work outside the home as an avenue to individual fulfillment. In fact, many endure their low-status, low-paid, factory, domestic, service, or office work as necessary for family economic stability, work they will readily abandon when economic conditions improve. Still other working-class women look to their outside work as a means of changing the daily routine and reducing the isolation of housework and childcare. Many blue-collar husbands resist their wives' desire for outside work on at least two grounds: first, because such work stigmatizes the husband as an unsuccessful provider; and second, because husbands fear their wives will become "too independent."

Within the working-class family, women traditionally have reached out to other female kin, particularly for important domestic help and emotional support. Rubin's research suggests that working-class wives are beginning to seek more emotional support and communication from their husbands, thereby escalating the confusion and conflict that accompany changing gender roles.[3] Working-class husbands participate in household chores and the care of older children somewhat more than popularized versions of working-class life suggest. Nonetheless, the physically tiring occupations of many working-class men make their women less likely than middle-class wives to expect their husbands to share domestic chores or childcare. Sociologists report that the working-class wife still expects to have a hearty meal ready for her hard-working husband at the end of a long day of usually heavy manual work. This was so in the early 1960s, and it remains true now, even when the wife also works outside the home.

Ironically, a recent Gallop poll revealed that among women who have not graduated from high school, cooking is the most disliked domestic chore. (But dishwashing remains the least liked household task among American women generally.) Working-class women and men agree that cooking, laundry, and dishes, as well as the care of very young children, are "women's work," but shopping, some housecleaning, and babysitting for older children are not considered off limits for working-class husbands. We might ponder why the tasks working-class women dislike the most are the same ones men shun completely, albeit with women's acquiescence. Does this mean that the more powerful group can choose to avoid altogether whatever tasks it perceives as most undesirable by labeling them "women's work"?

Maternal and domestic responsibility, then, remain at the heart of the working-class wife's gender-role repertoire, despite her paid labor force activity. Important components of the blue-collar wife's role in earlier generations—neighborly assistance, community and church work—are somewhat less central today.

Marital Sex Roles

Conjugal sex is an important, if difficult, part of working-class marital roles. A special enjoyment for some, sex is a recognized conjugal responsibility for all working-class wives. The variation in sexual expression that characterizes the middle-class and upper-class sex roles of married couples is something of a battleground among working-class husbands and wives. According to psychologist Rubin, contemporary working-class husbands may press their wives for more erotic sexual variation; the wives, however, remain caught in the conflict between their upbringing as "nice girls" and a desire to meet their husbands' sexual needs and desires. Repeated assurances from their spouses that normal marital sex may take many forms do not allay many working-class wives' fear of losing esteem in their spouses' eyes. They feel safely respectable with traditional sexual behavior. The marriage bed thus becomes the setting for a power struggle—with esteem, desire, affection, love, sexual satisfaction, domestic service, and authority the resources at stake.

Marital sex roles (that is, sexual behavior within marriage) are learned from the more sexually experienced partner, usually the husband. For some working-class spouses, same-sex friends offer concrete sexual advice. A more limited set of blue-collar couples look to books for guidance. Young wives may turn to their mothers for general information, including confirmation or consolation about their conjugal responsibilities. Young wives frequently seek more specific help, however, from their sisters and female friends. Despite this list of available resources for guidance, working-class spouses often feel serious inhibitions against discussing their sexual "problems" with anyone other than their partners. In fact, several research studies suggest that working-class partners report difficulty in exploring such sensitive issues even with each other.

Studies of working-class gender roles suggest that the males are socialized to an orientation toward things, rationality, and stoicism—as the control myths teach. They are taught to act, not to feel, much less to verbalize feelings—again echoing control myths. Females, by contrast, learn to explore and value relationships, emotionality, intuition, and expression of feelings. This is not so different from the gender-role socialization of females and males in other classes, rather a matter of degree.

More recent studies of interaction in blue-collar marriages reveal that wives increasingly look to their husbands for emotion, communication, and intimacy that is not simply sexual. Wives who measure love in terms of verbal expressions of affection and caring find it difficult to accept their husbands' sexual overtures, unaccompanied by verbal affection and communion, as evidence of the love they seek. Working-class husbands, unschooled in verbal expressions of affection, are equally bewildered by their wives' resistance to reconciling their nonsexual differences in the marriage bed, the setting the husbands perceive most appropriate for expressing love. Reticence to discuss sexual problems only diminishes the possibilities for clarifying changing expectations about sex roles.

The Male Circle of Buddies

After marriage, most working-class couples continue to live in their childhood neighborhoods. In the early years of marriage, the young husband spends much of his free time with his male "buddies," many of whom are childhood friends. Since many working-class couples have little money in the first few years of marriage, they commonly live with parents. This living arrangement tends to foster the illusion of continued bachelorhood for the husband.

Studies of working-class marriages report that the time the young husband spends with his male buddies in homosocial pursuits creates serious marital conflict in the early years.[4] Often the young wife turns to her mother-in-law to support her claim that free time is a family resource, a commodity not to be so freely spent in all-male activities. Rubin documents the difficulties 50 young, working-class families had in learning to become a couple (or as sociologists would say, "learning their marital gender roles").[5] Not only must the young wife combat the tight, wife-excluding hold of her husband's childhood buddies; she must also find a comparable group that she and her husband can join as a couple. In addition to their families, married couples handily serve this function.

Learning How to Be a Couple: Socialization to Marital Gender Roles

The circle of married couples with whom the blue-collar couple associates provides a social mechanism for socializing young husbands and wives to their couple roles. This clique, composed of a close-knit set of married pairs, creates a framework for married social activities that competes with the husband's all-male buddy network. Of course, there may be some overlap between the men in the husband's buddy network and the husbands of clique couples.

Working-class wives also have their female confidantes, often the wives of the clique couples. From these female confidantes, who may include a sister-in-law or sister, young working-class wives learn different dimensions of the wife and mother role. Matters of childcare, housework, and "husband-taming" may be discussed with a mother, mother-in-law, sister, or sister-in-law. Female relatives generally support one another's efforts to foster a family orientation among their married men. This eventually loosens the hold of the all-male buddy network. In the working class, then, learning marital and parental gender roles is very much a social process, distributed among kin and a tight circle of married friends.

Learning and Enacting Parental Roles

After children are born, the young working-class mother assumes primary responsibility for their care. Most young mothers learn childrearing practices from their mothers or mothers-in-law. Mothers remember their own childhoods, in which daughters were brought up more strictly than sons, but sons were also expected to adhere to a clear line of discipline. These young working-class parents tend to rear their own children very much the way they were brought up, except when childhood memories provide negative role models and events.

Working-class parents enforce strict gender roles. Young girls are expected home by a "reasonable" hour to protect them from physical harm, as well as from premarital sexual activity. Working-class sons are allowed far greater social latitude, particularly with regard to sexual and drinking mores. Daughters of working-class families commonly marry very young, because this is the only readily available escape from the strict parental home.

Increasingly, working-class daughters and sons are being encouraged to continue their education beyond high school; however, such encouragement usually means enrolling at the local community college, not "going away" to college. In fact, recent educational statistics reveal the greatest increases in women's higher education enrollments occurred in such community colleges, the mainstay of working-class students. Randour, Strasburg, and Lipman-Blumen report that the percentage of women's enrollments in two-year institutions of higher learning (community colleges) climbed from 36.9 percent in 1963 to 54.4 percent by 1979.[6] In addition, the working-class movement has prompted mature women, particularly older mothers and grandmothers, to complete previously abandoned high school educations, even continuing through community college programs.

Despite this growing emphasis on higher education for women, working-class daughters are still more likely than middle-class daughters to forego college for early marriage and babies. And working-class families continue to value children and home above education for women.

The Grassroots Movement and Gender Roles

The mass media's description of the renewed women's movement has largely ignored the involvement of working-class women's groups, referred to as the *grassroots movement*. The emerging grassroots movement emphasizes familial and community values, but still recognizes changing gender roles. It acknowledges the natural leadership strength of ethnic women, who have administered the complex, if informal, organization of extended families. The importance of education for working-class women, even later in life, is a value that the grassroots movement actively encourages, all within a family and community context.

The grassroots movement offers a compelling mechanism for integrating continuity and change in working-class gender roles. Its emphasis on family, community, and church, along with women's leadership and power in these domains, is slowly transforming working-class gender roles. Simultaneously, the grassroots movement is restructuring the underlying power struggle between working-class women and men.

The grassroots women's movement brings together grandmothers with daughters and granddaughters. As a result, the older generation, which traditionally resisted gender role changes, actually legitimates the new expectations and behaviors. In this way, working-class gender-role changes are occurring within a supportive, multigenerational context that integrates continuity and change. The power shifts created in this way seem a benign, more palatable, pill to swallow. This cross-generational alliance gently files down some of the sharp differences between working-class gender roles. Although the grassroots movement represents a small portion of working-class women, their numbers, and therefore their influence, are growing.

MIDDLE-CLASS FAMILIES

Across the social-class spectrum, middle-class gender roles are probably the least differentiated. Both parents, but mothers more than fathers, show considerable flexibility toward children who test the limits of gender role. The unisex trends in clothing and hairstyles of the 1960s and 1970s originated with middle-class youth seeking new definitions of sex and gender roles, including new ways of relating to one another.

Despite the greater similarity between female and male roles in middle-class families, a recognizable difference still exists. This differentiation of sex and gender roles is particularly marked in less urbanized areas, and is similar to that of the working-class family. Women are responsible primarily for children and housework, even if they work outside the home, and men are the principal breadwinners. Unmarried women are more sexually active than before, but still somewhat less so than men.

In the 1970s, a major shift in middle-class gender roles became apparent, particularly in the public sphere. For the first time since World War II, women were assuming a visible public presence, and this time because *they*, not society, were demanding it. As we shall see, women's educational level also began to rise, along with their expectations of winning more lucrative jobs.

Learning Middle-Class Gender Roles

Gender roles, more blurred in middle-class families, are learned from a somewhat more diverse set of sources. Family members are, of course, important agents of gender role socialization, but friends, teachers, books, TV, newspapers, the theater and films, as well as other aspects of twentieth-century life, create significant learning experiences.

Young middle-class adults usually marry after college or graduate school. Living in college dormitories, away from the nuclear family, introduces them to a diversity of values. The later first-marriage age of middle-class couples increases the likelihood of spending more time before marriage in adult nonfamily relationships. These extrafamilial relationships provide young middle-class adults with additional experience in the complex dynamics of male-female interaction and the power balance they represent. The current generation of middle-class college students explicitly struggles with women's issues, from the abstract level of power relationships and ideology to the pragmatic details of sharing expenses on dates and integrating careers and marriage.

Middle-class gender roles show considerable flexibility, particularly compared to those at the two extremes of the class spectrum. Young married couples are more likely to expect both husband and wife to work at professional careers and to share household responsibilities, at least until the arrival of children confronts them with more complex responsibilities and arrangements. Fewer and fewer aspects of marital gender roles are "taken for granted"; virtually everything is up for discussion and negotiation—a radical departure from their parents' experience. Of course, these young wives had middle-class parents, particularly fathers, who exerted some pressure toward gender-role conformity. Increasingly, however, middle-class fathers have encouraged their daughters to pursue higher education and fields of study previously reserved for sons.

The expanding educational choices facing middle-class females set them on more broadly defined gender-role paths. Middle-class young women with college and professional degrees expect to combine marriage and careers, an expectation relatively few of their mothers had when they were young. If popular magazines offer us any clues to the concerns of middle-class young women, the plethora of articles on integrating career and family points to a deep concern about these issues. The spate of new magazines—*Working Woman, Savvy, Ms.*—addressed to middle-class young and not-quite-so-young women bespeaks an audience seeking, if not solutions to these dilemmas, at least practical ways of "muddling through."

Middle-class couples look somewhat less to their parents for help and advice regarding marital gender roles than the working-class couples described earlier. More likely, they turn to friends and work associates, to books, even to psychologists and psychiatrists. Middle-class couples are less likely to live in their childhood neighborhoods, moving instead to accommodate the demands of graduate work and careers. Consequently, the all-male circle of childhood buddies that we saw in working-class circles is a less readily observable component of middle-class life. The clique of married couples serves here also to provide instruction, support, approval, or disapproval to young couples learning what it means to be married. Marilyn French's novel *The Women's Room* describes the intricate functioning of the suburban couples' network in the 1950s.[7] The children of that generation, today's more "liberated" couples, undoubtedly engage in somewhat different activities and articulate somewhat different values, but the couples' network continues to socialize spouses to their marital roles.

Middle-Class Sex Roles

Middle-class sex roles, entailing appropriate sexual behavior for females and males, are learned both formally and informally. Formal sex education occurs within the school and sometimes the church. Formal instruction in biology and physiology, as well as social science and sex education courses, broadens the sexual understanding of middle-class students in high school and college.

The family and the peer group provide major sources of informal learning. The family, from early childhood through young adulthood, offers informal verbal and behavioral lessons in appropriate sex roles. The peer group creates its own perspective and knowledge of sex roles and sexuality, sometimes in contradiction to family and church teachings. Within the peer group, sex is a serious and seemingly endless topic of informal discussion. Middle-class youth, immersed in college campus life, learn from their own and others' sexual experiences. Sex manuals, both scientific and erotic, are considered legitimate, if not mandatory, reading. Movies, TV, and theater, other sources of sex-role knowledge, explore sexual themes in increasingly explicit terms. From heterosexuality, to lesbian and gay sexuality, to pre- and extramarital sexual relationships, little is left to the imagination.

The technological breakthrough of the Pill catapulted many young couples into sexual relationships that the fear of pregnancy constrained in previous generations. Sparked by the Pill, the sexual revolution reportedly has broadened the range of acceptable sexual behavior, particularly among the middle class. Even 30 years ago, the famous Kinsey Report reported a wider middle-class acceptance of oral sex and other less traditional sexual practices.[8] Today that cultural acceptance has grown, and oral sex, particularly, is taken for granted as a standard sexual practice, even if one's individual tastes differ.

The sexual distinction between "good girls" and "bad girls" is less sharp, if it exists at all, within the middle class. Middle-class men and women rarely concern themselves with a woman's virginity. This more nonchalant attitude toward nonmarital sexuality sets the stage for greater sexual freedom, even innovation, among middle-class couples. But the devaluation of female virginity reduces its importance as a negotiating chip in the sex-gender power struggle. Not even the much-publicized herpes epidemic is likely to restore much of the negotiating value of female virginity.

The women's movement, with its emphasis on female sexuality, has brought new concern about female orgasm, an aspect of sexuality perhaps more easily discussed by middle-class than by working-class individuals. Female orgasm, conceptualized by feminists as women's sexual "right," heightens the power struggle between men and women. The reciprocal concern with men's alleged increasing impotence provides ammunition for the counterattack. Now that women's capacity for multiple orgasms is well recognized, both men and women, paradoxically, begin to insist that women should experience sexual climax. Some women argue that they have been deprived of orgasms by men whose single-minded concern with their own sexual pleasure prevented them from stimulating their partners in ways that would lead to female orgasm. The male response has been that women who do not actively participate in the sexual encounter (who are inorgasmic) deprive men of the sexual and psychological satisfaction of knowing they have satisfied their mates.

The debate about male impotence sounds a set of parallel concerns. Impotent men complain that women's new sexual aggressiveness, their demand for sexual satisfaction based on male performance, is the root cause of men's sexual problems. Women counter that male impotence is a hostile act designed to punish women. One might label this sexual debate "Whose orgasm is it anyway?" This is a serious topic of middle-class debate, but the issues, perhaps less openly discussed, plague working-class couples too. Across the social-class spectrum, the marriage bed sets the stage for the power struggle between women and men.

Division of Household Labor

The bedroom is but one scene of the gender power struggle among middle-class women and men. Perhaps more among middle- than working-class couples, the kitchen and nursery are critical battlegrounds. Some observers even suggest that the greatest change in middle-class gender roles involves the division of labor within the home, a shift closely tied to women's evolving public and occupational roles. Unlike the working-class division of family labor, where the struggle is less explicit, the middle-class family has begun to debate, if not actually reallocate, household responsibilities. The women's movement has encouraged a reexamination of housework and childcare as strictly "women's work." These responsibilities, feminists argue, should be shared. From a feminist perspective, men's household labor is their rightful duty, not their gift, to the family.

In many historical periods, housework has been women's major occupation. Nonetheless, the subject of housework has been systematically ignored by traditional historians. Not until contemporary feminist scholars reclaimed the importance of housework, both in women's lives and the social economy, was the contribution women have made through their unpaid domestic labor truly recognized.[9] (As noted earlier, economists too are beginning to calculate the contribution of women's unpaid domestic and community work to the gross national product.) To compound our ignorance of "women's work," traditional scholars failed to examine the changing nature of housework and the impact of that change on the adult female's gender role. Home economics, which does concern itself with domestic subjects, conventionally has been cut off from the elite arts and sciences, even in nonelite universities, and the high-prestige Ivy League colleges and universities have never even considered home economics a possible part of the curriculum. The concerns of home economists were patronizingly dismissed as the ramblings of second-rate female intellects in less-than-elite universities. Not that the subject matter of the fields of study within home economics was intrinsically unimportant. For example, once the field of nutrition, previously a subdiscipline within home economics, was recognized as an area of critical knowledge, high-status nutrition departments were established in Ivy League schools of public health and medicine. Home economics, however, remained behind with ever-diminishing status even within land-grant universities, their historical homes—another example of how female domains are coopted by males once they are perceived as a potential resource.

As we discussed earlier, when production was transferred from the home to the factory, the type of contribution women made to the economic unit of the family changed. That factory labor was paid and housework was not created a serious, if long unattended, difference in men's and women's roles and the power relationship between them. As Veblen noted, those middle- and upper-class wives who were "ladies of leisure" served as symbols of "conspicuous consumption," testifying to their husbands' elevated social status.[10] Being "not-working wives" made middle-class wives increasingly dependent on their spouses. It also silently reduced their power within the domestic relationship, while simultaneously increasing their husbands' power in the eyes of other men. The twin roles of consumer and homemaker became relentlessly depicted as "middle-class feminine," even though some working-class women always worked outside the home—witness the Lowell girls, whom we shall meet later. But housework remained woman's responsibility, whether she personally performed these tasks or engaged the services of domestic help—usually also female.

Those working-class women who worked for wages outside the home, sometimes as domestics in other women's houses, found their own housework awaiting them at home. With the advent of World War II, domestic workers sought higher-paid jobs in defense plants, leaving middle-class women, unassisted by men, to confront the laundry and dirty dishes. The home economics movement had previously undertaken to systematize women's housework and childcare, but the idea remained that this was women's—not men's work. And it was middle-class women who gave the home economics movement its warmest reception.

The socialist movement in many countries intermittently discussed the "equality of women"—a code phrase for "women's unequal role of unpaid household worker." But repeatedly, even in the early twentieth-century experiment of the Israeli kibbutz, where housework and childcare were made community responsibilities, the question of women's work became submerged in so-called larger social questions. Because the political and economic implications of housework were repeatedly brushed aside, middle-class women and upwardly mobile working-class women continued to regard the role of fulltime homemaker as women's appropriate—even status-conferring—role. Historian Nancy Schrom Dye suggests:

> There are still many questions left unanswered about housework and the social and economic role of the housewife. How did housewives in the past perceive their role and their work? How have they structured time around the rhythms of housework and child care? When did women become American society's primary consumers? By what processes did they internalize this role?[11]

These questions speak to women of all social classes, even upper-class women who merely supervise others' performance of household chores. But they are particularly relevant to the middle-class family's division of household labor. The answers could provide much insight into the power struggle between wage-earning men and love-earning women in the middle class.

The Daycare Debate

The 1970s witnessed a new public debate—most vociferous within the middle class—about the division of household labor, particularly childcare. Time budget studies worldwide produced findings similar to American surveys: women spent much more time working, both outside and inside the home, than their husbands did.[12] Demands for public solutions to housework and particularly childcare appeared in mass media, then echoed through political assemblies. By 1973, a national childcare program was designed in the United States, and legislation was crafted. The debate reached a crescendo as the legislation moved through Congress to the president's desk. But supporters' hopes were dashed by President Nixon's veto. His reason: The government should not interfere in the internal workings of the family. Some observers have interpreted this governmental inaction as one more example of society's use of women's childbearing power as a net in which to trap them and keep them from accruing economic resources.

Daycare centers were plentiful and effective in American defense plants during World War II, when the national crisis demanded more women factory workers. Daycare facilities still exist in limited numbers, but mostly on a private basis. Kamerman and Kahn's international studies of childcare attest to the utility and benign influence of such arrangements in other countries, without noticeable impact on American domestic policy.[13] Daycare, a more insurmountable problem for the middle-class nuclear family than the working-class extended family, continues to elicit heated argument. And middle-class families, lacking the network of readily available grannys and aunts provided by working-class extended families, feel the pinch. Both middle- and working-class single-parent families, particularly those headed by women, share this need.

The housework-childcare debate between middle-class wives and husbands, still unresolved, is at least recognized in the 1980s as a legitimate subject of disagreement. Feminist writers argue that until the husband "shares" the household burdens—including cooking, shopping, laundry, and childcare—rather than simply "helps" his wife with what he perceives to be *her* household responsibilities, women and men will have no chance for equality. This is particularly so if both wife and husband work outside the home. Nonetheless, the sharing, or helping, however one wishes to view the male housework role, is greater in American middle-class than in working-class families. In upper-class families, scarce domestic help still offers affluent couples a way to avoid narrowing this aspect of the gender-role gap within the home.

Family Eating Patterns

One major aspect of the female domestic role revolves around food. Working wives and middle-class wives spend many hours shopping, preparing, and serving food, and upper-class women still supervise the selection of menus. But the 1970s and 1980s have brought a startling revolution in eating out, especially in middle-class families. By 1980, 37¢ of every food-budget dollar went to eating out.[14] By 1978, there were 55,312 fast-food establishments in the United States, with annual receipts of $21 billion. Only two years later, their number had grown to nearly 67,000, and their receipts to more than $29 billion. U.S. Department of Commerce experts estimate that by 1990, Americans will be spending half of every food dollar on eating out, primarily in fast-food establishments. By 1990, the experts say, Americans will be spending equal amounts in restaurants and supermarkets. Such figures have given rise to the popular joke: "What do American women make best for dinner? Reservations." American mothers are pictured summoning their children for dinner by calling, "Get in the car, kids."

As middle- and working-class families eat out more, whether in fast-food shops or elegant restaurants, role expectations regarding shopping and cooking are changing. Cooking is becoming a less critical component of the middle-class female role. Clearly, much has happened since the introduction of instant coffee and cake mixes, which American housewives initially resisted, feeling they somehow were cheating their families. (The processed food companies solved the instant cake mix problem by requiring housewives to add two fresh eggs and a cup of water.) More men now consider themselves "gourmet cooks" and take command of the kitchen on special occasions. Few male gourmet cooks, however, routinely assume daily food preparation chores in the American family. As a result, middle-class debate continues to swirl around women's legitimate household responsibilities. The intensity of the argument flows in large part from the often hidden links between household and other gender-role responsibilities, resources, and power.

UPPER-CLASS FAMILY PATTERNS

The upper-class family—a relatively small slice of the American population—still revolves around comparatively traditional gender roles. Like the working class, the upper class fosters clear gender role differentiation: men in the public arena, women "at home." But "at home" has a broader meaning for upper-class wives. Labor force statistics point to the fact that as husbands' incomes increase, wives' labor force participation decreases. So it is not surprising that by 1980 less than one quarter of all working wives had husbands whose incomes exceeded $25,000.

Unlike their working- and middle-class sisters, upper-class wives leave domestic chores to housekeepers, butlers, and other household help. But these women, along with their middle-class sisters, contribute to the economy through unpaid community volunteer work. Without their voluntary labor, hospitals, schools, museums, and many other social institutions would lack the human and material resources to carry on.

Volunteer Roles for Women

Upper-class women enact clear-cut gender roles that often differ dramatically from those of their middle- and working-class sisters. For example, many upper-class women build unpaid "careers" in the volunteer world. Sociologist Arlene Daniels studied "a select group of 70 philanthropically inclined" upper-class women. This research describes the ways in which these women live daytime existences not only totally different from those of their husbands, but also at variance with the lives of their working- and middle-class sisters.[15] Leisure activities that fill the days of upper-class women are reported in fashion magazines and other mass media. And rather than inciting hostility or envy, upper-class women, particularly the wives of famous and powerful men, regularly appear on lists of "most admired" and "most influential" women.

Like sociologist Daniels's "society women," many upper-class women create meaningful—but gender-differentiated—careers for themselves in philanthropic organizations. In fact, philanthropic organizations were an early stepping-stone nineteenth-century women used to move beyond hearth and home to the public arena. Some sociologists argue that upper-class women's gender roles involve setting styles and acting as arbiters of culture. Through their activities with museums, symphony orchestras, charity balls, and other cultural-social events, upper-class women influence the taste and behavior of their middle-class sisters particularly, for whom they commonly serve as role models.

Male Power, Female Influence

The upper-class male role is characterized by control of major social institutions. Many upper-class men, sons of wealthy families, manage inherited banks, brokerage houses, and major industrial corporations. They often serve on interlinked corporate and foundation boards, making decisions that shape the entire society. Some seek high elected office where they control domestic as well as foreign policy. The upper-class male gender role includes the exercise of substantial social, financial, legal, and political power. Domestic power, based on major control of financial resources, belongs to the upper-class male as well. It is one form of power that few upper-class husbands have the time or interest to exercise. Still, anecdotal reports of women as "credit-card prisoners" reveal some affluent husbands' reluctance to give their wives disposable cash. This suggests that even some upper-class men are not ready to relinquish economic control over their wives.

For some upper-class women, gender-role differentiation does not necessarily lead to powerlessness, particularly if they remain married to their powerful and affluent husbands. Many, of course, are themselves the daughters of upper-class families, with social and economic power of their own. The world they inhabit as wives of prominent husbands is filled with power and influence. One route to vicarious power and influence for upper-class wives is at the side of their influential husbands, in whose company they meet and sometimes influence the movers and shakers of their own society, if not the larger world.

The Society Hostess Role

This considerable social influence is an important dimension of the upper-class wife's gender role. As a society hostess, she entertains key decision-makers in her home, where dinner party conversation may hover around tomorrow's decision about the money supply, foreign policy, defense spending, even Supreme Court appointments. Married to men who control the major institutions of society—from banks and airlines to steel mills, automobile plants, brokerage houses, and political assemblies—these women commonly are privy to important world events. Sometimes the knowledge proves perilous, as was the case for Martha Mitchell, outspoken wife of the attorney general during the Watergate scandal. After several late-night telephone calls to her favorite reporters, Martha Mitchell claimed she was beaten and given drug injections by unknown strong-arm men because she "knew too much." Some political analysts view this as an extreme example of brute male force used to quell a woman's efforts to offset unbridled male abuse of power. More commonly, such inside knowledge simply provides spice and excitement to upper-class wives' lives in their roles as companions to and hostesses for men of power.

Given the mores of the corporate world, powerful upper-class men rely upon the significant social contributions only their wives can make. Upper-class wives, freed from menial domestic chores and childcare responsibilities, are expected to play hostess for their husbands' associates and companion to their husbands on important business trips. The special cachet provided by a glamorous and elegant wife was typified during President Kennedy's famous trip to France, where he introduced himself as the "man who accompanied Jacqueline Kennedy to Paris." The upper-class wife contributes in real and symbolic ways to her husband's power position. In the process, she too may exercise influence, even vicarious power.

The Underside of the Upper-Class Female Role

Not all is chinchilla and caviar for the upper-class wife, however. Many upper-class and middle-class male roles are enmeshed in what sociologists Coser and Rokoff call "greedy institutions," which usurp the unpaid labor of the wife as well as the highly rewarded efforts of the husband.[16] Sociologist William H. Whyte, Jr. highlighted the importance of the corporate wife for her husband's career.[17] Even today, the wives of junior executives may be interviewed before their husbands are "brought on board." Many women, including wives of university and corporation presidents, diplomats, and politicians, share the dubious fate of having their own lives absorbed by their husbands' institutional connections and responsibilities. When their own time is not being usurped by social obligations connected with their husbands' careers, upper-class wives may find themselves isolated, waiting for their spouses to return from 18-hour days or international travel.

A special case concerns spouses of celebrities. People of great fame and celebrity—statistically more often males than females—create a spotlight around themselves that may not include their mates. The divorced wife of a famous TV personality has described the loss of identity suffered by wives whose only access to accomplishment is through their celebrated husbands.[18] On a late-night talk show, she and the wives of three other famous men—a symphony orchestra conductor, an author, and a talk-show host—compared notes about the "loss of self" they experienced as wives of famous husbands. They recounted a common experience: acquaintances who actually fail to recognize them when they appear in public unaccompanied by their well-known spouse. This vicarious existence, they agreed, left them with a deep sense of anomie and anonymity. Of course, men with famous wives may also encounter this, possibly with even greater pain, since the societal expectations for the "vicarious spouse" seems specifically tailored to women. Surviving spouses of celebrated husbands quickly learn that their wide-ranging vicarious status and power may fade quickly. For women and men too, this is but one of the many gender-role transitions in power and influence that the individual undergoes during the life span within the family.

SUMMARY

Social class affects the hues that color the landscape of the sex-gender system. Both sex and gender roles vary across social class lines. The division of labor, the expression of sexuality, and the degree and type of power exercised by men and women change dramatically as one moves up and down the social ladder.

The allocation of tasks both within the home and in the public arena reflects the values and attitudes of the family's socioeconomic status. Power within the family is closely linked to domestic as well as to occupational and community roles. This power balance, however, is further calibrated to the type and quantity of resources available to women and men as individuals and as members of families from distinctly different social classes.

In a closed society, individuals are locked into various social strata, as well as inescapable gender roles, from birth. In open societies, however, education is the most significant route to social mobility and alternative gender roles. So it is important to understand the relationship between education, gender roles, and power, the subject of the next chapter.

NOTES

1. Mirra Komarovsky, *Blue Collar Marriage* (New York: Random House, 1962).
2. Lillian Rubin, *Worlds of Pain* (New York: Basic Books, 1976).
3. Ibid.
4. Ibid.
5. Ibid.
6. Mary Lou Randour, Georgia Strasburg, Jean Lipman-Blumen, "Women in Higher Education: Trends in Enrollments and Degrees Earned," *Harvard Educational Review,* 52, no. 2 (May 1982), 189–202.
7. Marilyn French, *The Women's Room* (New York: Summit Books, 1977).
8. Alfred Kinsey, *Sexual Behavior in the Human Male* (Philadelphia: W. B. Saunders, 1948).
9. Nancy Schrom Dye, *As Equals and As Sisters: Feminism, the Labor Movement, and the Women's Trade Union League of New York* (Columbia, Missouri: University of Missouri Press, 1980); Mariarosa Dalla Costa and Selma James, *The Power of Women and the Subversion of the Community* (Bristol, England: Falling Wall Press, 1972); Margaret Benston, "The Political Economy of Women's Liberation," *Monthly Review,* 21, no. 4 (September 1969) 13–27; Renate Bridenthal, "The Family: The View from a Room of Her Own," in *Rethinking the Family: Some Feminist Questions,* ed. Barrie Thorne with Marilyn Yalom (New York: Longman, Inc., 1982), pp. 225–239; Ann Oakley, *Women's Work: The Housewife, Past and Present* (New York: Pantheon, 1974).
10. Thorstein Veblen, *The Theory of the Leisure Class* (New York: Modern Library, 1934).
11. Nancy Schrom Dye, *As Equals and As Sisters: Feminism, the Labor Movement, and the Women's Trade Union League of New York* (Columbia, Missouri: University of Missouri Press, 1980), p. 27.

12. Alexander Szalai, "Women's Time: Women in the Light of Contemporary Time-Budget Research," in *Women and the Future,* ed. Guy Streatfield (Guildford, Surrey: IFC Science and Technology Press, 1975); Michael Paul Sacks, *Women's Work in Soviet Russia* (New York: Praeger, 1976).

13. Sheila B. Kamerman and Alfred J. Kahn, *Child Care, Family Benefits, and Working Parents* (New York: Columbia University Press, 1981).

14. Bernie Ward, "Eating Out in the Eighties," *Sky,* May 1960, pp. 10–14.

15. Arlene Daniels, work in progress.

16. R. L. Coser and G. Rokoff, "Women in the Occupational World: Social Disruption and Conflict," *Social Problems,* 18 (1971).

17. William H. Whyte, Jr., *The Organization Man* (New York: Simon & Schuster, 1956).

18. Marilyn Funt, *Are You Anybody?* (New York: Pinnacle Books, 1981).

CHAPTER 10
EDUCATION AND GENDER ROLES

One need not be a Plato or Michelet to recognize the pervasive influence education—or its lack—imposes on every aspect of an individual's life.[1] From Third World countries to postindustrial nations, the role of education in politics and power is apparent. Educational systems change the destiny of groups that have differential access to the system. Education, which historically limited women's access, provides a potent mechanism for keeping the power relationship between women and men in balance.

Education is a radicalizing force. Beginning with its most basic ingredient, literacy, education fosters radicalism by enabling the less powerful to read and spread dissent. Education thus threatens the power establishment, whose power is enhanced by its control over knowledge. Early American slaveowners, recognizing education's radicalizing potential, passed laws that forbade teaching slaves to read or write. In America's first industrial sweatshops, straw bosses prevented immigrant workers from learning English, lest they communicate, then organize and revolt. If withholding education means withholding power, it is hardly surprising to discover the widespread efforts from one century to the next, and from one country to another, to insulate women from education's equalizing and radicalizing effects.

Even among the middle and upper classes, daughters everywhere customarily received less education than their brothers did, particularly at the university level. Limiting women's education hampered their ability to lead their sisters in revolt. And discouraging those more educated middle- and upper-class women's participation in the labor force also prevented them from radicalizing and leading the revolt of their less educated working-class sisters. Poorly educated women, on the other hand, could be encouraged to work, since their labor contributed to productivity without threatening revolution.

Middle- and upper-class women were often educated individually by tutors, isolated at home, safely separated from their sisters. This isolation was simply one more method for limiting the political leadership roles that educated, more affluent women were liable to assume. In Great Britain, for example, while the sons of aristocratic families studied the classics at Cambridge and Oxford, daughters, if they were allowed to study at all, did so secluded at home with a private tutor. Literary critic Jane Marcus reminds us "of Virginia Woolf's definition of reading and writing as radical acts and the irony of her (self)definition (as a) 'daughter of an educated man,' meaning one who is dispossessed of culture."[2] Both in *A Room of One's Own* and *Three Guineas*, Woolf decries women's forced educational isolation as insulating them from communing and bonding with their intellectual peers. The bonding that occurred among classmates at Oxford and Cambridge, and even earlier in all-male public schools, created a well-recognized foundation of tight homosocial networks (the "old boys club") that even now rules Great Britain. According to Marcus (1981),

> . . . it was Woolf's revolutionary goal to storm the gates of Cambridge to steal the secret of . . . "same-sex bonding," that brotherhood which appeared to own the means of production of culture—in law, politics, literature and life.[3]

Education, the potential equalizer and radicalizer, everywhere has been less available to women. Nonetheless, a few women have managed through the ages, and many more recently, to become educated. The French writer Simone de Beauvoir acknowledged the importance of education in her own admittedly atypical life. In a 1976 interview, de Beauvoir described her educational background:

> I had the luck to come from . . . the bourgeoisie, which could afford not only to send me to the best schools but also allow me to play leisurely with ideas. Because of that I managed to enter the man's world without too much difficulty. I showed that I could discuss philosophy, art, literature, etc., on a "man's level." I kept whatever was particular to womanhood to myself. I was then reinforced by my success to continue. As I did, I saw I could earn as good a living as any male intellectual and that I was taken as seriously as any of my male peers. . . . I then found that I could travel by myself . . . sit in cafés and write and be as respected as any male writer, and so on. Each stage fortified my sense of independence and equality.[4]

Simone de Beauvoir, however, was the exception, not the rule. Until quite late in the twentieth century, and even now, education has represented different worlds of knowledge and control for females. In fact, distinguished educators and scholars argued against formal education for women, lest it upset either their brains or their ovaries. Historian Carl Degler (1980) reminds us that

> As late as 1858 a report of the Board of Regents of the University of Michigan, which had for twenty years accepted on paper the enrollment of women, opposed instituting coeducation on the ground that it was "contrary to nature" and predicted that "young men would lose a proper sense of dignity of their pursuits" while "the delicacy of female character would be destroyed"[5]

AN HISTORICAL OVERVIEW

Throughout history, education has been a significant mechanism for shaping the populace in accordance with the views of state or church. From ancient Sparta to the postindustrial world, the education of males and females trained them for different adult roles. Male education was often pointed toward men's public roles as military and political leaders; girls were raised to be wives and mothers of outstanding men.

American Education

The story in the American colonies was not much different. After the American Revolution, women's education in the colonies was linked to the requirements of the fledgling republic, where educated women were needed to rear patriotic sons. A spate of books and articles championed the importance of comparable education for girls and boys.

In the first decades of the nineteenth century, the common school provided instruction to boys and girls alike. By midcentury, white girls attended publicly supported schools alongside their brothers. But women's education before 1830 stopped at the door of higher education; only males aspiring to the ministry, other professions, and political leadership could enter the "hallowed halls."

Social and economic changes encouraged several strong-spirited women to push for higher education for women. In the early nineteenth century, female seminaries began to spring up from New England to Alabama. Emma Hart Willard opened her first seminary for girls at Middlebury, Vermont, in 1807. In 1819, Willard published *Plan for Improving Female Education,* a bold design to provide females with a first-class education that would also fit them to be exemplary mothers or self-supporting teachers. She contended that women were entitled to the same dignities and freedoms as men, and thus should study mathematics, metaphysics, science, and geography. In addition, for the sake of domestic happiness they should also learn scientific "housewifery." Two years later, in 1821, Willard founded the Troy Female Academy, where she sought to implement her "radical" pedagogical notions.

Catharine Beecher, sister of Harriet Beecher Stowe and Henry Ward Beecher, sought to elevate housework in the public mind by infusing it with "qualities that put it on a plane with epistemology and differential calculus."[6] Beecher, imbued with the notion of "stations in life" and "separate spheres," also endorsed nursing and teaching as appropriate women's roles. In 1828, she founded a Female Seminary at Hartford, Connecticut, a short-lived avant-garde institution.

Both Willard and Beecher addressed their educational beliefs to *all* women, but paradoxically, their seminaries were available only to those who could afford the expense of a private education. Mary Lyon, born to a family of relative poverty, developed the design for educating middle-class women. In 1837, Lyon established Mount Holyoke Female Seminary in South Hadley, Massachusetts. Vying with established male institutions like

Harvard, Mount Holyoke gave only grudging attention to domestic subjects, to which Lyon attributed little intellectual worth.

In these early female seminaries, the seeds of women's colleges were planted, seeds that would suffer through a prolonged germination period. Georgia Female College in Macon, Georgia, declared itself the first American college for women in 1836. Unfortunately, this and several other women's colleges that appeared in the South and West failed to live up to the promise of a first-rate intellectual experience. It was not until Vassar opened its doors in 1861 that women had the kind of opportunity for higher education available to their male peers at Harvard and Yale. Other Ivy League women's colleges, including Wellesley and Smith, opened soon thereafter.

Coeducation: Formality or Reality?

Oberlin, founded in 1833, became the first coeducational college in America by including four women in its opening class. Here again, we see women's education promoted as a resource primarily for men. Degler (1980) notes:

> . . . even pioneer Oberlin . . . was moved less by egalitarian principles than by a desire to meet the needs of men . . . . the presence of women would give men an alternative to single-sex education and women would provide a social outlet . . . thus encouraging male academic concentration. . . . Moreover, the presence of women would have a civilizing and humanizing effect on the male students who, as future ministers, would profit from such influences.[7]

During the Civil War period, coeducational colleges proliferated, as non-Southern states began to establish public universities, and women students were officially included. Yet fears about what higher education would do to women persisted. Although feminist scholars would probably interpret these concerns as fears that women would accede to power through education, the doubts were couched in terms of women's health. The same "emotional and sensitive" nature that made women perfect mothers and wives was the source of an alleged delicacy that would break under the strain of higher education. As noted earlier, Harvard Medical School educator Dr. Edward H. Clarke asserted women had the intellectual capacity for university studies, but warned of the serious physical hazards they would experience from such efforts—an early proponent of women's "fear of success." Although Clarke's claims were refuted by male and female critics, they had a telling effect.

Despite such obstruction, the belief that women's education was important to others—their children and husbands—served to promote their access to higher education. North Carolina educator Charles McIver's pronouncement that to educate a man was to educate one person, while to educate a mother meant "you have educated a whole family" encapsulated an even stronger public attitude. Education was designed to serve, not interfere with, women's family roles. So the observation that late nineteenth-century college women were less likely to marry, and that even those who did had fewer children, evoked public alarm. Although the same fertility behavior characterized college-educated men, there was no parallel concern about men's education, since their "primary role was not fatherhood."[8] Feminist analysts would no doubt understand this outcry against education's effect on women's delayed or diminished marriage and fertility rates as a protest against diminishing societal (read "male") control over educated women. That education gives women power, first over themselves and then over society, is a fear not easily extinguished.

Women's entry into American colleges and universities was officially assured by the beginning of the twentieth century. Still, subtle unofficial forces, including fears and attitudes translated into policies and practices, continued to restrain women's higher educational opportunities. It was crisis, in the guise of both World Wars, that finally opened the doors to women students, if only to fill the university coffers, depleted by the absence of military-aged male students.

After each World War, however, women again were gently steered into marriage or postsecondary school employment, a situation later recognized by Betty Friedan as part of the "feminine mystique."[9] Those women who did enter higher education were guided by counselors, teachers, and parents into fields of study "appropriate" for their female role as wives and mothers.[10] As we shall see, only in the wake of the resurgent women's movement did women move into male educational preserves in significant numbers. Small wonder it took so long, given the male/female demarcation in education that begins in early childhood.

KINDERGARTEN AND ELEMENTARY SCHOOL

Kindergarten is the world of play, preparation for real school. Even now, kindergarten remains an extension of home, with a female teacher as the surrogate mother. Kindergarten is the world of the doll corner for girls, blocks and erector sets for boys. Kindergartners do not yet recognize the power differential between these distinct gender worlds, which they will sense later in elementary school. They do, however, understand which toys "belong" to which group, and which adult roles each may appropriately play. In the doll corner, girls play mother, nurse, or teacher; boys play builders, doctors, astronauts, or soldiers. Rarely, and only after much urging from girls, do boys play father. This reluctance to enact the father role mirrors the behavior of adult fathers, who spend from less than 1 minute to 20 minutes daily with infant sons or daughters.[11]

The invidious comparison between females and males remains ambiguous in kindergarten. That the female role is less valued than the male role is partly obscured by the fact that girls aged 3 and 4 comprise the majority of kindergarten students, a pattern that has persisted for more than a decade. According to the latest educational statistics,[12] in 1979, 35.6 percent of girls, compared to 34.6 percent of boys aged 3 and 4 years old, were enrolled in school. Girls generally maintain this slight numerical advantage until age 13; after that, from age 14 to 29, a larger proportion of the male population is enrolled in school. Females do not regain their enrollment advantage until age 30 and above, when, as mothers and grandmothers, they return to continuing education programs, often as part-time students.

The illusion that females are equally, perhaps more, valued than males continues during the early school years. It is fueled by the compatibility between the reward system of elementary school and control myths that suggest that: (a) females take care of other people, nurture them, put other people's welfare above their own; and (b) females are passive and docile, while males are aggressive and active. In the school setting, these two control myths translate into female compliance with socially established rules. Girls mind the teacher, do their homework, even help the unruly boys. Little boys are less compliant, less likely to hand in neatly and accurately completed homework assignments; they "act up" and generally push the limits of established rules. Researcher Raphaela Best's observations of elementary school children find little boys fighting, daydreaming, losing the page, and testing the limits of school discipline. Little girls often "mother" their male classmates, helping them keep up with the lessons, even bossing them around.[13] In kindergarten and elementary school, little girls are rarely the troublemakers; they are too busy doing what is expected of them and reaping the rewards of teachers' smiles and gold stars.

The "Feminization" of Early Education

The greater ease with which girls move through the early school years has led some observers to suggest that elementary education has been "feminized." Critics attribute most of this feminization to the preponderance of female elementary school teachers, who transmit female values and reward feminine behavior.[14] Educational statistics confirm the majority hold that female teachers have on elementary schools, although their numerical advantage has dwindled over the last half-century. In 1929–30, female elementary school teachers numbered 633,819, compared to 68,705 males, almost a 10 to 1 ratio. By 1975–76 (the latest available figures), women elementary school teachers still outnumbered men (1,139,992 versus 218,977), but their advantage had narrowed to slightly more than 5 to 1. And the number of female elementary school principals has also dwindled dramatically over the years.[15]

At first glance, this numerical preponderance of female teachers appears to support the "feminization" argument. But psychologist N. D. Feshbach's studies of student teacher preferences in personality characteristics of elementary school pupils suggest that a teacher's gender is irrelevant. Male and female teachers alike reported that they preferred pupils who were compliant, dependent, and passive—traditional female characteristics. Feshbach's student teachers were less favorably inclined toward active, independent, assertive students. Although male pupils most often warranted this description, active, independent, and assertive girl students were equally unattractive to student teachers of both genders. In fact, male and female teachers alike gave high ratings to conforming, "rigid" female pupils, but low evaluations to female students who displayed independence.[16]

Few proponents of the feminization hypothesis have considered other features of elementary education that may attract teachers—both male and female—who prefer docile, conforming students. Few critics have taken into account the substantial evidence that the structure of both elementary and secondary schools may be what fuels the teachers' desire for compliance and passivity in students. For example, large classes, so common in urban schools, are difficult to supervise under the best of circumstances. The additional disruption caused by nonconforming or rebellious students just adds to the teacher's burdens.

The influence of control myths in encouraging girls' and discouraging boys' passive, compliant behavior is also overlooked. The accusing finger remains stubbornly and inexplicably pointed at female teachers. This persistently negative attitude toward female teachers, who in their preponderant numbers do indeed represent considerable power and control in elementary school, begs investigation itself. Is this still another example of the dread of female power, even in situations or occupations ordinarily considered relatively low in status and power?

Physical Differences between Males and Females: How Do They Count?

During the elementary school years, distinctions between girls' and boys' gender roles are primarily physical. At recess, little girls play hopscotch and jump rope in clusters of twos and threes. Boys, by contrast, engage in rougher team sports. Even at this tender age, boys learn through team sports the complex dynamics of leadership, followership, and teamwork that social scientists are just beginning to recognize as valuable training for adult organizational and political roles. Teachers call on boys to help with physical tasks they believe are too difficult for girls—moving furniture and washing blackboards. Girls assist primarily with social and emotional tasks. In this way, girls gain experience with "people problems," learning to be experts in social-emotional issues. The gender worlds, even here, are beginning to diverge, setting the stage for adult, family, and work roles.

The homosocial worlds of adult men and women, each different, each exclusively single-gendered, begin in the classroom, on the elementary school playground, and in the school corridors. Teachers routinely line up girls and boys in separate columns for marching to the auditorium and to other activities. This physical separation of the genders, presumably according to differences in physical size and abilities, is taken as "natural" by the children, who see the adult world similarly separated according to gender. No one—teacher or pupil—seems to question the illogic of bigger girls being treated as smaller and weaker than smaller boys. This categorization by gender, rather than individual characteristics, lies at the core of stereotypes. It generates a process that pervades the educational system and spills over into the adult occupational world.

Mathematics Performance and Gender

Throughout elementary school, intellectual distinctions between girls and boys are blurred. Only later will alleged "aptitudes" affect their adolescent and adult destinies. In the elementary years, little girls excel in so-called male intellectual tasks, and vice versa. Over time, however, gender-linked differences appear. We see the workings of this process quite clearly in mathematics.

Contrary to common belief, in the early grades girls perform better than boys in mathematics. The National Assessment of Educational Progress, which evaluated the performance of 9-, 13-, and 17-year-old students in various academic subjects, concluded that girls aged 9 and 13 scored 0.2 and 0.6, respectively, *above* the mean national performance level in mathematical skills. Boys ages 9 and 13 scored 0.2 and 0.6, respectively, *below* the national mean. By age 17, however, girls were 2.5 below the national mean level in mathematics, and boys had risen to 2.6 above the mean.

How this transformation in mathematical performance comes about has yet to be systematically documented, although researchers Fox, Fennema, and Sherman have examined a variety of cognitive, affective, educational, and biological factors, including various aspects of gender-role socialization, to account for it.[17] They conclude that the differences in mathematical performance that emerge by age 17 result largely from boys taking more math courses. Why girls, even those with superior mathematical skills, take fewer math courses than boys is explained largely in terms of socialization, including stronger expectations for boys to continue with their mathematical studies. The loophole that "I won't need to use math when I'm an adult" is available to girls only. A control myth intones that males are more analytical and females more intuitive, and the process continues.

Johns Hopkins researcher Lynn Fox attributes girls' greater disinclination to study mathematics to a broader array of social influences: gender typing by parents, teachers, and counselors of mathematics as a boys' field; the dearth of female mathematical role models in the classroom, media, and textbooks, particularly math books; girls' more intense conflict between family and work roles; their greater lack of awareness of mathematics' relevance to various career fields; and their weaker "interest" in math-related occupations.[18] The end result, according to educator Sheila Tobias, is "math anxiety," a condition that causes more females than males to avoid mathematics.[19] Even easily accessible calculators do not offset the mind-set that insists the sufferer cannot handle math.

Some researchers contend that sociopsychological factors outweigh the influence of biological differences, including gender-linked differences in serum urate levels, estrogen effects, and X-linked characteristics. Spatial and problem-solving abilities, associated with earlier left cerebral dominance in females, have some bearing on females' mathematical performance in later years, according to some researchers. This influence, however, could be offset by additional training in spatial visualization. Presumably, boys learn spatial visualization by manipulating physical objects, first with erector sets and building blocks, and later in woodworking and other object-oriented activities.

In societies where females' mathematical ability keeps pace with males,' such as Japan, spatial visualization differences between girls and boys do not seem to materialize. Researchers have yet to determine what specific aspects of Japanese culture or biology account for this situation. No one has yet investigated, for example, the effect of Japanese children's early experience with origami, the traditional paper-folding craft, which teaches children how one dimension can be transformed into many.

The remediability of females' lagging mathematical interest and performance is becoming evident in national educational statistics. Since the mid-1970s, when sociologist Lucy Sells first called attention to mathematics as a "critical filter" in women's educational and occupational choices,[20] educators, parents, and researchers have taken preliminary steps to relay a new message: girls *can* do mathematics. Recent national statistics suggest the message has been received; more than ever before, females are studying mathematics and math-requiring fields in high school, college, and graduate school—evidence that the problem is more social than intellectual, or at least lends itself to social remedies. Mathematics illustrates how male and female twigs are bent differently in elementary school to conform with the adult gender roles expected of them. This process accelerates with the approach of puberty and entry into secondary school.

SECONDARY SCHOOL, ADOLESCENCE, AND GENDER ROLES

By secondary school, boys and girls are traveling the chaotic road to adolescence. Puberty marks the beginning of physiological adulthood; entry into secondary school signifies the beginning of social adulthood. The outlines of adult gender roles are visible, almost palpable. Some students, particularly from the working class, skip the last few years of high school to assume adult gender roles through marriage and work. Even for those who go on to higher education, imminent adult gender roles greatly influence adolescent social and academic activities.

Priorities and values begin to diverge more sharply for female and male students. Beauty and popularity, particularly popularity with boys, become increasingly important for girls—echoes of a familiar control myth. Athletic prowess and popularity head the male priority list. In adolescence, when "dating and mating" processes are gearing up, this is hardly unexpected. In fact, some social scientists would call these nonacademic concerns vital, even functional, for the biological perpetuation of society.

Academic choices are shaped by many factors, not the least of which is adolescent concern with popularity and social acceptance. For girls, social acceptance is a potent motivating force in academic achievement, according to motivation theorists McClelland, Atkinson, Clark and Lowell.[21] The work of psychologist Lois Hoffman also points to the critical role of affiliation in girls' academic behavior.[22] Girls, particularly, select fields of study that are "acceptable" for females, that will protect them from ostracism and ensure their popularity, primarily among boys. To study, much less to excel in, traditionally male subjects puts females on rather dangerous social ground, a position especially uncomfortable for self-conscious adolescents. Consequently, male-designated fields like mathematics and physics are studied by fewer high school girls than boys. Among American high school seniors in 1980, almost 30 percent of the boys and slightly less than 22 percent of the girls had taken a course in trigonometry. Calculus, taken only by advanced students, was reported by less than two-thirds as many girls as boys (6 percent versus 10 percent, respectively). And 39 percent of the boys, compared to 28 percent of the girls, reported they had taken mathematics for three or more years.

These statistics confirm that stereotypical "male" and "female" fields of study become self-fulfilling prophecies. More specifically, the stereotypes about male and female interests, aptitudes, and fields of study tend to channel students into the "gender-appropriate" courses, which in turn confirm the stereotype. Gender-linked curricular choices made in secondary school funnel male and female college students into increasingly divergent areas. For example, the "critical filter" of mathematics discussed earlier becomes extremely important during college, where advanced mathematics, physics, and chemistry courses are prerequisites for many science and mathematics programs.

Academic and adult career goals are established in secondary school. The gender-linked educational choices made by college-bound students follow them into institutions of higher learning. There students find it even more difficult to cross boundaries of traditional gender-linked programs. For those who enter the world of work directly from secondary school, gender-linked adult work and family roles seem even more sharply differentiated.

HIGHER EDUCATION AND GENDER ROLES

Channeling the genders into differentiated roles through education continues in institutions of higher learning. Despite the impressive political and legislative gains of women activists in the 1970s, the gender typing of educational fields persists. A recent analysis of 10- to 20-year trends in women's educational programs by Randour, Strasburg, and Lipman-Blumen notes that women are indeed entering higher education in greater numbers. Yet gender-role stereotypes and the structural barriers that maintain them are still far from eradicated.[23] For example, most women continue earning degrees in traditionally segregated female fields: education, fine and applied arts, foreign languages, health professions, home economics, and library science at the bachelor's level. As late as 1979, the percentage of bachelor's degrees awarded to women in home economics was 95.1 and in fine and applied arts, 62.5. Some previously gender-balanced fields, such as psychology and interdisciplinary studies, are becoming progressively female intensive. In 1971, psychology was a relatively balanced field, with men earning 55 percent and women 45 percent of all bachelor's degrees awarded. By 1979, psychology as an undergraduate field had "tipped," with women earning 61 percent of the bachelor's degrees. Male undergraduates still dominate traditionally masculine fields. More than 10 times as many men as women (57,201 versus 5,174, respectively) earned bachelor's degrees in engineering in 1979; men earned more than three times the number of undergraduate degrees earned by women in business and management (120,176 men versus 52,748 women).

At the graduate and professional levels, the segregation of men and women by field of study continues, notwithstanding increasing numbers of women in male-intensive fields (but not vice versa). Traditional professional degrees in dentistry, medicine, and law are still disproportionately conferred on males, despite some unprecedented inroads by women in the 1970s. In 1979, for example, men earned 4,794 of the dentistry degrees, compared to 649 for women; in medicine, men earned 11,381 MDs, while women earned 3,405; and in law, 25,108 degrees were conferred on men compared to 10,026 on women.

Despite this persistent segregation of men and women in dentistry, medicine, and law, the picture has changed perceptibly even since 1970, when these traditional professions were almost off limits to women. During the brief period from 1970 to 1979, women increased their share of dentistry degrees from 0.9 to 11.8 percent, in medicine from 8.4 to 23 percent, and in law from 5.4 to 28.5 percent. Although women are far from reaching parity in these fields, the figures reveal important changes. Gender-role stereotypes about "appropriate" fields for women and men, as well as structural barriers such as gender-segregating admissions practices, are beginning to give way.

Medical Education: Case Study of a Male Bastion

During the 1970s, strongholds of male power and control—particularly medicine and law—began to admit women, but not without personal struggle for the young women pioneers venturing into these male homosocial worlds. Elizabeth Morgan, a plastic surgeon, documented her struggle to enter that tightly guarded male world. Morgan, herself quite free from any feminist perspectives, writes:

> It is easier to be a woman in surgery during the internship and early residency years, because the men think it is sweet for a woman to try to be a surgeon. Later on it is harder, because most men don't like to be subordinate to a woman surgeon, who is telling them what to do, or who is right on a diagnosis when they are wrong. . . . I had been warned that surgeons did not want women in the field and that physically, women did not have the stamina needed for surgery.[24]

The "sacred" world of medicine has been protected from women in every society where the medical community controlled the highly valued key to health and thus sometimes to life itself. Only in the Soviet Union, where they were introduced into medicine specifically to dilute its elite status, have women been officially encouraged to enter the field. Entrance to medical education and practice has been a focus of virtually all women's movements in the United States and Europe, which recognize medicine's symbolic and practical importance as a bastion of male power. Often feminists pleaded women's case to enter medicine on several grounds that avoided the sensitive power issue: (1) women's alleged affinity for caring for the ill and wounded, a natural outgrowth of their maternal instincts and experience; and (2) women's special need for female physicians to treat those conditions, particularly obstetrical and gynecological, which they were embarrassed to present to male doctors. Between 1844 and 1890, women began to be admitted to the study and practice of medicine, but not everywhere.

Harvard researcher Karen Johnson Freeze documents the struggle of Czech women from the early 1890s to 1900 to gain entrance to medical schools.[25] Women activists presented petition after petition to the Reichsrat and the Ministry of Education. Emperor Franz Joseph tentatively unlatched the door to women's entry into medicine with his 1890 decision to permit Rose Kerschbaumer, a Swiss-educated, Russian-born opthalmologist, and her husband to open a clinic in Salzburg. But Czech women had to wait until 1900 before the Ministry of Education "approved a resolution permitting women to enter medical study as regular students with full rights to practice upon graduation."[26] Hints of the power struggle that women's efforts to enter this sacred male reserve aroused are seen in Freeze's description of the response of male medical students to the prospect of female medical students:

> Ironically, the very fact that women were now technically qualified for university study seemed to arouse hostility and opposition hitherto not so visible. In 1895, the male medical student society of the Czech University published a statement against admitting women. The argument was a common if indefensible one: for every job a woman takes, a man will lose one—and thus not be able to get married and take care of an unemployed woman. This vocal minority among Czech medical students also claimed that it was "unnatural" for women to want medical or other professional training, that women were "happiest being mothers." These students would continue to harrass their women colleagues after the latter finally did gain entrance to the medical facility.[27]

These male students were supported by a brochure, *Die Frauen und das Studium der Medizen*. Written by a "highly placed" government health official and prominent University of Vienna surgeon, Eduard Albert, the pamphlet insisted that women's small and inferior brains, as well as their interest in maternity and hair styles, prevented their making any contribution to knowledge and technology. The brochure depicted women as grown-up children whose emancipation would lead to insanity. As evidence, Albert cited a report by an American psychiatrist claiming that one-third of American women were insane.

Who Fears Academic Success?

The nineteenth-century Czech male medical students and Dr. Albert were not the last to insist that women had intrinsic weaknesses disqualifying them from high academic achievement. This approach, labeled "blaming the victim" by twentieth-century civil rights analysts, has seen its contemporary counterpart in a virtual avalanche of scholarly research investigating women's "motive to avoid success." More popularly known as women's "fear of success," this research thrust was provoked by the work of psychologist Matina Horner, who claimed that women's underlying motive to avoid success was at the core of their poor showing in traditional male academic pursuits.[28]

Horner's work itself was an effort to redress the lack of attention paid to women in earlier achievement motivation research. In 1963, David McClelland and his colleagues reported sparse and equivocal findings on women's achievement motivation.[29] Their theory of the origins and expression of achievement motivation seemed to hold only for men. Men, they argued, learn to be high achievers through early independence training by warm but somewhat detached mothers. Raised in this way, boys learn to internalize standards of excellence, against which they measure their academic and later their adult occupational accomplishments. In the experimental situation, boys responded to leadership and intellectual cues designed to elicit their achievement motivation. Girls, according to the McClelland research, seemed unmoved by these traditional male cues, and responded instead to social acceptability cues.

A doctoral dissertation by W. F. Field hypothesized that women's achievement motivation was keyed to social acceptance.[30] This frail research effort had serious consequences, since it created the basis for McClelland's group and other researchers to assume that women were motivated by a need for affiliation, and men by a need for achievement. Other research, demonstrating that women's need for affiliation was stronger than men's, grew much like the proverbial snowball hurtling down a snow-covered hill. Women came to be perceived as poor subjects for traditional achievement motivation research, and the Catch-22 was complete.

Horner's work, appearing after a virtual dearth of evidence on women's achievement motivation, incorporated notions of women's need for social acceptance. Her preliminary findings sent out seismographic waves, picked up by the media and telegraphed as the new "explanation" for women's failure to scale the ivy-covered walls of academe. Horner suggested that women's needs to achieve and to perceive themselves as "feminine" were contradictory forces. She concluded that many women tended to experience anxiety about the possibility of achieving, which they feared would make them unattractive to men. This result, Horner believed, was particularly strong in women actually capable of high academic performance and with high achievement motivation. The negative consequences these women envisioned, particularly social rejection, created an ambivalence about success, and a "motive to avoid success" (or a "fear of success"). A decade of work ensued in which researchers tried to replicate or disprove Horner's findings. Numerous methodological and conceptual criticisms appeared in subsequent research. Some researchers found that the degree to which both male and female subjects accepted gender-role stereotypes influenced their responses to achievement cues.

Psychologist Thelma Alper described an experiment in which women who held very traditional views about gender roles were more apt to write stories in response to laboratory cues that described physical danger to the achiever or danger to her social and emotional relationships.[31] Female subjects who rejected traditional gender roles also created danger stories, but less frequently than the traditionalists and more often in terms of the failure of the accomplishment attempted, rather than physical or emotional disaster for the achiever. After reviewing 61 "fear of success" studies, psychologist David Tresemer concluded that there was little consistent evidence that women exhibited more fear of success than men. In fact, he pointed to several studies in which the fear of success scores of males were not particularly different from those of female subjects.[32]

The entire fear of success research thrust has begun to recede in importance, but the question of women's supposedly greater need for affiliation continues to comprise part of the female stereotype, a stereotype channeling women into people-oriented occupations. In addition, gender-role stereotypes that coalesce into a belief system about appropriate social behavior for women and men have a strong influence on women's educational aspirations. For example, Lipman-Blumen found that among college-educated wives, those who accepted a traditional domestically oriented role were more likely to meet their need for achievement vicariously through their husbands' accomplishments and thus had lower educational aspirations for themselves. Women with contemporary gender-role ideology felt they had to accomplish directly on their own, not vicariously, and therefore aspired to higher educational accomplishments.[33]

What is it, we might ask, about contemporary gender-role ideology that guides women toward educational accomplishment? In this same study of college-educated wives, intellectual curiosity was at the apex of values held by wives with a contemporary ideology. By contrast, women with a traditional ideology gave top priority to emotional maturity, morals, and ethics. Interpersonal skill was much less important for contemporary women than traditionalists, who also were more likely than their contemporary sisters to admire their parents as successful role models. Women with contemporary views about gender roles were also less willing to accept their parents as role models and more likely to have broken with the religion in which they were raised. These contemporary women, valuing intellectual curiosity so highly, caring less about interpersonal skills, viewing their parents' achievements as less than successful, throwing off their childhood religious upbringing, rejecting vicarious achievement through their husbands' accomplishments, were far more likely than their traditional sisters to expect and plan to attain the highest educational levels.

Rejection of the power and authority of others—parents, church, husbands—is the hallmark of the women with contemporary gender-role ideology. Not unexpectedly, contemporary ideologists (in today's jargon, "liberated women") expect to carve out educational accomplishments on their own. These women seem to substitute their own efforts for the power and authority of male institutions, whether the family or the church. If we questioned these women today, the issues of male and female power would undoubtedly figure explicitly in their gender-role ideology, with even greater impact on their educational aspirations. And although a comparable study of male subjects has not been conducted, it is likely that men's gender-role ideology, keyed to a distinctive set of values and behaviors, forcefully shapes male educational aspirations as well.

STRUCTURAL AND POLITICAL FACTORS

Mentors and Role Models

Needs for achievement and affiliation, fear of success, vicarious achievement, and gender-role ideology all speak to individual factors that bind gender roles and education. Cultural definitions of masculinity and femininity are incorporated into the individual personality. Structural and political factors mesh with these individual components, solidifying the definition and enactment of gender roles.

Within the educational system, structural factors such as gender requirements for admission to certain courses or programs are powerful forces. They reinforce boys' and girls', then young men's and women's, internalization of culturally defined gender roles. For decades, only boys could take shop; only girls could enroll in home economics. Only since the 1970s has new legislation provided the legal basis for protesting this channeling of educational interests by gender.

From kindergarten to graduate and professional schools, formal rules and practices in educational institutions lead to a gender-segregated educational system. The mathematics or science courses required for certain academic programs blend with gender-role stereotypes, forming a significant part of the complex processes now recognized as sex discrimination. Informal norms and practices also contribute to sex discrimination, creating a matrix of forces particularly difficult to detect and therefore to eliminate. For example, unwritten norms guide the "old-boy network," which moves aspiring males into higher-level academic posts; male professors tend to recommend promising male students when their colleagues inquire about candidates for available positions.

Mentors are central figures in the male homosocial network. The mentoring process can begin quite early in the education system, with the mentor protecting and shaping the protégé's course from undergraduate through graduate school and even beyond. More often, the process begins in graduate school. These homosocial senior mentors, adept at placing their protégés in desirable educational and occupational posts, act as gatekeepers to important positions. Even without formal rules and regulations barring women from the highest ranks of educational administration, the informal practices of the "old boy" network manage to reserve the lion's share of these roles for their own and their colleagues' protégés.

Women rarely penetrate this network in the higher reaches of academia. The 1970s witnessed repeated, usually unsuccessful, tenure battles by women faculty members in American colleges and universities. Feminist scholars in particular have had a difficult time. Novelist and critic Carolyn Heilbrun illustrates the fate of such women academics in *Death in a Tenured Position*.[34] Even in the late 1970s (the latest available data), women continued to be underrepresented on college and university faculties. In 1978, only at the lowest academic rank (below assistant professor) was the proportion of women faculty close to that of men.

In a detailed review of women's educational progress from 1975 to 1980, Lipman-Blumen and Strasburg reported:

> In 1978, women comprised 9.5 percent of the full professor rank, down from 9.8 in 1975. At lower levels, women have made slight progress. At the associate professor level, women increased from 17.0 percent in 1975 to 18.2 percent in 1978. The assistant professor level rose from 28.9 percent in 1975 to 31.6 percent in 1978.[35]

Overall, the proportion of women faculty members is higher at women's colleges and small schools. Even so, in academia generally women tend to predominate in lower faculty positions. Projected declining enrollments forecast diminishing opportunities for women to infiltrate the higher faculty levels, particularly at elite coed or all-male colleges and universities.

Nor is women's underrepresentation in institutions of higher learning simply at the faculty level. Among the 2,722 colleges and universities accredited by major regional educational associations, by latest count only 231 have female chief executive officers or presidents. Approximately 40 percent of these women are in all-female colleges, institutions relatively limited in resources. Only 16 women head state colleges or universities. Of the 231 women chief executive officers, 107 head religious educational institutions, 12 lead colleges with student enrollments greater than 10,000, and 7 of those 12 head two-year public colleges. That such a small proportion of women head higher educational institutions is suspiciously indicative of some informal process, such as sex discrimination, at work. It is particularly curious, given that approximately one-third of all doctoral degrees awarded to women are in education, thus providing a sizable pool of candidates for such positions.

The lack of women role models in professorial and high administrative positions in medical, law, and business schools, as well as in university math and science departments, creates a dearth of live examples whom female students might emulate. Male students, too, lack male role models in a variety of female-intensive fields. As a result, the possibilities for either men or women to move into cross-gender educational roles are limited. The presence of female role models in male-intensive fields conveys a message to female students that such a role is feasible for them; male role models send a comparable message to males. Unfortunately, potential role models all too often conform to gender-role stereotypes—understandable because the male establishment more readily rewards both men and women who model traditional gender-role norms. Special leadership qualities may be required to enter cross-gender educational fields for both male and female models.

Leadership Training through Athletics

Since ancient Sparta, young men have been trained for political and military leadership through physical education and sports. Women's athletic training, even when viewed as a prelude to healthy motherhood, has been less rigorous. Some observers attribute women's underrepresentation in leadership to exclusion from sports that provide leadership training for adult professional, organizational, and political life.

Young women's exclusion from team sports became the focus of concerted efforts by the women's movement during the 1970s. According to Lipman-Blumen and Strasburg, the later years of the 1970s brought impressive results:

> At the high school level, female athletes number more than two million, a 26 percent gain (between 1978 and 1980) in sports such as basketball, track and field, as well as in softball, tennis and volleyball.

> The number of women participating in intercollegiate athletics (63,375 in 1977) has more than doubled since 1972, so that they now account for somewhat less than one-third of all students actively engaged in sports. By 1977, approximately 576,600 women were competing in intramural sports, representing a 100 percent increase since 1972. (The comparable male figure was an increase of 23 percent).[36]

Despite these gains, athletic budgets, including scholarships, still reveal large disparities. During the late 1970s, however, more funds than ever before were being spent on women's athletics. For example,

> In 1973–74, the average budget for women's athletics in *small* colleges was $23,000 (compared to $207,000 for men's): by 1978–79, the figure has jumped to $60,000 (vs. $259,000 for men's).

> In *large* colleges, average athletic budgets for women grew from $35,000 to $259,000 in the same period.[37]

These figures encourage those who see athletics as the training ground for leadership. Yet recent cutbacks in federal spending undoubtedly will restrain the important strides that women had begun to make.

SOCIAL POLICY: EDUCATIONAL LEGISLATION IN THE 1970s

The 1970s saw political activists narrowing the gap between women's and men's educational and life opportunities. Most of those advances resulted from changes in educational legislation that opened doors to minorities, including women. Some legislation was aimed specifically at women; Title IX of the Educational Amendments of 1972, for example, prohibited any federally funded educational program or activity from discriminating on the basis of gender.

These legislative initiatives created the formal basis that women could use to press for equal access to educational institutions and programs. Of course, compulsory elementary and secondary school attendance for both sexes has generally been the case in the United States for more than a century. Nonetheless, discriminatory practices still existed through high school and beyond. The decade of the 1960s brought legislation—the

Equal Pay Act of 1963, Title VII of the Civil Rights Act of 1964, and the Public Health Services Act as amended by the Comprehensive Health Manpower Training Act of 1971, prohibiting sex discrimination in employment and training—which opened the door for women's legal equality in selected areas. Four pieces of legislation—Title IX, the Women's Educational Equity Act of 1974, the Vocational Education Act of 1976, and the Career Education Incentive Act of 1977—completed the major legislative cornerstone supporting women's equal access to all academic levels. Several Executive Orders, including E.O. 11246, as amended by E.O. 11375, strengthened women's legal claim to educational equality. Title IX embodied the civil rights authority prohibiting discrimination in federally funded educational institutions and programs; the other three laws established programs designed to promote educational equality for women. Many political observers credit Title IX with the major educational advances made by women in the 1970s. The fact that it safeguards those rights not covered by the Civil Rights Act underscores the importance of Title IX, especially in light of the defeat of the Equal Rights Amendment, the constitutional amendment proposed to provide umbrella prohibition against sex discrimination.

Three additional pieces of educational legislation played a part. First was the Women's Educational Equity Act (1974), whose congressional intent was to secure women's educational equity through financial assistance enabling educational agencies and institutions to meet Title IX requirements. These companion laws formally acknowledged sex discrimination in education, a reality whose impact has been felt primarily by women. They also provided the legal means for creating programs to redress this pervasive inequality, which reinforced both traditional gender roles and the gender power balance. The Vocational Education Act of 1976 required the appointment of full-time personnel ("sex equity coordinators") to assist the states in implementing the legislation's intended equal access for women. Here, Congress sought to integrate sex equity issues into all vocational education policies, programs, and procedures. In addition, the Career Education Incentive Act of 1977 established a grant program to increase career awareness and planning, including monies for projects specifically designed to eliminate sex bias and stereotyping in career education.

It is apparent that the 1970s generated a major legislative thrust to ensure educational equity for American women. Even then, however, activists complained that Title IX, the key bulwark against sex discrimination in the educational system, was not sufficiently enforced. Almost immediately, institutions of higher learning asserted that a more evenhanded allocation of financial resources between men's and women's programs would prove disastrous. The critical battle was waged over athletic programs, where major resources had traditionally been allocated to male sports, popular among generous male alumni and regarded as a source of revenue at the fieldhouse gate. This offers us a clear example of the powerful protecting their institutional resources.

The widespread conflict over Title IX might serve as the microcosmic example of the power struggle between the genders within the educational system. Earlier in this volume, we suggested that the gains women have made in their power struggle with men usually occur because women's initial efforts receive scant attention, and thus the implications for longer-range advantage are not immediately recognized by the males in power. When subsequent events reveal the real power gains, the male establishment characteristically mounts an impressive, often effective, counterattack. Such has been the case with Title IX, which sailed to legislative victory on a quiet tide. Once in place, women activists used Title IX to seek educational equity.

Resistance from the male athletic and university establishment came in a flood of newspaper editorials, as well as TV sports commentaries (not to mention efforts to lobby the Congress). The argument: Title IX would eviscerate male collegiate sports, if not the entire university system. The battle was joined. Using Title IX as its legal rationale, the major national women's athletic association (The Association for Intercollegiate Athletics for Women—AIAW) began to move its troops into position. Previously disdained and ignored by the male-dominated National Association for Intercollegiate Athletics (NCAA), the AIAW soon became the object of serious takeover attempts after Title IX's ripple effect enhanced its political leverage. More recently, observers note a backlash embodied in lawsuits filed by males claiming "reverse discrimination" and the rising conservative tide of the 1980s. Recent court decisions will limit Title IX's broad-gauged impact to selected programs within educational institutions. These events jeopardize Title IX and other legislation created to safeguard women's educational equity. Budget cutbacks further threaten women's laboriously won educational gains, and the motif echoes again: an ebb and flow of women's efforts to equalize the gender-role power balance.

SUMMARY

Through the centuries, the educational system has maintained gender-role segregation. Through formal structural mechanisms, such as admissions policies and curriculum-tracking requirements, women have been excluded from critical power-producing fields like medicine, law, business, and math-related scientific disciplines. Through differential allocation of critical resources, the educational system has denied women learning opportunities readily available to men. This has been particularly true with respect to higher education, a potential arena for radicalization. Witness the radicalization in the 1970s of female faculty in higher education, who filed class action suits against universities. This radicalization could lead to a reevaluation of wifehood and motherhood by women, who would then insist on restructuring the traditional roles, placing the gender-role power balance in serious danger. This radicalization also threatened to produce gender bonding among women, which might offset the long-standing and powerful male homosocial hold on institutions.

Through informal processes and practices that integrate control myths and related gender-role stereotypes, women have been guided into restricting, low-level fields of study and employment. By contrast, marriage often poses a clearly preferable alternative. Through other informal processes and mechanisms, such as the "old-boy network" and the mentoring system, men thread their way through the educational system to positions of affluence and power.

Some might consider female educational inequality as the archetypal example of male efforts to limit female power. Not during innocent, powerless, asexual childhood, but only at the first hint of immanent adulthood's promise of female sexuality and power does the male establishment act to suppress females. Such an interpretation would shed additional light on an educational pattern evident from ancient Sparta to contemporary America: educational equality during the childhood years, followed by increasingly limited educational access as adulthood approaches. This might also explain why the most stringent inequalities are structured into the institutions of higher education, which potentially could radicalize and empower women, in the world outside the family. The lesson is clear; limit women's education, lest it incite them to radicalism and transform them into powerful leaders who would call for an adjustment of the gender power balance.

This pattern of male dominance and female subordination has been rationalized through the ages as the ideal system for preparing individuals to assume their rightful "functions," "spheres," or "places" in life: women as wives and mothers, albeit educated; men as the powerful and dominant controllers of society's major institutions. The motif of gender-role differentiation, so clearly elaborated in the educational system, is then perpetuated by the occupational system.

NOTES

1. In *The Republic,* Book 4, 425-B, Plato comments on the life-long influence of education: "The direction in which education starts a man will determine his future life." And centuries later the French philosopher Jules Michelet, in *Le Peuple* (1949), noted, "What is the first part of politics? Education. The Second? Education. And the third? Education."

2. Jane Marcus, "Liberty, Sorority, Misogyny" (paper presented at the Radcliffe Institute, Radcliffe College, Cambridge, Mass., 1980), p. 25.

3. Ibid., pp. 10–11.

4. Simone de Beauvoir, "The Second Sex: 25 Years Later," *Society,* 13, no. 2 (January/February 1976), pp. 79–85.

5. Carl N. Degler, *At Odds: Women and the Family in America from the Revolution to the Present* (New York: Oxford University Press, 1980), p. 311.

6. Adolphe E. Myer, *An Educational History of the American People,* 2nd ed. (New York: McGraw-Hill, 1967), p. 214.

7. Degler, *At Odds,* p. 310.

8. Ibid., p. 314.

9. Betty Friedan, *The Feminine Mystique* (New York: W. W. Norton, 1963).

10. J. S. Pietrofessa and N. K. Schlossberg, "Counselor Bias and the Female Occupational Role," in *Counselor Bias and the Female Occupational Role,* N. Glazer-Malbin and H. Y. Waehrer, eds., (Chicago: Rand McNally, 1972), pp. 219–21.

11. Urie Bronfenbrenner, testimony before the Senate Subcommittee on Children and Youth, September 25, 1973, in *American Families: Trends and Pressures* (Washington, D.C.: Government Printing Office, 1974), p. 151.

12. National Center for Education Statistics, *Digest of Education Statistics* (Washington, D.C.: Government Printing Office, 1981), p. 12.

13. Raphaela Best, *We've All Got Scars: What Boys and Girls Learn in Elementary School* (Bloomington, Indiana: University of Indiana Press, 1983).

14. Patricia Sexton, *The Feminized Male* (New York: Random House, 1969).

15. *Digest of Education Statistics,* p. 12.

16. N. D. Feshbach, "Sex Differences in Children's Modes of Aggressive Responses toward Outsiders," *Merrill Palmer Quarterly,* 15 (1969), pp. 249–58.

17. Lynn Fox, Elizabeth Fennema, and Julia Sherman, *Women and Mathematics: Research Perspectives for Change,* NIE Papers in Education and Work, no. 8 (Washington, D.C.: Government Printing Office, 1977).

18. Lynn Fox, "The Effects of Sex Role Socialization on Mathematics Participation and Achievement," in *Women and Mathematics: Research Perspectives for Change,* NIE Papers in Education and Work, no. 8 (Washington, D.C.: Government Printing Office, 1977).

19. Sheila Tobias, *Overcoming Math Anxiety* (Boston: Houghton Mifflin, 1980).

20. Lucy W. Sells, "The Mathematics Filter and the Education of Women and Minorities" (paper presented at American Association for the Advancement of Science, annual meeting, Boston, Mass., February 1976).

21. David McClelland, G. W. Atkinson, R. A. Clark, E. L. Lowell, *The Achievement Motive* (New York: Appleton-Century-Crofts, 1953).

22. Lois W. Hoffman, "Early Childhood Experiences and Women's Achievement Motives," *Journal of Social Issues,* 28, no. 2 (1972), pp. 129–55.

23. Mary Lou Randour, Georgia Strasburg, and Jean Lipman-Blumen, "Women in Higher Education: Trends in Enrollments and Degrees Earned," *Harvard Educational Review,* 52, no. 1 (May 1982), 189–202.

24. Elizabeth Morgan, *The Making of a Woman Surgeon* (New York: G. P. Putnam's Sons, 1980), pp. ix, 36.

25. Karen Johnson Freeze, "Medical Education for Women in Austria: A Study in the Politics of the Czech Women's Movement in the 1890s" (paper presented at the Sino-Soviet Conference on Changes in the Status of Women in Eastern Europe, George Washington University, Washington, D.C., December 4–6, 1981), p. 16.

26. Ibid., p. 19.

27. Ibid., p. 16.

28. Matina Horner, *Sex Differences in Achievement Motivation and Performance in Competitive and Non-Competitive Situations* (unpublished Ph.D. dissertation, University of Michigan, Ann Arbor, 1968).

29. David McClelland, G. W. Atkinson, R. A. Clark, and E. L. Lowell, *The Achievement Motive* (New York: Appleton-Century-Crofts, 1953).

30. W. F. Field, *The Effects of Thematic Apperception upon Certain Experimentally Aroused Needs* (unpublished Ph.D. dissertation, University of Maryland, College Park, 1951).

31. Thelma G. Alper, "Achievement Motivation In College Women: A Now-You-See-It-Now-You-Don't Phenomenon," *American Psychologist* (1974), pp. 194–203.

32. David Tresemer, "Current Trends in Research on 'Fear of Success,'" *Sex Roles,* 2, no. 3 (September 1976), p. 211.

33. Jean Lipman-Blumen, "How Ideology Shapes Women's Lives," *Scientific American,* 226, no. 1 (1972), pp. 34–42.

34. Carolyn Heilbrun, *Death in a Tenured Position* (New York: Dutton, 1981).

35. Jean Lipman-Blumen and Georgia Strasburg, "U.S. Country Paper: The Educational Status of Women" (paper prepared for the U.S. Office of Education and the U.S. Department of State for presentation at the U.N. Conference for International Women's Year, Copenhagen, 1980), p. 69.

36. Lipman-Blumen and Strasburg, "U.S. Country Paper," p. 78.

37. Ibid., p. 80.

CHAPTER 11
GENDER ROLES AND EMPLOYMENT

In his classic work on the division of labor in society, French sociologist Emile Durkheim (1858–1917) eloquently dissected its underlying dynamics. For Durkheim, the division of labor is the connecting fiber of an advancing society, the structure from which morality, happiness, and organic solidarity grow. In this organic view, society is composed of interdependent parts. Like the human organism, each component fulfills its specialized function, thereby contributing to the life of the whole. Individuals and groups offer their labor to society in an interdependent way, with labor assigned according to the abilities, or "nature," of the workers. Durkheim's radical focus concentrates on the division of labor among men outside the home, casually accepting the division of labor within the family as a natural interdependence creating domestic solidarity.

In a trenchant argument that predates the sex discrimination debate, Durkheim contends:

> . . . the division of labor produces solidarity only if it is spontaneous and in proportion as it is spontaneous. But by spontaneity we must understand not simply the absence of all express violence, but also of everything that can even indirectly shackle the free unfolding of the social force that each carries in himself. It supposes, not only that individuals are not relegated to determinate functions by force, but also that no obstacle, of whatever nature, prevents them from occupying the place in the social framework which is compatible with their faculties.[1]

Durkheim's concepts continue to color discussions about the division of labor both within the home and in the paid labor force. Contemporary economists recognize *occupational segregation* as the process whereby most current societies divide or assign paid labor outside the home largely on the basis of gender. Durkheim's caveat that the division of labor should be "spontaneous," without obvious or subtle external forces barring individuals from occupations for which they have the ability, is relevant to problems of contemporary occupational segregation.

Although Durkheim focused on the division of labor in more advanced societies, anthropological evidence suggests that work allocation by gender characterizes preliterate societies as well. Anthropologist George Murdock's study of 224 preliterate societies revealed that even structurally less differentiated social groups distributed economic activities or functions strictly along gender lines.[2] Although the gender segregation of occupations outside the home is striking across these 224 preliterate societies, equally striking is the fact that a male-dominated occupation in one society may be female-dominated in another. This gender segregation of occupations, we see, has been visible from preliterate through postindustrial societies.

Sociologist Alex Inkeles' recent work suggests that, particularly within the family, men and women do not perform the same work. And of special relevance to our concern with the gender power balance is the fact that men's work in all societies is more valued, more respected, more highly paid than women's.[3] The type of work one gender performs in a given society has often changed from one generation or century to the next, but prevailing norms, stereotypes, and control myths create the illusion that the current division of labor has always existed. Both classicists and social historians tell us otherwise.

AN HISTORICAL OVERVIEW

Classicists remind us that women worked in Greece and Rome, and that their work was surprisingly varied. Mary R. Lefkowitz indicates that upper-class educated Roman women owned and managed property, while "lower-class women and women slaves lived in many respects the same kinds of life as men, with set occupations and professions, some segregated, but fewer than we might have expected."[4]

Centuries later, the agrarian society of colonial America, according to social historian William H. Chafe, knew little occupational segregation by gender, nor was there life or time enough for a leisure existence. Chafe writes:

> Women from all classes were centrally involved in the mainstream economic activities of the community. Crops had to be planted and harvested, animals tended, clothes made, gardens cared for, and food prepared.[5]

It was only during social rituals, such as funeral eulogies, that women were described as practitioners of delicate "feminine pursuits." Only then was formal tribute paid to otherwise fictitious norms of the leisurely feminine life style. For the most part, these norms remained simply ideals presented by normative literature such as *The Spectator,* a weekly periodical.

During the colonial period, a small urban population began to develop. Many, but not all, urban women filled numerous occupational roles traditionally considered male territory: silversmiths, papermill workers, distillers, woodworkers, leatherworkers, and barbers. Degler notes certain of these "she merchants . . . actually issued, at one point, public protest against sex discrimination."[6] He suggests that most women were catapulted into these occupations and activities by some personal crisis, most often widowhood. Again, we see that crisis offers prime conditions under which roles, especially gender roles, change.[7]

The ease with which women, in the face of crisis, assume new roles attests to their intimate knowledge of, in fact their own latent socialization for, such activities. Their obscured contribution to the economy, their unnoticed activities side-by-side with their husbands, characterized women's participation in the occupational life of society. It is this hidden nature of women's economic and occupational life that has engendered surprise at women's ability to assume roles left vacant by men in crisis. Major societal upheavals, such as war, provide additional examples of the part crisis plays in breaking down the barriers of occupational segregation.

In the colonies, as elsewhere, the Industrial Revolution wrought a serious and complex change in the division of labor. Before industrialization moved the manufacture of many commodities from the home into the factory, women and men engaged in a common economic enterprise, often geared toward sustenance of the family rather than cash returns. Industrialization carved a sharp distinction between men's and women's economic conditions. Factory labor that resulted in manufactured goods was recompensed with money; home activity that produced goods and services remained unpaid. During this period, the domains of masculine and feminine work became more sharply differentiated, and beliefs in "masculine" and "feminine" spheres put down new roots.

Social Class and Ethnic Differences in Women's Roles

Despite the popular stereotype, not all colonial women engaged in similar activities. Work and life style among women of different social classes, as well as ethnic and racial groups, became clearly differentiated. Only those who managed to achieve middle- or upper-class levels could indulge themselves, or be indulged by their husbands, in full-time homemaking or leisure activities. Black women who labored as slaves continued to work in the paid labor force after emancipation. Chafe reminds us how they worked at nondomestic tasks indistinguishable in difficulty from those of black men.[8] They did the same field work, and in addition they worked inside the home as domestic servants.

Newly built factories, promising good wages and safe conditions for women and children, lured young unmarried farm women from the New England states to the Lowell textile mills along the banks of the Merrimack River. Aged 12 to 30, these "Lowell girls" lived in all-female boarding houses provided by the mill owners, where they were "protected" from the dangers of city life. Once confident of an adequate labor pool, the textile industrialists increased both hours and productivity demands, while lowering wages.

The segregation of these women in exclusively female boarding-houses and in indistinguishable oppressive jobs enabled them to experience a commonality as women and workers. Not separated from one another by relationships with men and free from consciousness of different social class loyalties, the Lowell girls developed strong bonds of personal and political solidarity. With developing economic and political awareness, the Lowell girls defiantly protested. They registered their objections to the oppressive hours and decreased wages by organizing strikes, or "turnouts," first in 1834 and, undaunted by less than total success, again in 1836.

The Lowell girls' ability to organize for economic and political purposes was met with hard-nosed resolve by mill owners, who replaced them with recently arrived immigrant women. Unlike the original Lowell girls, these new workers did not require promises of educational and healthy surroundings. When black, poor, and immigrant women became field-hands and factory workers, native-born white women began to view these occupations as "beneath them," another example of how women's emerging political strength was sapped through social class differentiation among women.

> By the end of the 19th century . . . a clear line had been drawn between the appropriate activities of "proper" white middle-class women and the activities associated with black, poor and immigrant women. For the first time in the nation's history, women from the former group were not centrally involved in what the dominant culture defined as mainstream economic activities. Their less-well-off sisters, by contrast, provided a major source of cheap and marginal labor.[9]

The shift from white, native-born to ethnic, immigrant female factory workers is reflected in several statistics. First, in 1836, 96 percent of the women textile workers in a large Lowell textile factory were native-born, compared to 40 percent by 1860. Historian Thomas Dublin and others suggest that after 1850, most women factory workers claimed Irish heritage.[10] By 1900, 17 percent of all white women were in the paid labor force, most of them from abroad. Forty-one percent of all nonwhite women also were counted as part of the labor force in 1900. In the last half of the nineteenth century, American women's presence in manufacturing increased 500 percent, yet comprised slightly less than 20 percent of that sector, which was expanding at an even faster rate. Unlike their entrepreneurial Northern French sisters who owned factories, American women were predominantly mill workers.

American women's influx into manufacturing as factory hands was indeed great, but not as great as their numbers in an occupation they gave great evidence of abhorring: domestic service. During the nineteenth century, domestic service was the single largest female occupation. In 1850, female domestic servants outnumbered women in teaching and manufacturing combined. The 1900 census reports more than 1 million female servants and waitresses, among whom 26 percent were second-generation white women, 19 percent were first-generation white females, and the remainder approximately equal proportions of black and foreign-born women (27 and 28 percent, respectively). Despite the fact that factory work

paid better, domestic service claimed the lion's share of female workers—
45 percent in 1880, 40 percent in 1900—simply because the female labor
pool was growing even faster than the expanding industrial economy. This
is similar to the picture in manufacturing, where just somewhat below one-
quarter of all women workers were employed from 1800 to 1900.

Class and ethnic background played a large part in occupational
"choice." Many middle-class and upper-middle-class women engaged in
the "more respectable" homebound profession of writing. Harriet Beecher
Stowe, Catharine Sedgwick, and Mary Wollstonecraft are some of the better-known women writers who worked within tbe confines of their own
homes. Teaching was such a favored middle-class female occupation that
90 percent of all professional women counted themselves teachers in 1870.
In the quarter-century before the Civil War, the teaching profession shifted from a male-dominated occupation to a female-intensive field. Here too
a crisis—this time a teacher shortage—led to the gender transformation of
an occupational category. Here too we see the "tipping" procedure at
work—a "contamination" process by which a field is overtaken by a lower-
status group, while the former higher-status group flees into less stigmatized occupations.

Growing urbanization and increased mechanization of jobs in the late
nineteenth century did lead to expanded employment opportunities for
women. This burgeoning economy, however, did not keep pace with the
faster-growing female demand for jobs. As a result, paid employment outside the home characterized only a relatively small proportion of the total
female population, a condition that persisted through the early twentieth
century.

Marital Status and Labor Force Participation

At the turn of the century, most women in the paid labor force were
single. Among white women workers, most were young and single, expecting to marry and subsequently leave the labor force. In 1900, not even 4
percent of white married women were in the paid labor force. By 1920,
their proportions had edged up to 8 percent. By the eve of World War II,
only 12 percent of white married women were paid workers. Norms about
married women working, particularly mothers, kept many women at
home, as opinion poll data show.

For women and men alike, a married woman's working outside the
home labeled her husband an economic failure. Such attitudes held married women hostage to their husband's status and power relative to other
men. The validity of Veblen's notion that the unemployed wife symbolized
her husband's affluence[11] is seen in the fact that married black women
have always had employment rates far greater than married white women
in the United States (although recent studies of nineteenth- and twentieth-
century black women workers suggest that lower incomes do not fully
explain their greater labor force participation). Furthermore, black women
professionals of the 1970s often reported desires to become full-time
homemakers, a luxury rarely dreamed of by their female forebears.

In the interwar period, 1920–1940, white married women's labor force participation rates increased in the United States, while their black married sisters' rates decreased. Even so, by 1940, black married women were twice as likely as their white counterparts to be in the paid labor force. Still, not quite 25 percent of black married women worked outside the home right up to World War II.

World Wars: The Archetypal Crisis

Both World Wars and every subsequent more limited war have redistributed men and women in the workplace. War is the archetypal crisis in which the stratification system, that social grid which channels individuals into hierarchical positions, weakens sufficiently to enable people to assume previously unobtainable roles.[12] In war, as in other crises, norms and values undergo radical, if only temporary, shifts, accommodating a new division of labor unthinkable in stable periods. Roles previously differentiated by gender, race, age, or any other admission criterion become "dedifferentiated" in the face of a crisis that threatens survival. Ability to accomplish the task becomes the overriding consideration.

During both wars, women, blacks, and other stigmatized and stigmatizing groups were actively recruited into jobs previously reserved for white males. In both postwar periods, unions and management acted to oust them. Once crisis opens the door to formerly unacceptable role applicants, it is difficult to slam it shut again. Once abrogated, norms rarely snap back to their precrisis tension. A small proportion of the new role occupants remain after the crisis is resolved, changing the baseline ratio of traditional and nontraditional role occupants. Accordingly, in 1940, just before World War II, women comprised 24.4 percent of all employed workers. That figure rose to 25 percent in 1941, 26.3 percent in 1942, 32.1 percent in 1943, and 35 percent in 1945. It receded to 28.3 percent in the 1948 post-war period. By 1949, the percentage of women began to edge up once again to 29.3. The next minor peak came with the onset of the Korean war. These figures demonstrate how crisis creates a "window of opportunity" in occupational role de-differentiation that may close in the postcrisis period. But the level of role de-differentiation rarely regresses to the precrisis baseline, creating a permanent, if slight, change.

Not only did World War II create gross fluctuations in women's participation in the labor market; it also brought internal change in the gender balance of previously segregated roles. Some fields that were just beginning to admit women opened their doors even wider. Other occupational categories that were formerly off-limits to women made initial overtures to female workers. In 1940, women held 21.2 percent of all clerical jobs; by 1945, their share had increased to 25.4 percent. Operatives and kindred workers shot up from 18.4 percent in 1940 to 23.9 percent in 1945, later declining in the postwar period (1947) to a new baseline of 21.7 percent. Craftworkers, floor supervisors, and kindred workers showed similar patterns. According to labor economists Wool and Pearlman, nearly 15 percent (1,500,000) of the women employed prior to the war changed occupational roles by March 1944.[13] In 1940, there were only a few thousand women in skilled or semi-skilled jobs in production plants; by 1945, women workers showed impressive gains.

Women's labor force participation diminished somewhat in the immediate postwar period, but never receded to pre-World War II levels. In fact, women's share of the total labor force has increased quite systematically ever since, with sudden spurts in times of national crisis. Total employment itself felt the impact of an expanding economy for much of the 35-year period following World War II, until the most serious economic downturn of the early 1980s.

POST-WORLD WAR II TRENDS: WOMEN AND MEN IN THE LABOR FORCE

Total employment in the United States has grown steadily since World War II, despite no less than eight postwar recessions, rising from 58,920,000 to 98,313,000 between 1950 and 1981. Along with this increase has come what economist Ralph E. Smith has labeled "the subtle revolution"—a steady increase in the number and percentage of women in the paid labor force.[14] Women's labor force participation grew from 3.7 million in 1890 (the earliest useful statistics) to 45.8 million by the end of 1981. In 1890, women workers comprised 17 percent of the total labor force and 18 percent of women ages 14 and over. As we saw in the historical overview, "all but a million of these working women were single," and "only 4.5 percent of married women were in the labor force at that time."[15]

According to U.S. Department of Labor statistics, by 1981, 42 million females were in the labor force, representing more than half of all adult women, and approximately 43 percent of the total labor force. Against a backdrop of combined social, political, and economic forces, increased female labor force participation occurred not only because the general population expanded, but because women in all age and marital status groups continued to enter paid work roles.

Young as well as older women swell the ranks of U.S. workers. As Table 11–1 indicates, in 1981, 51.8 percent of all women 16 to 19 years old and 22.7 percent of women 55 years and over held paid jobs. Even in the short period from 1971 to 1980, adult women increased their labor force participation, while men's participation rates declined. Thus, between 1971 and 1980, among women 20 years and over, the participation rate for

TABLE 11-1   Labor Force Participation Rates, December 1981 (Labor force as percentage of population)

Women 16 years and over	52.1%
16 to 19 years	51.8
20 to 24 years	69.6
25 to 54 years	65.3
55 years and over	22.7

Source: U.S. Department of Labor, Bureau of Labor Statistics, "Employment in Perspective: Working Women," *1981 Annual Summary,* Report 663, p. 2.

TABLE 11–2   Civilian Labor Force Participation Rate, 1971–1980

	PARTICIPATION RATE		
DEMOGRAPHIC GROUP	1971	1975	1980
Total	60.2	61.2	63.8
Teenagers (16 to 19 years)	49.7	54.1	56.9
Adult men (20 years and over)	82.1	80.3	79.4
Adult women (20 years and over)	43.3	46.0	51.4
Never married	68.1	68.7	71.8
Married	41.3	44.8	50.5
Widowed, separated, divorced	39.0	38.8	42.4

Source: U.S. Department of Labor, "Employment and Training Report of the President," (Washington D.C.: Government Printing Office, 1981), p. 13.

never-married women rose 3.7 percent, compared to a 3.4 percent increase for widowed, separated, or divorced women, and a 9.2 percent rise for married women.

Table 11–2 documents this change for women and also indicates that men's participation rates dropped 2.7 percent during this period. A longer-range view reveals that between 1890 and 1980, the male labor force participation rate dropped from 84 to 79.4 percent. This decline is not the result of a shrinking male population, which in fact has grown at approximately the same rate as the female population; rather, the drop is associated with protracted education, earlier retirement, and increased longevity, according to labor market analysts.

Women in all marital status categories continue to enter the paid labor force, as Table 11–2 suggests. By 1981, 51.2 percent of married women living with their husbands were paid workers, along with 60.6 percent of women maintaining families without husbands. Single, separated, divorced, and widowed women have always demonstrated strong labor force participation, but even their rates have increased over the years. Between 1890 and 1980, the single woman's participation rate grew from 37 to 71.8 percent, while the rate for previously married women rose from 29 to 42.4 percent. These increases notwithstanding, it is married women whose rates have risen most noticeably since World War II. Although some married women left their jobs during the postwar period, many remained. In fact, there is ample evidence that the postwar female attrition rate was largely attributable to not-so-gentle union and management efforts to persuade women factory workers to demonstrate their patriotism by relinquishing their jobs to returning servicemen. Nonetheless, from 1947 to 1981 nearly 17 million more women, mostly married, swelled the ranks of paid workers.

Mothers in the Labor Force

Many of the married women in the labor force are also mothers. In fact, by early 1981, economist Allyson Grossman reported that 54 percent of all American children below 18 had working mothers or mothers seeking employment.[16] In many families, mothers are the sole economic support of their children. More specifically, one-quarter of all children in the United States (14.8 million) live in families where the father is absent or not in the paid labor force.

According to Grossman, since 1970, 6.2 million more children have working mothers, even in the face of a 6.6 million overall decline in the number of children. In the single year from March 1980 to March 1981, the number of children below age 6 with working mothers rose from 7.4 to 8.2 million (from 43 to 45 percent of all preschoolers). Among mothers of children under 6, women aged 25 to 34 showed the greatest labor force participation increase. This particular group of women, born during the post-World-War-II baby boom, has tended to postpone marriage and children and eventually to have fewer children than did women of comparable ages in previous generations. Unlike women their age in earlier cohorts, these women have a longer prematernity history of labor force attachment. They rarely leave the work force, except for the briefest period immediately before and after childbirth.

Despite this increase among mothers of very young children, older children are still more likely to have mothers in the paid labor force. According to Grossman,[17] among all children aged 14 through 17, 60 percent have working mothers, versus 56 percent of those 6 through 13 years old and 45 percent of children below 6. In female-headed families, the figures are expectedly higher: 66 percent of 6- to 17-year-olds and 50 percent of children under age 6 have mothers in the paid work force.

With more mothers entering the labor force, the picture of the traditional American family with the father as sole wage earner has quietly, but significantly, changed. By 1981, in 60 percent of married-couple families with children under 18 both parents were in the paid labor force. These two-earner families, incidentally, also tend to have somewhat fewer children than single earner families. Paid employment outside the home seems to be an increasingly strong expectation for both parents, particularly in difficult economic times.

Attitudes toward Working Women

Documentation of changing expectations about women's work patterns comes from opinion polls that have tracked American attitudes during the last half-century. In the 1930s, less than 20 percent of women surveyed in a national opinion poll agreed that married women should have full-time jobs outside the home; 41 percent answered an emphatic "No." By 1964, when queried about a working mother's ability to establish a close relationship with her children, 54 percent of the female respondents felt that such an outcome was entirely possible; by 1970, 73 percent of the women respondents in a repeat survey expressed this opinion. Still, as pollsters Deborah Durfee Barron and Daniel Yankelovich report, the public retains ambivalent feelings about mothers working.[18]

Several polls point to these mixed feelings about women's work roles. A 1978 poll revealed that 61 percent of a mixed male and female sample felt that "women should have an equal role with men in running business, industry and government." That same year, however, 48 percent of the respondents in a national poll still felt that "woman's place is in the home"—only 1 percent less than in 1973. This same poll also revealed that 48 percent no longer believed that "marriages are stronger when the wife stays at home and doesn't go to work." In fact, 72 percent of a 1978 national sample said they approved of a "married woman earning money in business or industry (even) if she has a husband capable of supporting her"; this represented just under a 50 percent increase from the response to that same question in 1938.[19]

To add to the confusion, 77 percent of the respondents in a 1978 poll felt that "a wife should put her husband and children ahead of her own career." Although women surveyed in the 1930s and again in 1964 and 1970 felt increasingly optimistic about a working mother's ability to establish a close relationship with her child, the general public is somewhat less confident about this issue. A 1977 National Opinion Research Center (NORC) General Social Survey of both men and women revealed that only 48 percent agreed, while 50 percent disagreed that a working mother could develop such a relationship with her children.[20]

Working mothers of preschool children are most likely to be viewed negatively by the American public. Fifty-seven percent of the respondents in several 1978 surveys reported that they completely believed a "woman with young children should not work at a job outside the home unless it is financially necessary," and another 20 percent said they partially believed this. In the 1977 NORC survey, 66 percent of a national sample agreed that a "preschool child is likely to suffer if his or her mother works."

Despite these conflicting attitudes, women, including married women with and without children, are increasing their labor force participation. How much changing attitudes prompt more women to work and how much increasing numbers of working women change public attitudes is hard to determine. As external circumstances change, particularly as the economic picture becomes more threatening, the question of whether married women and mothers of young children should work may become moot.

WOMEN'S EARNINGS

Economists suggest that the benefits derived from paid labor outweigh the advantages of remaining outside the marketplace. Since real wages have increased as the overall economy has expanded, working without pay within the home, studying full time, engaging in volunteer work, or participating strictly in leisure activities fail to offer comparable benefits. In economic jargon, the *opportunity cost* of engaging in unpaid activities has grown too expensive for the majority of women to resist the attraction of the paid work force. For many married women, rising wages increased their husbands' incomes, and thus their standard of living. Many women chose to reduce, rather than increase, their own unpaid domestic work by purchasing labor-saving devices and services and then entered the paid work force. The increased educational levels women have attained in recent years are another factor contributing to their labor force participation, although education does not necessarily bring women the same economic rewards as men.

In stormy economic periods, more women enter the paid work force because of family income. Even today, most women are in the paid labor force because of economic need, whether they live with husbands or head their own households. Almost two-thirds of all women in the work force in 1980 were married to men earning less than $10,000 or were single, divorced, or separated. Among all families living in poverty, half were supported by women in 1979, and among poor black families, three-quarters were what census analysts call "female-headed families."[21] Economic necessity clearly is a major force behind most women's labor force activity. Rising divorce rates add momentum to this pattern.

Recent fundamental changes in American family law have eroded previous assumptions that divorce entitled former full-time homemakers to alimony and child support, even child custody. Emanating from an ideology of marriage based on power and dependence, past assumptions encouraged many women to neglect labor market skills in favor of full-time motherhood and homemaking. Rising divorce rates and recent legal decisions combine to suggest that "displaced homemakers" may well have to fend economically for themselves and their children after divorce. According to marital property law specialist Susan Westerberg Prager, as the full import of these trends becomes clear, many women will be forced to reconsider their willingness to forego labor force participation during marriage.[22] This creates still another factor certain to influence the power and dependency dynamic of traditional marriage.

Earnings and Domestic Power

Traditional male control over the family flowed mostly from the father's role as the sole economic supporter of his wife and children. He who controlled the purse strings determined all aspects of family life. The breadwinning father's economic contribution to the family purchased not only groceries, but also domestic power over his wife, whose labor within the home remained unpaid. Sociologists tracing the influence of women's paid labor force participation on the domestic power relationship suggest that as women's contributions to family income increase, so does their power in family decision-making.

Recent earned income figures reveal that wives' earnings, on average, account for 26 percent of total family income, and that the median contribution of wives working full-time year-round is as high as 38 percent. In 1981, for example, 14.5 million working wives holding full-time jobs had median (average) weekly earnings of $230, and those working part-time averaged $96 weekly. In black families, working wives contributed one-third of the total family income.[23]

Families in which wives work find themselves with higher incomes and improved standards of living. For example, in all families where both husbands and wives worked in 1981, the median weekly earnings of $560 was nearly 50 percent higher than the $379 median income for those families in which the husband was the sole earner. This difference was even larger among black and Hispanic married couples. The wife's economic contribution to the "better life" thus becomes a valuable bargaining chip in the domestic power struggle, particularly among families with borderline finances.

The U.S. Department of Labor reports that the wife's earnings frequently lift the family above the poverty line. In married-couple families in 1979, 14.8 percent lived in poverty when the wife did not work, compared to 3.8 percent who were poor when the wife was employed. Nonetheless, although women's earnings raise their families above poverty, improve living standards, and augment the wife's marital power, on average, working women earn less money than men (a 60 percent salary gap) in the same occupational categories. This salary and power gap remains despite the Equal Pay Act of 1963, which requires equal earnings for women and men engaged in the same work.

The Earnings Gap between Women and Men Workers

Comparisons of median earnings of year-round, full-time workers reveal that a significant gap remains between men and women. Throughout the decade of the 1970s, women's earnings as a percentage of men's hovered between 57 and 59 percent, reaching 60.2 percent in 1976, but then dropping slightly in the remaining years of the decade. In 1980, women's earnings rose to 60.2 percent of men's, with women workers' median earnings leveling out at $11,197, compared to $18,612 for men's. Economists calculate that the resulting earnings gap in constant 1967 dollars was $3,004. By the end of 1981, women's earnings had moved up to 65 percent of men's (Table 11–3), with considerable variations from one occupational category to another.

TABLE 11–3 Median Usual Weekly Earnings of Full-Time Wage and Salary Workers, by Sex and Occupation Group, Third Quarter 1981 (Workers 16 years of age and over)

OCCUPATIONAL GROUP	WOMEN	MEN	WOMEN'S EARNINGS AS PERCENT OF MEN'S
Total	$225	$346	65%
Professional and technical workers	323	436	74
Managers and administrators (except farm)	285	476	60
Sales workers	194	371	52
Clerical workers	221	326	68
Craft and kindred workers	238	367	65
Operatives (except transport)	187	298	63
Transport equipment operatives	239	315	76
Nonfarm laborers	191	242	80
Service workers	167	233	72
Farm workers	141	180	78

Source: U.S. Department of Labor, Bureau of Labor Statistics, News Release # U.S. D.L. 81-551, December 8, 1981.

Professional and technical women workers earned 74 percent as much as men in the same fields, but female sales workers managed to earn only 52 percent of male salespersons' wages by the third quarter of 1981. Certain female blue-collar workers narrowed the gap by garnering 72 to 80 percent of the wages earned by men in the same fields (see Table 11–3). Some analysts argue that the salary gap occurs because women enter these fields at lower levels, thus pulling down women's overall earnings; however, entry level is presumably related to educational level, and even when women have higher educational levels, they still have difficulty earning salaries equivalent to men's.

As late as 1979, women with four years or more of college earned less than men with one to three years of high school. Incomes of such women averaged $9,928 in 1979, compared to $11,000 median income for men with one to three years of high school. According to the U.S. Department of Commerce, the median income of men with four years or more of higher education was more than twice the median income of women with the same educational level (21,538 versus $9,928).

By 1981, the U.S. Department of Labor reported that "although some of the better paying occupations for women were the same as for men, the earnings of women remained far below those of men"; for instance, median weekly wage and salary earnings for male lawyers were $574, 40 percent more than that for female lawyers ($407).[24] Median weekly earnings of women lawyers were about the same as the average earnings for male post office mail carriers, an occupation that ranked roughly fortieth in men's earnings.[25] In another government report, the median weekly earnings for female computer systems analysts was $422, compared to $546 for their male peers; for female physicians, dentists, and related practitioners, $401 versus $561 for men; for female personnel and labor relations workers, $330 versus $514 for men. The highest paid job for women in a field employing 50,000 or more in 1981 was operations and systems researchers and analysts, where women earned $422, compared to male counterparts who earned $515.[26]

In 1981, the four occupations with the highest median weekly earnings for full-time women workers were operations and systems researchers and analysts ($422); computer systems analysts ($420); lawyers ($407); physicians, dentists, and related practitioners ($401); and social scientists ($391). Registered nurses and secondary school teachers, traditional and still popular occupational roles for women, had median weekly earnings of $331 and $321, respectively. For men, the three highest-ranking jobs (here no female counterparts were statistically significant) were aerospace and astronautical engineers, stock and bond sales agents, and chemical engineers. Their median weekly earnings topped the earnings list at $619, $589, and $583, respectively. Of the 20 leading occupations of employed men, civil engineer was the lowest paying, with a weekly median income of $507.

These earnings present a clear message. Although women are gaining important educational prerequisites for top-level jobs, they still experience difficulty in earning wages comparable to men's. Women are not yet able to convert their increased educational levels into systematic occupational and economic gain. For women, education and even occupational achievement seems to represent less valuable chips in the power struggle in the labor force, although within the domestic relationship they seem to make some power difference.

Occupational Segregation of Women and Men

Serious students of men's and women's differential labor force rewards lay much of the blame at the feet of occupational segregation, as alive and well in modern postindustrial America as in anthropologist Murdock's 224 preliterate societies.[27] Partly the end product of educational tracking that leads females and males into different fields of study, occupational segregation remains a serious problem. Channeling women and men into different fields is a sociological phenomenon with many implications, as suggested earlier. Once socialization, with its many facets and institutional barriers, successfully tracks women and men into different fields of study, occupational segregation occurs naturally. Women who have avoided studying mathematics and science in secondary school and college face monumental barriers in their quest to enter occupational fields requiring quantitative and scientific backgrounds.

Even the most casual review of the distribution of women and men in the American labor force in 1981 reveals a consistent pattern of occupational segregation. Although women represented 42.9 percent of all workers, men and women dominated different fields, with very few occupational categories shared equally by the genders. Despite recent legislation designed to eliminate structural barriers, subtle practices still prevent occupational distribution, just as Durkheim warned. In terms of occupations that are direct conduits to institutional and economic power, there can be little doubt that men predominate in both.

Women's Recent Gains

Women, nonetheless, have made discernible occupational advances in recent years, assisted by legislation such as the Equal Pay Act of 1963, the Equal Employment Opportunity Act, the Comprehensive Employment and Training Act reauthorized in 1978, Title VII of the 1964 Civil Rights Act, and the Pregnancy Discrimination Act of 1978. In addition, the educational legislation described in Chapter 10 not only helped crack formal barriers, but also provided funds for programs to change informal gender-role stereotypes that so powerfully shape educational and occupational choices.

The results of these legal changes are just beginning to appear in statistics. In 1970, women comprised 37.7 percent of all professional and technical workers. By 1981, their share had risen to 44.7 percent. Of course, much of women's apparent strength in the professional and technical categories stems from their traditional concentrations in the roles of librarian, registered nurse, and elementary and secondary school teacher—fields where they represent respectively, 85.2, 96.5, 83.7, and 52.1 percent of all those employed in these jobs. Nonetheless, even between 1974 and 1980, women's share of several traditionally male-dominated fields increased substantially. For example, during that time, women's foothold in medicine grew from 9.8 to 13.4 percent and in law from 7 to 12.8 percent. Women engineers were so scarce in 1974 that their percentage of the field was not even recorded in official government statistics; by 1980, they were 8.6 percent of all individuals employed as industrial engineers. These are impressive gains in a relatively short period of time. Finer analysis of these categories usually reveals, however, that *within* these fields, women are again segregated to specific—usually lower-paid and low-status—subfields.

If we look at the distribution patterns for all employed women, we see occupational segregation from still another perspective. Most women, despite their demographic diversity, are still clustered in just a few categories. Over one-third (34.7 percent) of all employed women in 1981 were still clerical workers, and approximately one-quarter of female workers were concentrated in education (except higher education), health care (except medicine), and food and domestic service. Seventeen percent of all women workers were classified as professional and technical workers, including 4.9 percent health workers, 5.3 percent noncollege teachers, and 6.8 percent other professionals and technical workers. Although women have made concerted efforts to enter the higher-paying blue-collar fields, in 1981 only 13.5 percent of all employed women were counted among blue-collar workers. Among these, most women worked as nontransport operatives (91.7 percent), 0.7 percent were employed as transport equipment operatives, 1.9 percent as craft and kindred workers, and 1.2 percent as nonfarm laborers.[28]

This occupational concentration exists despite the fact that women workers exhibit diverse demographic characteristics. Younger and older women, less educated and more educated, married and unmarried, mothers and nonmothers all participate in the paid work force. Through some complex pattern of forces, this diverse group of women workers is still channeled into a relatively limited range of occupational categories, even the 75 percent of all employed women who are full-time, year-round workers. Social scientists and political activists have labeled this complex set of forces "sex discrimination," a phenomenon not yet fully understood.

Durkheim, who insisted that the spontaneous division of labor "supposes not only that individuals are not relegated to determinate functions by force, but also that no obstacle, of whatever nature, prevents them from occupying the place in the social framework which is compatible with their faculties,"[29] would have characterized this pattern as the "forced division of labor." Forced labor, according to Durkheim, cannot produce the socially desirable result of solidarity that is the expected outcome of a natural division of labor in society:

> . . . if the institution of classes or castes [read "women as an occupational caste"] sometimes gives rise to anxiety and pain instead of producing solidarity, this is because the distribution of social functions on which it rests no longer responds . . . to the distribution of natural talents. . . . [D]ifferences which originally separated the classes must have disappeared or grown less. Through changes produced in society, some must have become apt at functions which were at first beyond them, while the others lost their original

superiority. . . . In accordance with these transformations, the agreement between the aptitudes of individuals and the kind of activity assigned to them is found to be broken . . . constraint alone, more or less violent and more or less direct, links them to their functions. Consequently, only an imperfect and troubled solidarity is possible. . . . The forced division of labor is . . . abnormal.[30]

What is it then that maintains the division of labor according to gender even in contemporary, postindustrial society? Although the norms that tell society how to carry on its business change slowly, they do change. One index of evolving norms is changes in attitudes evident in opinion polls taken at different points in time, such as those described earlier. Often, there is a time lag between a significant change in norms and attitudes and a modification in laws that represent their official legal expression. Yet a change in the law does not mean that everyone in the society concurs with the new norm. As a result, there is still another lag, less noted by sociologists, between the time such laws are changed and the moment when the more universal acceptance and implementation of those laws occur.

Traditionally ingrained control myths keep the division of labor by gender from giving way to a more natural division of labor by ability and expertise. The control myths exert their powerful hold by signaling gender-linked messages: men are more intelligent than women; women's nature is best suited to helping, not leading; men will take good care of women. These control myths are at the core of gender-role stereotypes that help to maintain occupational segregation. As Durkheim reminds us:

> When the regime of castes has lost juridical force, it survives by itself in customs, and thanks to the persistence of certain prejudices, a certain distinction is attached to some individuals, a certain lack of distinction attached to others, independent of their merits. Finally, even where there remains no vestige of the past, hereditary transmission of wealth is enough to make the external conditions under which the conflict takes place very unequal. . . .[31]

Durkheim's analysis of the difficulty with which castes, once stigmatized, eventually emerge into a division of labor that more truly represents their actual abilities is applicable to the current condition of American women in the labor force. In fact, he foreshadowed the 1970s affirmative action efforts for women and other minorities when he analyzed how society is forced to address the inequality of castes:

> Finally, even this last inequality which comes about through birth . . . is at least somewhat attenuated. Society is forced to reduce this disparity as far as possible by assisting . . . those who find themselves in a disadvantageous position . . . [and] by aiding them overcome it. [Society] thus shows that it feels obliged to leave free space for all merits and that it regards as unjust any inferiority which is not personally merited. But what manifests this tendency even more is the belief . . . that equality among citizens becomes ever greater and that it is just that this be so. A sentiment so general cannot be a pure illusion, but must express, in confused fashion, some aspect of reality. But as the progress of the division of labor implies, on the contrary, an ever growing inequality, the equality which public conscience thus affirms . . . is equality in the external conditions of conflict.[32]

The "external conditions of conflict" to which Durkheim refers may be interpreted as external resources, which today still remain unequal between men and women. Women's attempts to escape occupational segregation have been seriously impeded by their traditional lack of control over external and institutional resources. And their relegation to low-paid, low-opportunity jobs further keeps them from accruing resources that might lead to the redistribution of the division of labor. The unequal external conditions that women encounter—customary family obligations, which they fulfill without salary—make their situation within a gender-segregated labor force even more difficult.

Feminist critics argue that a more equal division of labor or at least equal pay for comparable work is a necessary condition for women to begin to equalize the power balance between the genders.[33] But many important islands of institutional and societal power still remain essentially off-limits to women, including the military. The history of legislative "reform" of occupational conditions enlarges our understanding of this stubborn phenomenon.

EMPLOYMENT LEGISLATION: A TRANSITION FROM PROTECTION TO EQUAL STATUS

Employment legislation has played a major, if uneven, role in women's labor force participation and their ability to develop economic resources. In the early twentieth century, employment legislation was designed to protect women from exploitative labor conditions, including substandard pay, long hours, and work thought to exceed women's physical capacity. In addition, many states had laws requiring women to cease working for at least two weeks prior to and four weeks after childbirth. By custom, if not by law, employers resisted hiring pregnant women in a mix of chivalry and economic self-interest.

It took almost half a century before many of these protective laws were even recognized as the legal, yet insidious, means of excluding women from profitable occupational positions. Not many had the foresight of feminist Susan B. Anthony, who, even in the 1860s, objected to protective legislation, recognizing that it would make women workers a special case, set apart from their male peers. Many feminists insisted that the unions' indifference to women workers made it mandatory for women to rely upon statutory protection. Feminist labor organizer Fannia Cohn enunciated the "fundamental principle" of protective legislation in 1927 when she wrote: "Considering that very few women are as yet organized into trade unions, it would be folly to agitate against protective legislation."[34]

During the Progressive era, women and labor collaborated to bring the case of *Muller* v. *Oregon* (1908) before the Supreme Court. Justice Louis Brandeis defended women's health and safety.

Louis Brandeis argued . . . that special protective legislation [was] justified in order to protect women's health and safety. In distinguishing its position from that which it had taken only three years before, the Court fell back upon the special dependence of women upon men. A woman "is properly placed in a class by herself". . . . "It is impossible to close one's eyes to the fact that she still looks to her brother and depends upon him."[35]

During the Progressive period, the fact that young, unmarried women were the mainstay of the female labor force raised concern about maternal health. The yet-unborn children of these female workers led to a legitimate worry about the nation's future. "Many unions supported protective legislation for women because it could advance the special interests of men."[36] This familiar strategy—men supporting women's claim to equality to enhance their own position—became evident again in the 1970s, when the Fair Labor Standards Act, previously passed to provide a minimum wage for women, was extended to cover men as well. Nor does this phenomenon deny the sincere support of many individual men and male groups who readily accept and work for the advancement of women's equality in all social domains.

Laws passed early in the twentieth century to protect American women workers came under new scrutiny with the resurgence of the feminist movement in the late 1960s. The previous struggle resumed, with traditionalists clinging to existing "protective" legislation as women's only sure means of protecting themselves from even greater inequities at work, and feminists arguing that the safeguard was merely from better-paying jobs and equal opportunity. In the ensuing struggle, much of the "protective" legislation was struck down by court decisions.

The 1960s and 1970s brought new legislation designed to eradicate sex discrimination, particularly in employment. Title VII of the Civil Rights Act of 1964, as amended, prohibits discrimination in employment "based on sex as well as race, color, religion or national origin." According to this landmark legislation, it is illegal for employers, unions, or employment agencies to act in a discriminatory manner in matters of hiring, firing, wages, fringe benefits, classifying, assigning, or promoting workers. It also covers issues of training and retraining, apprenticeships, and other employment terms. Employers with 15 or more workers are subject to the provisions of Title VII, amended in 1978 to prohibit discrimination on the basis of pregnancy, childbirth, or related medical conditions. Two Executive Orders (11246, as amended by E.O. 11375) make it unlawful for any federal contractor to discriminate against employees or employment applicants on the basis of sex, race, color, religion, or national origin. Furthermore, federal contractors must pledge to develop affirmative action plans to guarantee nondiscriminatory treatment of workers. Affirmative action strategies, foreshadowed by Durkheim, include a wide range of activities designed to help eliminate occupational segregation. Coupled with the Equal Pay Act of 1963 and more recent concerns with equal pay for comparable work, these legislative efforts represent legalized norms, a major advance for women.[37]

These legislative initiatives all deal, in one way or another, with resources that can be invested to sustain or build economic independence and thus provide opportunities for adjusting the power balance between women and men. Retirement pensions, which offer critical economic resources, have been a focus of attention, particularly among the elderly, most of whom are women. In accordance with sex-based actuarial tables, women have been obliged to contribute more money to their pension plans or have received lower benefits—a solution actuaries allege flows from women's greater longevity. Too complicated an issue to be treated in this context, the myriad facets of pension inequalities as applied to male and female workers deserve special attention to untangle their economic and symbolic importance in the gender power balance within the world of employment. Taken together, pensions, equal pay, and equal opportunity legislation form a powerful political-legal basis for gender equality.

Cross-national studies reveal that many other countries have taken similar steps, some long before the United States. Austria in 1958, Belgium in 1975, Canada in 1971, the Federal Republic of Germany in 1949, France in 1972, and the United Kingdom in 1970 assured their male and female workers equal pay. Equal opportunity legislation or constitutional assurance currently exists in Canada, Belgium, France, the United Kingdom and Sweden; Austria, Belgium, and the Federal Republic of Germany are currently preparing to take similar action.

SUMMARY

The rising power of women often evokes a strong negative response from males, who rightly perceive that they are being asked to share what is recognized as a limited pie. Labor force participation, particularly under conditions of equal opportunity and equal legal protection, is a major source of economic, political, and domestic power. Recognition that the fruits of their labor could indeed help women equalize their private and public relationships with men is both heartening and threatening to men and women alike.

Widespread economic problems of the early 1980s provide the rationale, as did earlier erupting revolutions in many socialist countries, for setting aside women's need for equality in the name of the greater societal good. Alexis de Tocqueville's notion of "self-interest rightly understood," whereby individuals set aside their personal self-interest for the larger social good, is an argument heard again today: women should not press their claim for equality in the marketplace; the times are too dangerous. The work of labor historians is replete with examples of women bowing to the greater societal need, even when that meant putting aside their own potential economic and political power.

The rising tides of women's employment, coupled with their increased educational levels and family support responsibilities, make it unlikely that the call to redefine gender roles will diminish. More likely, efforts will continue for women to use their economic and political power as ammunition in the struggle to reset the gender power balance. The political arena is one in which the employment battle has been assiduously waged in the last two decades. An examination of the intricate connection between gender roles and politics, to which we now turn, should amplify our understanding of the centuries-old power contest between the genders.

NOTES

1. Emile Durkheim, *The Division of Labor in Society* (Glencoe, Ill.: The Free Press, 1947), p. 377.

2. George Murdock, "Comparative Data on the Division of Labor by Sex," *Social Forces,* 15, no. 4 (May 1937), pp. 551–53.

3. Alex Inkeles, "Modernization and Family Patterns: A Test of Convergence Theory," in *Conspectus of History,* eds. Dwight W. Hoover and John T. Koumoulides, 1, no. 6 (Muncie, Indiana: Ball State University Press, 1980), pp. 3–63.

4. Mary R. Lefkowitz, *Heroines and Hysterics* (New York: St. Martin's Press, 1981), p. 141.

5. William H. Chafe, *Women and Equality: Changing Patterns in American Culture* (New York: Oxford University Press, 1977), p. 23.

6. Carl N. Degler, *At Odds: Women and the Family in America from the Revolution to the Present* (New York: Oxford University Press, 1980), p. 365.

7. Jean Lipman-Blumen, "Role De-Differentiation as a System Response to Crisis: Occupational and Political Roles of Women," *Sociological Inquiry,* 43, no. 2 (1973), 105–29.

8. Chafe, *Women and Equality.*

9. Ibid., p. 23.

10. Thomas Dublin, "Women, Work and the Family: Female Operatives in the Lowell Mills, 1830–1860," *Feminist Studies,* 3 (Fall 1975), pp. 30–39; also Thomas Dublin, "Women, Work and Protest in the Early Lowell Mills: The Oppressing Hand of Avarice Would Enslave Us," *Labor History,* 16 (Winter 1975), 99–116.

11. Thorstein Veblen, *The Theory of the Leisure Class* (New York: Modern Library, 1934).

12. Jean Lipman-Blumen, "Role De-Differentiation," pp. 105–29.

13. Harold Wool and Lester M. Pearlman, "Recent Occupational Trends," *Monthly Labor Review,* 65 (August, 1947), 139–47.

14. Ralph E. Smith, ed., *The Subtle Revolution: Women at Work* (Washington, D.C.: The Urban Institute, 1979), p. 3.

15. Ibid.

16. Allyson Sherman Grossman, "More than Half of All Children Have Working Mothers," *Monthly Labor Review,* 105, no. 2 (February 1982), 41–43.

17. Ibid.

18. Deborah Durfee Barron and Daniel Yankelovich, "Today's American Woman: How the Public Sees Her" (manuscript prepared for the President's Advisory Committee for Women, December 1980).

19. Ibid.

20. Ibid.

21. U.S. Department of Labor Statistics, Women's Bureau, "Facts on Women Workers" (Washington, D.C.: Government Printing Office, 1980), pp. 1–3.

22. Susan Westerberg Prager, "Shifting Perspectives on Marital Property Law," in *Rethinking the Family: Some Feminist Questions,* ed. Barrie Thorne with Marilyn Yalom (New York: Longman, Inc., 1982), pp. 111–30.

23. Ibid.; also Nancy F. Rytina, "Earnings of Men and Women: A Look at Specific Occupations," *Monthly Labor Review* (April 1982), pp. 25–31.

24. U.S. Department of Labor, Bureau of Labor Statistics, "Employment Perspective: Working Women," *1981 Annual Summary,* Report 663, pp. 1–4.

25. Ibid., p. 2.

26. U.S. Department of Labor, Bureau of Labor Statistics, "1981 Weekly Earnings of Men and Women Compared in 100 Occupations." Washington, D.C.: Government Printing Office (March 7, 1982).

27. Murdock, "Comparative Data," pp. 551–53.

28. U.S. Department of Labor Statistics, *Employment and Earnings,* 29, no. 1 (January 1982), Table 21 (pp. 163–64) and Table 23 (pp. 165–66).

29. Durkheim, *The Division of Labor in Society,* p. 377.

30. Ibid., p. 376.

31. Ibid., p. 378.

32. Ibid., p. 379.

33. Donald J. Treiman and Heidi I. Hartmann, eds., *Women, Work, and Wages: Equal Pay for Jobs of Equal Value* (Washington, D.C.: National Academy Press, 1981).

34. Degler, *At Odds,* p. 401.

35. Ibid.

36. Ibid.

37. Treiman and Hartmann, *Women, Work and Wages.*

CHAPTER 12
POLITICS
AND
GENDER ROLES

POWER AND THE POLITICAL SYSTEM

The capacity to impose one's own will on others, despite resistance, lies at the heart of power, according to Max Weber and Peter Blau (influenced by Talcott Parsons). This definition of power implies the promise of reward or the threat of punishment, yet neither necessarily need be invoked. Power is formally structured in political systems, which establish the social order. Law, in turn, expresses this accepted social order, which a society expects its members to uphold, upon threat of force.

Max Weber's definition of power (*macht*) is

the probability that one actor within a social relationship will be in a position to carry out his own will despite resistance, regardless of the basis on which this probability rests.[1]

Peter Blau's definition of power is

the ability of persons or groups to impose their will on others despite resistance through deterrence either in the form of withholding regularly supplied rewards or in the form of punishment. . . . Three further implications should be noted. First, following Parsons . . . power is used to refer to an individual's or group's ability *recurrently* to impose his or its will on others, not a single instance. . . . Second, the punishment threatened for resistance, provided it is severe, makes power a compelling force, yet there is an element of volunteerism to power—the punishment could be chosen in preference to compliance, and it sometimes is—which distinguishes it from . . . direct physical coercion. Finally, power is conceptualized as inherently asymmetrical and as resting on the *net* ability that remains after the restraints . . . impose(d) . . . have been taken into account. Its source is one-sided dependence. Interdependence and mutual influence of equal strength indicate lack of power.[2]

In one sense, power relationships are the essence of politics. Power is practiced not only through governmental politics, but also through political interactions between individuals and among groups. Indeed, a power dynamic is embedded in all relationships—familial, social, economic, and political—where one party can make its will prevail and other parties follow, ostensibly voluntarily, but often reluctantly. When complex networks of power relationships exist within the public sphere, they are conceptualized as the political structure; within the private sphere, such networks may be understood as interpersonal relationships.

The major thesis of this text has been that the basis of most power relationships is the private, domestic relationship between individual women and men. It is echoed in the public relationship of male and female groups, as well as in power relationships among social groups, classes, and nations. The historic asymmetry in the relationship between women and men, both in the family and the body politic, provides a blueprint that the power relationships among generations, castes, colonies, and nations have followed.

As the dominant group, men have determined the major outlines of women's lives through formal legal systems, as well as through informal customs and mores. To complete the picture, women, along with men, have been socialized to accept these mores, based on control myths stereotypically depicting men as strong, aggressive protectors of less intelligent, dependent, selfless women. As a result, women's presumed acquiescence to male domination has had an appearance of being voluntary. For example, those women who have argued against mandating women's equality through the Equal Rights Amendment seem to choose voluntarily to remain unequal. For some, this "choice" is based on control myths about the "natural" differences between women and men. For others, this voluntary inequality rests on the belief that remaining legally dependent ensures protection and support from men, who may or may not be willing to defend women's best interests without a legal mandate.

There have been exceptions, of course, but as Blau stated, the consistent and recurrent ability to impose one's will on others, based on one's own world view, is a genuine mark of power. Such persistent power implies, at the very least, an asymmetry of control over the resources that may be used to punish or reward the target of one's power efforts. Some observers note that women who tenaciously defend female dependence on men do so believing that to free themselves from male support, without adequate training to generate their own resources, is an act of misplaced ideology. Thus, lack of access to and control over life-sustaining resources perpetuates the seemingly voluntary submission to male power.

This power asymmetry that leads to the domination of one individual or group by another rests upon many other factors, only several of which can be treated within the limits of this chapter. The society's values, norms, and legal system, buttressed by the political system, the social rankings of the stratification system, and the possibility of individual or institutional force all combine to create the twin conditions of domination and subordination among both individuals and groups.

CONTROL MYTHS AND POWER

In earlier chapters, we examined the values and norms articulated in control myths, which serve to structure the power relationships in which women and men have been locked throughout much of history. The value of perpetuating society through new generations is a widespread sentiment that has preserved the concept of the family everywhere. Control myths depicting females as suited for domesticity and dependence and males for support and dominance have guided the allocation of private roles to women, public roles to men.

Within families, the differentiation of roles by gender and age, girded by control myths and norms, provides two major power axes. The result is a family pattern recognizable across many cultures: Men dominate women, parents control children. Significantly, the individual private, domestic power relationship created the central rationale for the public power balance between male and female groups. If it were necessary, or even natural, for wives and daughters to be protected, supported, and thus dominated by men within the home, it followed that this relationship was even more imperative within the larger public domain.

Women's dependence on more powerful men was based, partially at least, upon limited resources: physical, economic, political, legal and social. Sociologists Joan Acker, Gunnar Myrdal, and others have compared women's dependence to the subordinate positions of racial and ethnic minorities, castes, classes, and colonial nations.[3] Although these parallels do not hold in every detail, as Chafe's comparison of women and blacks in the United States demonstrates, the main outlines provide striking similarities.[4] Most important, these comparisons highlight the critical power differences between the groups.

Norms suggesting differences between women and men, which support the gender power distribution, are articulated informally in control myths and formally in law. Social historians have emphasized these differences and, in descriptions of nineteenth-century life, have linked these dissimilarities to the concept of men's and women's "two spheres." Functionalists and sociobiologists have perpetuated this concern with studies of gender-role differentiation to the present day.

Two Spheres: The Polity and the Family

The exaggerated emphasis on the notion of the "two spheres" as a feature of the postindustrial era introduces slight confusion. Long before the Industrial Revolution and its accompanying urbanization, the public sphere—particularly politics and the military—belonged to men. In ancient Greece, Spartan and Athenian boys were raised to be military and political leaders, girls to rear sons who would fill these powerful roles. During the preindustrial period, however, economic responsibility was shared by men and women, as well as children, within families. Each family was an individual economic unit, dependent for its sustenance on its own members. When industrialization made factories and offices the sites of income-producing work, the paid economic functions of the family became uniquely part of the male sphere. With the industrialization of work, social policy emerged as a means of buttressing the economic requirements of new entrepreneurs. Legislation subsequently drafted and enacted by the new industrialists in their political roles reinforced male economic power. The result: the merger of the economy and the political/military realms under exclusive male control, with a clear separation from women's domestic, nurturant, spiritual, and moral domain within the family.

In the face of incipient, competitive industrialization, the family came to be perceived as the only remaining haven from the harsh realities of a mechanized society. Acting through control myths, norms specified women's and men's expected roles and statuses in the new industrialized, urban era. Control myths that described woman as more selfless, morally superior, less aggressive, and more religious led both women and men to believe in the appropriateness of her private, domestic role as childbearer and rearer, nurse, helpmate, moral guardian, and community benefactress. The control myth expressing the male's concern with women's "best interests" and protection, linked to the related myth describing men's greater intellectual and physical prowess, provided the rationale for males to control the public arena, often in the name of women and children. Exaggerated under competitive capitalist conditions, men's natural aggression could be tempered only by the nurturant, moral nature of women. Moreover, fusing these two sides into one coin produced the ideology of a natural fit, a preordained integration of the genders' personalities and roles. This neat division of public and private responsibility, however, was less perfect, even less rigid, than it appeared on the surface.

Religion: An Avenue from Private to Public Policies

The notion of two spheres linked to gender-differentiated characteristics contained the seeds of the rationale women eventually would use to move beyond the confines of the domestic walls. Time and again, in the name of moral guardianship, religious practice, and selflessness, women stepped out of the boundaries of hearth and home to influence, if not directly participate in, the political life of the community. This political activity was often aimed at controlling male behavior.

Women's enthusiastic church attendance initially was perceived as perfectly innocuous—in fact, even seemly. Yet their strong religious orientation paved the way for women to enter the political realm in the name of religious and charitable concerns.

But at least two paradoxes are evident in the religious roles women enacted through their church attendance. First, despite their spiritual and moral superiority, women found themselves not in the ranks of church leaders, but primarily among religious followers. Thus, women's fervent religious beliefs paradoxically bound them in even greater servitude, obedience, and devotion to God and church. Like other potential powers of women (for example, reproduction), their religious and moral "superiority" was transformed into a source of subordination.

The second paradox emerged from the first. This additional source of women's servitude provided an opening, a rationale, for entering the larger political world beyond the home. The quintessentially feminine concern with religious and moral issues would become the vehicle women ultimately would use to gain entrance to the public sphere, in the name of protecting the morality and spiritual sanctity of the home. Fighting prostitution, alcohol, and other social and moral ills, women entered the political realm, moving to control men's behavior—often their sexual behavior. Their appetites whetted by success, women eventually sought to formalize their newfound power through universal suffrage in the early twentieth century.

Women's Organizations and Associations

Initially at the urging of their ministers, married women, even more than their single sisters, undertook to care for the poor. From there they branched out to all manner of community work, which eventually spilled over into political action. The Sunday School movement, which promoted religious education, was followed by other charitable and religiously oriented societies. Historian Donald Mathews suggests that Southern women's route to public life started on its way through prayer meetings, which eventually evolved into benevolent societies with a reformist bent.[5]

Through their predominantly female membership, such associations offered women an important public arena in which they learned, without male competition for leadership roles, how to organize for collective, and eventually political, action. In addition, the experience of socializing and working together with women outside their own family or kin group created the medium in which female solidarity, identity, organization, and political skill could develop. The psychological, social, and organizational support women received from women outside the confines of their families provided a potential alternative to total dependence on their husbands. Economically, however, the reliance on husbands, fathers, and brothers remained intact.

The list of women's religious and benevolent societies with a reformist orientation is impressive: from the New York Female Moral Reform Society and the Philadelphia Female Anti-Slavery Society of the 1830s to the Women's Christian Temperance Union, still a powerful force in the early twentieth century. The majority of these organizations boasted memberships composed of well-educated, middle- and upper-class matrons who, in a newly industrialized society, saw their duty as helping less fortunate working-class women. With few exceptions, these lofty motivations rarely led to organizational coalitions between working-class women and their more affluent sisters.

Reacting to stereotypes of one another, both groups feared assimilation, an example of the contamination control myth setting women against women. The social-class divisions of the larger society were too deeply embedded to be overcome by these organizations. Women faced social-class divisions similar to those which frustrate the efforts of present-day middle-class feminist groups to reach out to working-class women of different ethnic and racial backgrounds, and vice versa. The inability to forge coalitions across class lines failed to discourage these more affluent matrons from pursuing religiously-motivated civic activity, which inevitably moved them from quasi-political to overtly political action. Women's participation in the social purity, temperance, abolition, and suffrage movements represents a direct path from early charitable and benevolent societies to organizations designed to bring about fundamental social and political reform.

The Antislavery Movement

Women's participation in the antislavery movement exemplifies how a moral orientation led women to hold up the mirror of social conscience. They eventually recognized their own image in that same mirror; there women began to see both their own powerlessness and their potential collective strength. Women's experience in the abolition movement is particularly relevant, since its main outlines were repeated over a century later in the civil rights movement of the 1960s.

Initially, the abolition movement provoked women's concern with the moral and religious injustices of slavery. When women sought to articulate their religiously based objections to slavery, they encountered important male abolitionists who refused their request to speak out publicly. To their dismay, Angelina Grimke and other female abolitionists found that their own efforts to speak from the pulpit were denied, even by the most radical male abolitionists. Female abolitionists began to understand this male resistance as a symbolic effort to thwart women's power, literally to deny them their political voice. (Echoes of Sparta and Athens, where boys, but not girls, were trained as public orators!) The more radical female abolitionists responded by uniting to press for their own equality.

WOMEN'S ALTRUISM AND THE LARGER SOCIAL CAUSE

The control myth that describes women as selfless has repeatedly deflected women from working to promote their own cause, regardless of its justness. Repeatedly, this ingrained selflessness and the twin guilt that accompanied expressions of self-interest have been mobilized to keep women from protesting their lack of power, status, and societal resources. Historically and cross-culturally, whenever women's awakened awareness of their own needs for a greater share of society's resources on which power is based emerged, women were chastened to relinquish self-interest in the name of the greater social good. From one historical time and place to another, "social good" traveled under different names: abolition, civil rights, nationalism, socialism, and Zionism. The sacrifice of women's issues for the "greater cause" has been surprisingly consistent. Eighteenth-century Czech women were admonished that the "women's question" should not be pushed, lest it jeopardize the greater social cause of nationalism. In the American abolition movement, women urging their own rights were advised that women's emancipation would obstruct the antislavery movement.

In the early twentieth century, European Jewish women pioneers, the *halutsot,* emigrated to Palestine to seek a Zionist homeland where socialism promised to eliminate class and gender power differences. Buoyed by dreams of tilling the soil as equals with their socialist brethren, they were disillusioned to learn that the "women's issue" would be addressed only within the larger issue of socialism—not separately. Israeli poet Rachel Blaustein, who took the dream of gender equality seriously, expresses this disappointment in her famous poem "Perhaps":

> And perhaps it was only a dream after all?
> And perhaps I never really went forth with the dawn
> To toil with the sweat of my brow?[6]

In the pre-*kibbutz* years at Degania and Kinnereth, women "comrades" were disheartened to discover that only male workers earned monthly wages from the Palestine Office of the Zionist movement, which had not included women in the contracts they wrote with the pioneers. Psychologist and journalist Lesley Hazleton reports that "when they insisted on being included, the women were told pointblank that they were working for the men and not for the Palestine Office."[7]

In Russia, women in the Bolshevik revolution were given the familiar pledge: women's equality would be addressed as soon as the revolution created a new social order. And in the tumultuous 1960s, American women, who saw their long-denied self-awareness first sparked and then denied within the "larger" of the civil rights movement, experienced a similar fate. Repeatedly, women's efforts in major causes on behalf of others opened the window to a view of their own inequality and powerlessness. And repeatedly, promises that the gender power relationship would be addressed remained unkept.

Paradoxically, the occasions on which men did join women in their efforts to promote women's equality were specifically when such moves offered additional benefits for men. For example, the Prohibitionists encouraged American women's suffrage primarily in the belief that women's votes would be cast against drink. Nor was that the case only in the United States. In Finland and Norway, too, women's suffrage was promoted primarily to advance nationalism during foreign domination.[8] Unions have taken a similar tack. Only when male unionists' interests would be served did unions press for improvement in the working conditions of women. Nor, indeed, are such coalitions to be dismissed lightly; coalitions built on diverse interests are precisely what Charles Dudley Warner meant in his oft-quoted observation that "politics makes strange bedfellows."[9] Women, frequently accused of an ideological purism that prevented their benefiting from such political strategies, have become increasingly sensitive to the need for coalition building, particularly since the 1970s.

THE BACKLASH AGAINST FEMALE POLITICAL AND PROFESSIONAL SUCCESS

If women's moral and religious orientation first led them to political participation, it would be inaccurate to interpret their efforts as merely naive attempts to create an ideal kingdom of heaven on earth. Their activities in various social and political movements can be equally well read as actions designed to influence, if not change and control, men's behavior, particularly their sexual behavior. Women's activity within the antislavery movement was fueled in part by their belief that the white male masters frequently fathered children by their female slaves. The prohibition movement received strong support from the Women's Christian Temperance Union, which sought to eliminate drinking, particularly in saloons, where family money and time were squandered on alcohol, gambling, and prostitution. By limiting men's sexual behavior to the marital bed, women could ensure that their husbands would continue to provide economic support. Economic support was rarely recognized as a double-turning key that locks both women and men into the dependency trap.

These initially successful political actions on the part of women were not without a price, the price of political setback and sometimes backlash. Many attempts to control male behavior and reset the power balance met with unexpected initial success when the male establishment failed to take seriously female political activity. Once the weight of women's political success became apparent, their efforts frequently were squelched, their gains reduced or eliminated. The 1980s rollback of political, legal, and economic advances feminists won in the 1970s is only the most recent example of an old pattern.

A case in point: In 1982, a decade after women in the Maryland General Assembly formed the first women's legislative caucus in the United States, women legislators were taken aback by new opposition to seemingly elementary legislation. Washington *Post* staff writer Alison Muscatine filed the following report on March 29, 1982:

> The intensity of male camaraderie, which surfaced rarely during the heyday of feminism in the 1970s, has seldom been more apparent than it was two weeks ago. Then the House of Delegates defeated a bill requiring the state to give the details of state employees' pension plans to their spouses—half of whom are women. . . ! 'We have not heard that kind of debate in years,' said an angry Del. Bert Booth (D-Baltimore County), chair of the women's legislative caucus and a member of the legislature since 1975. . . . Although women legislators, aided by sympathetic male colleagues, managed to pass the pension bill a few days later on a vote of reconsideration, the episode left many wondering whether a decade of accomplishments was suddenly about to vanish . . . after their hard-fought successes on more controversial legislation in past years . . . women now find extraordinary reticence in the legislature on issues that seem simple by comparison.[10]

That women's success promotes a strong backlash is a political fact of life for which new strategies are required.

HOMOSOCIAL WORLDS

In one sense, women's occasional political success in controlling male behavior may be viewed as an effort to penetrate the male homosocial world, with its control over the major institutional resources of the society. By *homosocial* we mean "the seeking, enjoyment and/or preference for the company of the same sex,"[11] as we have indicated earlier. Homosociality does not necessarily involve explicit sexual interaction between members of the same gender group, nor is homosociality limited to males. Women too live in their own largely homosocial world. The critical, but surely not the only, difference between the homosocial worlds of men and women is the control over institutional versus domestic or personal resources and the relative power each connotes.

The homosocial network is a major tributary whose waters carry important resources to favored members of the in-group. In the male homosocial world, political, economic, legal, and professional support glide along homosocial currents. Until quite recently, the only resources ordinarily distributed in the female homosocial world were those related to personal nurturance and emotions—tender loving care, understanding, empathy, and reassurance. Even now, only a relatively minute fraction of the female population has significant economic, legal, political, or professional resources to bestow on or withhold from others. The ability to distribute resources that count marks one as a wielder of power.

Because men control institutional and thus massive societal power, they are more highly valued. Their contribution of resources is central to their valuation in the eyes of those less able to provide such help. The stratification system, which ranks individuals and groups in terms of their value to society, systematically places males in more desirable roles than females.

Because men control resources that they can then contribute to the general society, they are rewarded by being placed in positions in which they control even more resources. Women, without a strong purchase on societal resources, rarely penetrate the male inner circle, within which they might receive, and then possibly control and redistribute, societal goods. As a result, women are valued derivatively, through their association with powerful men. Supportive evidence comes from the Gallup Poll's annual survey of America's "most admired women," which consistently lists more wives of powerful, important men than women who have achieved prominence by their own accomplishments. Perhaps this simply reminds us that the greatest achievement for a woman is to marry a prominent man. The latest available poll (December, 1981) ranked Nancy Reagan, wife of the president, in first place, above both British Prime Minister Margaret Thatcher and U.S. Supreme Court Justice Sandra Day O'Connor.[12]

The dominance order within the male homosocial world is based on ability to control resources and, through the use and withdrawal of resources as rewards and penalties, to impose one's will on others. Psychologists long ago documented the processes whereby individuals within contexts as diverse as families and concentration camps identify with resource controllers. This process of identifying with those able to bestow rewards and inflict punishment is equally apparent in relations between women and men. Feminist theorists undoubtedly would argue that women with "raised consciousness" no longer identify with such power figures, but rather recognize their power and resent their control over the powerless. Nonetheless, the dominance order, reflected in the stratification system, continues to be based on access to and control over major resources. And despite recent female advances, the majority of women continue to have more limited access to the institutional levers of power than their male counterparts.

As long as any individual or group manages the distribution of resources, they have power, whether or not they use it. As Max Weber wrote:

> Patriarchal power . . . is rooted in the provisioning of recurrent and normal needs of workday life. Patriarchal authority thus has its original locus . . . in those branches of the economy that can be satisfied by means of normal routine. The patriarch is the 'natural leader' of the daily routine . . . the bureaucratic structure is only the counter-image of partiarchalism . . . fashioned to meet calculable and recurrent needs by means of normal routine."[13]

The image of patriarchal power, generated in the sex-gender system and applied to the economy, emphasizes the subtle blueprint influence of the gender-power balance. This control of resources is the source of an individual's or group's power to impose its will on others. During times of stability, the stratification system acts as a social grid, keeping everyone in appropriate social, economic, and political niches. During such periods, it is difficult for those who lack resources and power to impose their will on others.

This is not to deny the importance of influence, persuasion, and subtler forms of manipulation which the powerless use to ease the bonds of dominance. Slaves as well as wives and children learn to "read" the master's moods and adjust their behavior to exert subtle influence and offset domination. Earlier, we described macromanipulation, the influence men wield through government policy. Women's interpersonal influence on male power—whether their husbands' or Congress'—we described as "micromanipulation," the alternative women have been socialized to use to offset the controlling effects of male power. In times of stability, when the stratification system keeps a tight lock on roles and their associated resources, women and other power groups are forced to fall back on micromanipulation. In times of crisis, however, the situation changes drastically.

CRISIS AND SOCIAL CHANGE

As we intimated earlier, crisis periods are renowned for the relative ease with which massive social changes occur. During a crisis, highly differentiated or segregated roles, including gender roles, undergo rapid shifts that would be unimaginable over long decades of stability. The wartime redistribution of occupational roles described in Chapter 11 is a clear example. Much of this "role de-differentiation" occurs because crisis impairs the stratification system.[14] During stable periods, the stratification system demands specific characteristics and credentials—gender, race, education, family lineage, and wealth—for entry into certain roles. In times of social equilibrium, the society's goals are diffuse, long-range, and difficult to rank. As a result, means become more important than ends or goal attainment, and the focus is on who is performing or allowed to perform a task, rather than on which task and how well the task is being executed. As a result, in stable periods the stratification system is robust; individuals and groups are rigidly controlled with regard to the roles they may occupy and the resources they may govern.

Crisis, by contrast, creates a situation that participants recognize as a serious threat to the status quo, if not to survival itself. Ordinary coping mechanisms and resources are perceived as inadequate. Crisis demands maximum rational use, even reallocation, of resources, including resources often held in reserve or deliberately repressed. Perceived as resources, social roles, including gender, generational, occupational, and political roles, often prove critical in these periods.

Consequently, during crisis, the stratification system weakens. The boundaries between previously differentiated roles become increasingly permeable. Goals are easily identified, tied as they commonly are to survival. Sociologically speaking, the criteria for participation in various roles change, with decreased emphasis on the formal characteristics of individuals or groups and increased recognition of their ability to achieve crisis-related goals.

In crisis periods, then, roles are no longer clearly limited sets of expectations, tasks, attitudes, rights, and responsibilities, separated from one another by distinct norms for entry. Therefore, it is not particularly surprising to discover that crisis is a time when gender roles, along with other types of social roles, are most likely to undergo change. In every major war, roles change. The shortage of nurses during the Crimean War, for example, led to the differentiation of the previously all-male nursing role to include females. More recent evidence comes from the Great Depression of the 1930s and both World Wars, which brought major changes in the allocation of occupational roles. In the postcrisis period, a new baseline is evident, not necessarily set at the peak of crisis-induced role change, but essentially above the precrisis level. The thrust toward the precrisis role pattern is a common post-crisis event.

Large-scale shifts in the wartime labor force may be explained by some as the response to a human resource shortage. Unlike overall labor force shifts, the phenomenon of de-differentiation of legislative roles during war cannot be explained simply in terms of a shortage of male candidates. To understand the underlying process, it is instructive to examine the case of women's wartime entry into national legislative roles, involving as they did too few numbers to be explained by the supply factor alone. During World War II, women's presence increased significantly in this most carefully guarded sanctum of male political power, not only in those countries most centrally involved, but even among neutral nations.

The majority of national legislatures during World War II had memberships that hovered around 700, and women's prewar share of that membership was stable worldwide at approximately 1 percent. During the war, in the United States and other involved nations, women's representation virtually tripled, although their absolute numbers were still quite small. In most legislatures, women gained no more than an additional 14 seats during World War II, a figure important because of its limited size. More specifically, with such a small increase in absolute numbers, we cannot lay the blame on the shortage of men. This is particularly so since legislators' modal age of 41 made it unlikely their replacements would come from the servicemen's cohort, whose age ranged from the late teens to mid-twenties.

Clearly, processes other than shortage are at work in crisis periods, as reflected both in the massive labor force statistics reported earlier, as well as in the numerically more limited situation of national legislatures. The stratification system, the permeable boundaries of roles, the shift from formal credentials to crisis-solving abilities, and the reallocation of resources, including social roles, are all crisis-engendered processes that promote the de-differentiation of gender roles within the family, the labor force, and the political system.

Although crisis provokes periods of sharp and swift social change, less dramatic social change occurs between crises peaks as well. In the wake of crisis, the residual changes in norms, values, and roles offer a new baseline from which social change continues to move. In subsequent periods of stability, the enduring recollection of crisis-induced social change creates the understanding that social structure is not immutable. Growth and change, quietly spurred by this recognition, continue in the intercrisis period.

WOMEN IN PUBLIC SERVICE

After their eye-opening participation in the 1960s American civil rights movement, increasing numbers of women engaged in more comprehensive political action. The National Organization for Women (NOW), founded in 1966, grew dramatically in the 1970s. Conceived as a national action organization, NOW was originally little more than an East Coast superstructure with few skilled organizers and a spate of activists among its members, according to political scientist Jo Freeman.[15] A short decade later, NOW's ranks were filled with politically knowledgeable women and men, taking up volatile political causes, including abortion and the Equal Rights Amendment. The Women's Equity Action League (WEAL), a more conservative outgrowth of NOW, devoted itself to legal and economic problems, particularly employment and educational issues. Since the early 1980s, more politically concerned women have joined these and other organizations, which they perceive as the only bulwark against the vociferous conservative assaults on women's political equality. NOW, for example, gained 117,000 new members within two months of the inauguration of the Reagan Administration.

The National Women's Political Caucus, established in 1971, explicitly aimed to increase the number of American women elected and appointed to political office. Since its founding, NWPC has developed a genuinely national structure, with caucuses in almost all 50 states. The success of such organizations, as well as politically active women outside these groups, can be read in the slowly growing numbers of women holding all levels of public office. (The increasingly familiar backlash against women's political success, nonetheless, could be seen in the small proportion of female candidates elected in the interim election of 1982.) Another index of the success of women's political organizations is the willingness of presidential candidates to address their conventions.

The Center for the American Woman and Politics at Rutgers University reports that women are moving into political positions in increasingly greater numbers. By 1981, women held 11.8 percent of appointed positions in governors' cabinets (112 women out of a total of 949 appointed state cabinet officials). Only Arizona, South Carolina, Texas, and Utah had no women appointed to state cabinet positions. Occupational segregation, however, still exists in the functional areas of appointment. Twenty percent of women in state cabinet positions serve in health and human services areas, compared to 10 percent in labor and industrial relations, 8 percent in finance, budget, and fiscal management, and 4 percent in commerce. But women have made impressive gains in balancing the political power structure. In fact, between 1975 and 1980, the percentage of women holding elective office nationwide more than doubled, with an additional 10,370 women elected to public office. Thus, from a 1975 baseline of 5,765 women officeholders representing 4 percent of all elected offices, women officeholders increased to 16,136, or 12 percent by 1980. At the state level, by 1981, 908 women had been elected to legislative positions; they comprised 12.1 percent of all state legislators in the country. The Center for the American Woman and Politics indicates that women hold 64 (8.3 percent) of the 808 state legislative leadership positions, up from 7.2 percent in 1979. By 1980, two women had been elected governor, 55 lieutenant governor, and 11 secretary of state.[16]

On the less optimistic side, as late as 1981 there were no women in leadership positions in either the House or the Senate in 24 states, and only two states—Connecticut and Rhode Island—had more than one female in leadership posts in each house of the state legislature. Viewed differently, women still hold fewer leadership positions in state legislatures than their male counterparts do (7.4 percent vs. 11.3 percent in 1981). The picture at the national level is equally instructive. Between 1975 and 1981, the number of women in the U.S. House of Representatives seesawed between 17 and 20 (out of 535 total members). In 1981, 20 women (4 percent) served in the U.S. House of Representatives, and 2 women (2 percent) were in the U.S. Senate.

In many state legislatures, women have worked together in bipartisan fashion via congresswomen's caucuses to push for women's equality and political clout. There was considerable optimism in the 1970s, and many congressional women hoped they could leave the ghetto of women's caucuses and join the mainstream. More recently, however, unexpected opposition to supposedly innocuous legislation targeted for women has prompted new concern for the strength of the caucuses. At the national level, the Congresswomen's Caucus, with 14 female members and 114 males, recently changed its name to the Caucus for Women's Issues to reflect the participation and resources brought by the male members. A recent news report of this change read: "The caucus, which is supported by contributions from the lawmakers' office budgets, will now have more resources to devote to legislation of particular concern to women, say members of the caucus."[17]

Some believe this slowly growing political strength that women are demonstrating is simply the tip of the iceberg. Recent research suggests that the potential pool of interested and qualified female candidates is much greater than our control myths would have us believe.[18] Even so, prejudice against women's leadership still exists, as exemplified in a West German official's description of Prime Minister Margaret Thatcher's handling of the Falklands crisis as "ridiculous overreaction, and typical of a woman."[19] The routes open to women seeking political careers are demonstrably more difficult than those followed by men and thus impede women's ability to compete with men for political roles.

Sociologist Cynthia Epstein underscores myths related to female candidates' political socialization and their roles as wives and mothers.[20] She notes that, contrary to earlier research reporting that boys are more likely than girls to be socialized to take greater interest in political events, more recent work by Orum and his colleagues reports no significant gender differences between the political orientation and attitudes of school children.[21] Socialization is seen as less important than women's domestic roles, which confine them to home. Men's occupational roles, by contrast, tend to draw them into politics. Women's more limited participation in politics, suggested much earlier by political scientist Seymour Martin Lipset, rests on the belief that women's home responsibilities are too demanding to permit the time commitment political activity requires.[22] Epstein argues instead that it is not so much a question of expendable time, but the norms controlling how women *should* spend their time that is at the heart of women's politically weaker presence. She bolsters this argument with two facts: first, many women officeholders are single, widowed, or have adult children; and second, among the few women in public office who do have young children, their activity level in outside organizations is as great or greater than those without young children. Nonetheless, Epstein's analysis reveals that by 1974 the political tide apparently turned for women, with an upsurge in the number of women elected to political office. This change undoubtedly mirrored a shift in public attitudes toward women in political life.

Public Opinion Changes

Although old beliefs about women's and men's roles change slowly, they do change. Not, however, without ambivalence. So it is with attitudes toward men's and women's political participation. The 1937 Gallup Opinion Index revealed that only 31 percent of those polled would vote for a qualified woman for president of the United States. Responding to the same question in 1980, a resounding 77 percent indicated they would[23]. Even in the short period between 1972 and 1978, pollsters detected changes in attitudes toward women's political participation. For example, 51 percent of those polled in 1972 still agreed that "women should take care of running their homes and leave running the country up to men"; by 1978, only 31 percent gave that response. In 1972, 62 percent felt that "most men are better suited emotionally for politics than are most women"; again, by 1978 only 42 percent agreed with this position. By 1978, 70 percent of those interviewed in a Harris Survey agreed with the resolution passed by the National Women's Conference in Houston that more women be elected to public office. And even by 1976, 71 percent of those answering a Gallup Opinion Index replied that they thought the country would be governed better or no differently if more women held political office.[24] Despite this hearty endorsement, as late as 1980, 58 percent of the respondents in a Virginia Slims poll felt it was rather unlikely that a woman would be elected president of the United States by the year 2000; 68 percent, however, felt it was fairly or very likely that a woman would be elected vice-president. This large discrepancy between acceptance and expectations for women at the highest political level suggests an unresolved ambivalence toward female leadership and power.

Cross-cultural studies of the nine member countries of the European Community—Belgium, Denmark, France, West Germany, Ireland, Italy, Luxembourg, the Netherlands, and the United Kingdom—reveal that perceptions of politics as a masculine field have begun to change around the world. Well-educated and younger people, particularly younger women, are less likely to stereotype politics as a masculine preserve. On this point, gender differences were less than the differences between age groups, according to political scientist Donna S. Sanzone.[25] Sanzone reports a 1975 poll conducted by the Commission of the European Communities in which only 35 percent of the respondents believed that politics "should be left to men." Preference for male representatives in the national assembly was reported by 42 percent of the males and 33 percent of the females polled. Citizens of countries in which women have had the vote and participated in politics the longest were more likely to express positive attitudes toward women's political activity.

Voting Patterns

Just as attitude changes are evident among younger people, so too are variations in voting patterns, at least in the United States. Approximately half a century after American women won the vote in 1919, younger women for the first time went to the polls in slightly larger numbers than their male counterparts. Beginning in 1972, American women between 18 and 44 years old outvoted males of the same age, the difference increasing with each national election. In 1972, 58.7 percent of eligible female voters aged 18 to 44 voted in the national election, compared to 57.9 percent of same-aged eligible male voters. And by 1980, although a smaller proportion of eligible male and female voters participated in the national elections than in 1972, female voters outnumbered males by a clear and growing margin (54.2 versus 51.3 percent). This represents a marked departure from earlier voting patterns of American women, one concerned politicians have labeled the *gender gap*. Previously, political savants criticized women's weak voting record in light of their century-long struggle to obtain the vote. Many complained that those women who did vote simply followed their husband's choice, although there is little systematic evidence for this claim.

Age, however, is an important factor in female voting patterns. Women over age 45 remain less likely than their male age-mates to vote, although gender differences in this age group have diminished consistently. Since their 7 percent voting advantage over women in 1964, men aged 45 and over have gradually lost this edge. By 1980, only a 4 percent difference remained between these men and women (70 percent vs. 66 percent).[26] Although the privacy of the voting booth makes it difficult to detect whether a wife has voted with or against her husband's political choice, it is abundantly clear how women and men as groups have voted over the years. Women often differed from men on issues of peace, nuclear power, and the environment, but voted like men for every American president from Dwight D. Eisenhower to Jimmy Carter. During the 1970s, according to the Gallup poll, men and women indicated similar party affiliation.

An important change occurred in the 1980 presidential election, where more men than women voted for Ronald Reagan (55 percent versus 47 percent). In 20 polls measuring approval of the president's job performance taken within President Reagan's first year in office, the median gender gap was 9 percent, almost twice that of any president since Gallup began this polling procedure during the Eisenhower administration.[27] The Reagan administration's opposition to the ERA, abortion, and other social programs for women, children, and the poor is seen as motivating women's political disaffection. Many observers interpret women's greater dissatisfaction with foreign policy and economic decisions to mean that they have begun to examine and evaluate politics and politicians in terms of their own self-interest—a departure indeed from control myths that maintain women would always put their own needs last. Still other political savants see a widespread effort to transform cultural values to reflect women's more "moral" concern with peace and preservation of life. American women's growing disenchantment with their political representatives' decisions appears to be a sign of women's declining belief in another control myth—that men have women's best interests at heart.

The history of the women's movement, beginning with the Seneca Falls Convention of 1848 and rekindled in the 1960s by Betty Friedan's *The Feminine Mystique*, is sufficiently well known not to bear repeating here. Subsequent political advances made by women, followed by recent setbacks, represent the latest stage in the power struggle between the sexes. Political power, backed by military might, is society's quintessential power, which men have always taken as their right. Yet now women are demanding their due. Although women have made serious inroads, setbacks notwithstanding, into the political life of the nation, the military—the physical might buttressing political power—has become the focus of a renewed power struggle.

The Case of Women in the Military

The military lies at the core of institutional power. In Sparta and Athens, from a tender age, young boys were honed for military service; their female age-mates were shaped, instead, for future roles as mothers of military leaders. Although women in some ancient societies assumed military leadership roles, modern history knows few female generals or admirals. Those very few who have succeeded in rising through the military ranks have remained quite invisible to the general public.

A brief look at the current debate about women in American military service might serve as a case study of the virtually exclusive male control over military resources. Two volatile issues are central: (1) danger to women in combat, and (2) the "combat readiness" of units. The background of this concern is instructive. From a minimal 1 percent in 1971, women's presence in the all-volunteer American military had "soared" to 8 percent by 1981, with a recruiting goal of 12 percent by 1985 (250,000 women). In 1981 the Army, with moral support from the other services, called for a pause in women's recruitment in order to reassess the whole impact of women in the military and subsequently to reevaluate its policy on female recruitment.[28] Even before the reassessment began, the assistant secretary of defense for manpower predicted that the proportion of women in all services would probably be "leveled out" at 10 to 12 percent, possibly lower. Field commanders have argued that women in the army present numerous problems, some significant, others less so: female uniforms, childcare, pregnancy, married military couples, sexual harassment, single parenthood, a high attrition rate, female urinary tract infections under difficult field conditions, and "insufficient" upper-body strength.

Despite the formal exclusion of women from the combat zone, women are assigned to military occupational specialties and units that place them there, nonetheless. For example, women serve in units assigned to combat support duties, such as the medical corps, equipment maintenance units, communications, electronic warfare, and some artillery units. Units with specifically designated combat functions, including infantry and tanks, however, are technically off-limits to women. Pragmatically, this means that nurses and medical officers work within the combat zone, as do women communications officers who monitor the enemy's foreign language radio communiques. *U.S. News and World Report,* in a featured story on women in the armed forces, reported that "on one division exercise, a commander found that 30 percent of his female troops were in the forward battle area, even though present regulations prohibit combat duty for them. On another, a commander discovered that the division reserve unit he was about to send forward consisted almost entirely of female soldiers."[29] The article explained that "what has sparked the administration's decision to re-examine the female defense role are worries that the armed forces may be becoming too dependent on women in combat situations."[30] Could we tolerate this reallocation of dependency?

A pregnancy rate of 10 percent (approximately 6,900 of the Army's 69,600 female troops) is cited as another problem. The military does not perceive male disability as comparably alarming, despite the fact that pregnancy rarely requires female recruits or officers to leave their assignments for more than a few weeks. An analysis of the effect of pregnancy on one division by Army policy specialist Cecile Landrum examined military occupational specialties with high and low female density rates. Landrum found the only specialty where the pregnancy rate had a significant effect was among the piccolo players in the Army band.[31] This does not deny the potential problem in specialties where high pregnancy rates could conceivably impair a unit's combat readiness.

Other arguments have been raised about women in combat. For instance, the fact that females average 86 to 98 percent of "male bulk and volume, and even when size is held constant, women are only 80 percent as strong as men," is an alleged major deterrent to women's inclusion in combat units.[32] Differences in male and female aggression levels provide another related concern about the possible role for women in combat. Proponents of women in combat do not dispute the average differences in size, bulk, and strength between men and women; however, they argue, first, that not all women are smaller or weaker than the average man, and second, that even physical differences may be offset by the "superior mental aptitude and educational background of average female recruits."[33]

More subtle, and perhaps more pernicious, concerns about women's contamination of the military have also surfaced. In 1981, Dr. David Marlow, Chief of the Department of Military Psychiatry at the Walter Reed Army Institute of Research, still relied on World War II studies relating performance of military units to soldiers' perception of the unit to argue against female soldiers. According to Marlowe: "Many male soldiers who currently train in sex-integrated units suffer a loss in self-esteem, feeling that they have been subjected to less intensive training than soldiers in exclusively male units, even when objective examinations show otherwise. If women could do all the things they could do, how challenging could those things be? This self-doubt could take its toll in combat effectiveness."[34] Others caution that a potential enemy's perception of our military might is weakened by the women's presence (more evidence of cross-cultural views of women as weak and contaminating). Yet these same observers admit that many of the arguments currently cited to justify excluding women from combat roles have been used in the past to "prove" that they should not be doctors, voters, property-owners—or, indeed, independent, strong, autonomous persons. Such unpalatable conclusions make the arguments that generate them suspicious.[35]

The charge that chivalry and sexuality would undermine United States military strength echoes the dangerous female seductive qualities expressed in control myths. Many who protest women's combat zone presence argue that chivalrous male soldiers would endanger themselves and others by protecting their female comrades, rather than resolutely battling the enemy. Little mention is made of the historically acknowledged comradeship and protection male soldiers offer their wounded male comrades-in-arms. This proud sign of male bonding and homosociality most recently was described in Falkland Island combat communiques reporting soldiers jumping into the South Atlantic to rescue their floundering comrades.

Sexuality presents still another concern, translated into complaints about pregnant military personnel and the increasing numbers of married military couples, sexual harassment, and single parenthood (ironically, five-sixths of the single parents in the U.S. Army are fathers). Perhaps General William Westmoreland, Commander of the U.S. Army during the Vietnam war, articulated the implicit fears of many who see women's entry into the combat zone as the first sign of military deterioration. In a recent newspaper interview, General Westmoreland was quoted as saying that if a man and woman occupied the same foxhole, "They're going to be making love, not war," and that "Any man of gumption does not want women to fight his wars."[36]

Given these expressed concerns, no doubt communicated to military women, it is hardly surprising that the female attrition rate is higher than men's. According to one Army study, among 1980 recruits, 48.5 percent of the females do not intend to reenlist for a second tour of duty, compared to 34.1 percent of the males. This is true even among the "cream of the crop," women cadets at the U.S. Air Force Academy. Officials report the 1980 pioneer class of female cadets' attrition rate was 38.2 percent. Within one year, their attrition rate had jumped to 58.3 percent, compared to 39.8 percent for male cadets. Military officials attribute the high female dropout rate to changing career goals, dissatisfaction with military life, a desire to marry, and a loss of the "pioneer spirit" that strengthened the first women cadets. An alternative explanation might interpret these attrition rates as the outcome of an inhospitable male environment based on a rigid social structure that echoes old control myths.

New School of Social Research philosopher Sara Ruddick suggests that the "right to fight and command fighters, when qualified to do so, is a right conferred upon citizens and cannot be denied them because of their membership in a class or group."[37] Nonetheless, a recent Supreme Court decision upheld a lower court's exclusion of women from combat duty. Even without the Supreme Court decision, an inhospitable, if not hostile, climate within the military can influence women to curtail their efforts to assume their rights as citizens, including expectations to enter leadership roles in the military. Durkheim's concern with subtle external forces that drive groups away from valued and important occupations is still relevant a century later.

Despite these serious difficulties, 95 percent of all Army specialties are open to women, although a new Army report recommends closing an additional 26 job categories. Defense analysts predict that the all-volunteer force cannot survive unless women continue to play an increasing role. In the short run, the scarcity of civilian jobs is making military recruiters' efforts to fill quotas solely with men a veritable "piece of cake." Nevertheless, several longer-term issues compound the problem: first, a predicted scarcity of military-age males, and second, women's growing recognition of attractive military benefits—including educational, health, and employment benefits (for example, veteran's status allows any government employee a 10-point "preference" edge in recruitment and retention procedures). With announced government plans for expanding the military by as many as 200,000 new troops in the next few years and an expected drop in the pool of eligible males to 1.6 million by 1992, the gender role power struggle in the U.S. military promises to continue.

SUMMARY

For centuries, the political world was the scene of exclusive male leadership and control. Only circuitously, through religious and then social organizations, did women enter the American political arena. Restricted by control myths describing women as selfless and nurturant, but prompted by others depicting them as more moral than men, women initially entered the political realm seeking justice for others. Their political efforts on behalf of others sparked women's recognition of their own need for equality.

National crises, particularly World Wars I and II, set in motion sociological processes, such as a weakening stratification system and goal-linked criteria for role occupancy, that generated new political possibilities for women and other minorities. Other national crises focused on issues of equality and morality, such as the civil rights movement and Vietnam, created a climate of opinion that fostered women's quest for their own political voice. The resurgent women's movement of the late 1960s spawned national organizations to promote economic and political equality. These organizations fostered the cause of women political candidates as well.

Gradually, women have increased their legislative numbers at the state and national levels, although the threshold to the U.S. Senate seems to be a serious stumbling block for most female candidates. Perhaps the most significant political sign of the times is the growing gender gap—that is, women's stronger voting activity. Concerned politicians are beginning to woo female votes since the gender gap, signaling women's political muscle, has caught media attention. Nonetheless, the military services, the physical representation of political might, remain under unequivocal male control.

NOTES

1. Max Weber, *The Theory of Social and Economic Organization* (Glencoe, Ill.: The Free Press, 1947), p. 152.

2. Peter M. Blau, *Exchange and Power in Social Life* (New York: John Wiley & Sons, 1964), pp. 117–18.

3. Joan Acker, "Women and Social Stratification: A Case of Intellectual Sexism," *American Journal of Sociology,* 78, no. 4 (1973), pp. 936–43; Gunnar Myrdal, *An American Dilemma* (New York: Harper, 1944).

4. William H. Chafe, *Women and Equality: Changing Patterns in American Culture* (New York: Oxford University Press, 1977).

5. Donald G. Mathews, *Religion in the Old South* (Chicago: University of Chicago Press, 1977).

6. Rachel Blaustein, "Perhaps," in Sholom J. Kahn, "The Poetry of Rachel," *Ariel,* 38 (1975); trans. S. J. Kahn.

7. Lesley Hazleton, *Israeli Women: The Reality Behind the Myths* (New York: Simon and Schuster, Inc./ Touchstone Books, 1977).

8. Carl N. Degler, *At Odds: Women and the Family in America from the Revolution to the Present* (New York: Oxford University Press, 1980).

9. Charles Dudley Warner, *My Summer in a Garden* (1870); quoted in John Bartlett, *Familiar Quotations,* 14th ed. (Boston, Mass.: Little, Brown, 1968).

10. *The Washington Post,* March 29, 1982, pp. B1, B2.

11. Jean Lipman-Blumen, "Toward a Homosocial Theory of Sex Roles: An Explanation of the Sex Segregation of Social Institutions," *Signs,* 1, no. 3, part 2 (Spring 1976), 15–31.

12. "Annual Survey of America's Most Admired Women," Gallup Poll, December, 1981.

13. Max Weber, *Wirtschaft und Gesellschaft,* Part III, p. 753, trans. H. H. Gerth and C. Wright Mills, in *From Max Weber: Essays in Sociology* (New York: Oxford University Press, 1946).

14. Jean Lipman-Blumen, "Role De-differentiation as a System Response to Crisis: Occupational and Political Roles of Women," *Sociological Inquiry*, 43, no. 2 (1973), 105–29.

15. Jo Freeman, *The Politics of Women's Liberation* (New York: David McKay, 1975).

16. Center for the American Woman and Politics, "Fact Sheet" (New Brunswick, N.J.: Rutgers University, 1981).

17. *The New York Times,* December 14, 1981, section IV, p. 10.

18. Cynthia Fuchs Epstein, "Women and Power: The Roles of Women in Politics in the United States," in *Access to Power: Cross-National Studies of Women and Elites,* eds. Cynthia Fuchs Epstein and Rose Laub Coser (London: George Allen and Unwin, 1981), pp. 124–46.

19. *Time* Magazine, June 21, 1982, p. 31.

20. Epstein, "Women and Power."

21. Anthony M. Orum and others, "Sex Socialization and Politics," in Marianne Githens and Jewel L. Prestage, eds. *A Portrait of Marginality: The Political Behavior of the American Woman* (New York: David McKay, 1977), pp. 17–37.

22. Seymour Martin Lipset, *Political Man* (New York: Doubleday; London: Heinemann, 1960).

23. Deborah Durfee Barron and Daniel Yankelovich, "Today's American Woman: How the Public Sees Her" (Manuscript prepared for the President's Advisory Committee on Women, December 1980), p. 123.

24. Ibid., p. 122.

25. Donna S. Sanzone, "Women in Politics: A Study of Political Leadership in the United Kingdom, France, and the Federal Republic of Germany," in *Access to Power: Cross-National Studies of Women and Elites,* eds. Cynthia Fuchs Epstein and Rose Laub Coser (London: George Allen & Unwin, 1981), pp. 37–52.

26. U.S. Department of Commerce, "Voting and Registration in the Election of 1980," *Current Population Reports,* Series P-20, no. 370 (Washington, D.C.: Government Printing Office, 1980), p. 5.

27. "Women Shifting Sharply away from Reagan Republican Party," *Washington Post,* March 29, 1982, p. A3.

28. Office of the Deputy Chief of Staff for Personnel, Department of the Army, "Women in the Army Policy Review," Washington, D.C., November 12, 1982.

29. *U.S. News and World Report,* July 20, 1981, p. 44.

30. Ibid., p. 44.

31. Cecile Landrum, "Pregnancy Data on the 25th Infantry Division by Military Occupational Specialty" (unpublished study, September 1981).

32. *QQ: Report from the Center for Philosophy and Public Policy* (College Park: The University of Maryland, Center for Philosophy and Public Policy, Summer 1981), p. 3.

33. Ibid.

34. Ibid.

35. Ibid., p. 4.

36. Ibid.

37. Ibid., pp. 3–4.

CHAPTER 13
WHAT LIES
AHEAD?

STILL AT THE CENTER OF THE STORM

Will the powerless revolt? Will the gender power balance change dramatically? The answers to these and many other questions about the future of gender roles still elude us. That sex and gender roles remain at the eye of the darkening social storm is obvious to the most casual observer. For as we have seen, when a society solves the basic biological and technological issues threatening its survival, social problems emerge as the key to future development. Gender roles, the blueprint for all other roles and relationships, predictably have surfaced as the next major social problem pressing to be solved. This blueprint signifies the potential power balance embedded in all human relationships. Gender roles are central to contemporary life. Their diffuseness colors all other roles they touch; their influence flows into every cranny of social reality.

Existential anxiety, generated by the awareness that we are not in total control of our destinies, prompts us to create for ourselves and others the illusion that we are indeed safe. We do this by structuring power relationships—as individuals, as families, as private organizations, as professional groups, as unions, as nations. Western gender roles, imbued with an aura of sacred immutability from Judeo-Christian imagery, serve as a Weberian "ideal type" of power relationships.[1] All other roles, with their power infrastructures, are judged according to the model of gender roles.

Currently, in the United States and elsewhere around the world, gender roles are caught in a crossfire. They are simultaneously under attack by women, who see themselves locked into subordination within the framework of traditional gender roles, and by men, who wish to preserve the power position institutionalized through the sex-gender system. Naturally, there are women and men in the "enemy" camp. In general, however, both gender groups look to their own resource reservoirs to maintain or change their power positions. The power reserves of women and men were previously drawn from different sources, replenished by ancient religious images and literary and media stereotypes of culturally acceptable masculine and feminine behavior. These images, in turn, generated control myths, which guided the socialization processes by which society prepares its members to assume adult roles and responsibilities.

Reminiscent of other polarities—dark and light, good and evil—through which earlier civilizations understood their world, gender roles too evolved as differentiated, but presumably complementary, roles. Built upon the framework of biological sexual differences, social definitions of masculinity and femininity exaggerated both the differentiation and the complementarity of gender roles. Only belatedly has the complementarity of gender roles been recognized as a painful disguise for a serious, but not inevitable, power imbalance between women and men, both as individuals and groups. This power struggle, kept in place by subtle and blatant, formal and informal negotiations, is centuries old. Although some observers still find academic satisfaction in debating the origins of gender role differences, changing life conditions make the more central question not "*from* where?" but "*to* where?" in the decades ahead. Once again, demography offers us a useful social telescope.

DEMOGRAPHIC TRENDS

In the United States as elsewhere, women have become the majority population group. Demographers predict their population advantage will continue into the next century. With the longevity gap between women and men probably on the increase, demographers predict women's population advantage is assured past the year 2000. What will a growing number of older women in a generally older population mean in terms of the gender power struggle? Other demographic trends offer some clues.

After the demographic turbulence of the 1960s and 1970s, when birth, marriage, and remarriage rates were plummeting and the divorce rate was escalating, the situation seems to be leveling off. In the last several years, both the overall marriage rate and the divorce rate have been fluctuating over a very narrow range. American demographers, who not too long ago despaired about the possible disappearance of marriage, have begun to breathe a sigh of relief. Still, alternative explanations and predictions abound. Either the divorce rate will continue to stabilize, possibly even decline, as age at first marriage and educational level (both predictors of divorce) increase; or divorce will increase as the birth rate goes down, since fewer children will lower the costs of divorce and child support; or divorce will increase as women enter the paid labor force, since their economic dependence on men will decrease and the tensions of two-career families will put greater pressure on marriage; or the marriage rate will increase and the divorce rate decrease as the neo-conservative orientation grows and the existential anxiety generated by geopolitical tensions encourages women and men to seek comfort and meaning in more intimate relationships. Take your choice.

The birth rate, fickle as love itself, spreads its own uncertain influence throughout society. The low birth rates of the 1960s should lead to less competition for jobs among youth in the 1980s; however, a troubled economy in which jobs and entire industries may be permanently altered or lost could offset this easing of job competition. For young minority males and females particularly, the forecast is even more difficult, since they tend to live in concentrated urban areas where unskilled job opportunities are more limited. Labor force analysts predict that competition for entry-level jobs, especially in technical, professional, administrative, management, and craft occupations, will wane. The shrinkage of the school-age population will reduce the demand for teachers, but the expanding older population will create increased need for health care and other services.

The occupational outlook for specific fields depends on actual growth in the number of jobs within a field, as well as on replacement needs for workers who leave the field through retirement, death, or other reasons. Through 1990, replacement needs are expected to be double the number of job openings created by employment growth, although this will vary from field to field. The highest replacement needs are anticipated among fields requiring the least training, since in those occupations it is easier to move from one job to another. Occupational roles that demand long and specialized training, such as engineers, physicians, and bank managers, tend to have lower turnover and thus lower replacement rates.

At the same time, competition for higher-level jobs probably will increase between now and 1990. A college education, previously a dependable avenue to a promising job, is less valuable now than a decade or two ago, and that trend is likely to continue. Although the employment of college graduates increased 76 percent between 1968 and 1978, so did their proportion among clerical, low-level sales, and blue-collar occupations. During this period, 25 percent of college graduates entered jobs previously held by less-educated workers. Nonetheless, college graduates were still more likely than their less-educated peers not only to be employed, but to have the highest-paying managerial and professional jobs. Of course, much depends on one's field of study, and college graduates trained in quantitative and scientific fields will continue to have a decided edge over those with degrees in the humanities and education.[2]

Educational analysts point out that the overall educational level of the American population has increased steadily, and much of this advance is attributed to women's—particularly older women's—growing participation in higher education. As noted earlier, more women than ever before are enrolled in college and university programs, but the major enrollment growth has come from women studying in community or two-year colleges. The educational segregation of women in traditional "feminine" fields, such as the humanities and education, is gradually changing; women have made serious inroads in medical, law, and business schools. In growing numbers, females are enrolled in quantitative and scientific programs, but they remain far below their potential enrollment levels in terms of their population size.

Women's increasing labor force participation has been heralded as the "subtle revolution," a phenomenon many interpret as the most significant social change of the twentieth century. More than 43 million women, or 51 percent of all women over age 16, are in the paid labor force. And most analysts agree women will continue to enter the labor force in even greater numbers over the next few decades. Even if a low economic growth rate persists and the birth rate increases, the labor force participation rate among women aged 20 to 24 is expected to increase to the 75 percent level. For women 20 to 54, labor analysts predict an increase, with their participation rate ranging between 66 and 70 percent during the decade of the 1980s. The opportunity cost of remaining at home, compared to the benefits derived from working in the paid labor force, will encourage many more women to seek paid work. High current unemployment rates for women and men notwithstanding (9.5 percent and 10.2 percent, respectively), long-term trends of increased female labor force activity, particularly for women aged 20 to 54, seem likely.

Not only are more women working, but even women with young children are taking paid jobs. More mothers—including never married, currently married, and no longer married—are in the labor force now. Even more are expected to enter the marketplace in coming decades. The dramatic increase in women's labor force participation has given them a 42 percent share of the nation's total labor force.

By 1978, approximately 15 million people were part-time employees. Almost half of these part-time workers were women between ages 20 and 44. The U.S. Department of Labor reports that most of these female workers were employed as clerical workers, bookkeepers, receptionists, retail sales clerks, teachers' aides, childcare workers, bus drivers, beauticians, real estate agents, teachers, and nurses. Part-time workers, both male and female, tend to receive less pay, as well as fewer, if any, fringe benefits. In fact, part-time workers on the average earn 29 percent less per hour than full-time employees, a difference attributed to the predominance of part-time workers in low-paid sales, clerical, and service occupations. Even women who work in professional occupations confront a similar earnings deficit. Women who are part-time professional and technical workers are also economically handicapped, but their numbers increased by 36 percent even in the short period between 1970 and 1979.[3]

Technological and economic factors combine to produce a changing picture of work in the coming decades. Secretarial and other traditional female occupations are becoming obsolete in the wake of word processors and minicomputers. At the same time, technology creates opportunities for skilled work, much of which requires manual dexterity—presumably a feminine stronghold. Whether the growth of technological fields will help or exploit female workers remains an open question. The service sector of the economy, experts agree, will continue to expand, particularly as greater geographical mobility of the American population builds population density in previously underpopulated areas.

Demographers forecast considerable geographic mobility between now and 1990. Such population shifts are expected to weaken the demand for jobs in some areas and increase the need for workers in others. According to these predictions, more than half the United States population will be living in the West and South by 1990. Movement into previously less-densely populated areas will require more community services, including police and fire protection as well as health care and other services.

Political scientists call our attention to still another aspect of change: participation in the political process. They point particularly to the greater numbers of women, compared to men, who turn out to vote, as well as to women's growing inclination to vote differently from men. This is especially the case among younger voters. For instance, in the 1980 American presidential election, among 18- to 24-year-old voters, 3.1 million women versus 2.8 million men went to the polls. That represented 37.5 percent of the eligible women voters in that age group, compared to 35.3 percent of the eligible male voters in the same age cohort. Not since 1944, when 12 million of the 42 million eligible male voters were overseas with the armed services, had women cast more votes than men.

As younger women with greater political interest, sophistication, and activity replace older, less politically active women in the population, women's political clout will probably grow. As these younger women age, they will become a politically active cohort of older women. In Chapter 12, we saw that women are claiming a larger proportion of legislative seats at local, state, and national levels. The gender gap suggests that women voters might be mobilized to vote as a bloc, a potential resource for women candidates who emphasize women's concerns. The dramatic increase in women students in law and business schools, congenial backgrounds for political careers, enhances the possibility that women will have a stronger hand in shaping political, legal, and financial policy in coming decades.

Public opinion polls show that stereotypes about women, as well as about other minority groups, are gradually weakening. These polls indicate growing support for women's participation in the mainstream of society at all levels. Expectations for women's labor force participation are bolstered by widespread support for women to control their own fertility through contraception and abortion, despite the vociferous opposition of a well-funded minority. All these trends, some complementary, others contradictory, create a complex picture, one that leaves us asking: "What does it all mean?"

WHAT DOES IT ALL MEAN?

What do all these conflicting trends portend for the social context and the gender power balance within it in the coming decades? The overwhelming conclusion is that strong cross-currents make precise predictions difficult. Forces such as higher educational levels, increasing labor force participation, and lower birth rates suggest that women will continue to move into the mainstream of economic and political life. Countervailing factors, such as a no-growth economy, the devaluation of a college degree, the high level of divorce, the threat to feminine occupational strongholds through advances in technology, the development of foreign labor force pools to offset rising domestic labor costs, all becloud the picture of women's future resource base and the potential restructuring of the gender power balance.

A necessarily oversimplified interpretation of these trends would predict women as the majority population group, but with a difference. The dramatic rise of female-headed families, many below the poverty line, suggests that there will be a large pool of women with greater economic and family responsibilities but few resources. At the other end of the spectrum, women's increasing educational and occupational achievements, if they continue, will inevitably produce a growing number of women with more economic and political resources. The political participation of women in expanded voting activity and candidacy for public office suggests that women will indeed make their political voices heard and heeded.

Women's access to educational and occupational resources will strengthen their hand in personal heterosexual relationships, although that very hand-strengthening may well lead to increased divorce, at least under certain circumstances. One recent sociological study by Hiller and Philliber indicates that the divorce rate is higher among women in male-dominated fields than among those in traditional female occupations.[4] This is particularly so if these women are married to men whose own jobs are below what their educational backgrounds would predict. So the trade-offs may be difficult, at least in the short term.

With rising educational levels, control myths and stereotypes that separate women of different social classes and racial-ethnic groups have a strong chance of losing their hold. The likelihood increases for women— majority and minority, middle-class professional and working-class—to join forces, or at least to coalesce around certain shared political issues. Even now, pollsters report that stereotypes about women and other minorities are on the wane. As stereotypes and their control myths weaken, the barriers to coalitions among the powerless will begin to crumble. Coalitions among women, particularly older and younger women, women from all social, racial, ethnic, and religious groups, as well as coalitions between men and women, will have a strong chance of resetting the gender power balance.

We have noted throughout this volume the pattern of male support for female causes when those causes simultaneously benefit men. The breakdown of stereotypes, combined with the growing likelihood that women will sacrifice political purity for pragmatic coalitions, suggests that women might be more receptive in the years ahead to joining forces with men whose institutional resources could help them produce a mutually beneficial solution.

We have documented how women have been urged in the past to set aside their own needs for equality for the larger social good. Women's majority population advantage ironically suggests that the larger social good is whatever will benefit no less than 51.3 percent of the population. Moreover, the women's movement has helped men and women alike to understand that all social issues—not simply abortion, childcare, and maternity leave—are primarily women's issues. The rise of female-headed families has prompted more Americans than ever before to recognize that housing, transportation, and energy, as well as a host of other policy issues, most seriously affect the growing numbers of women who support themselves and their families on meager economic resources. It has become increasingly evident that defense policies, which require reallocation of national resources away from social programs benefitting women and their families to nuclear arms, are also women's issues. That foreign policy, which potentially threatens women with the loss of children and mates, is important to women should not be too difficult for policymakers to appreciate, particularly if those policymakers more often are women.

The demographic forecasts suggest that it will be more difficult to deny that the larger social good cannot be achieved without attending to the needs of women. With women's 51.3 percent population advantage, it seems somewhat absurd to continue telling them that we must try to solve the world's ills without directly building women's needs into the solution.

DEMOCRATIC IDEOLOGY AND REALITY

The issue of the larger social good takes on special meaning within the context of a democratic society. The centerpiece of the ideology of democracy is the belief that *all* members of the society are entitled to equal freedoms and equal opportunities. Whenever a disparity exists between any ideology and the reality it purports to describe, social and political tensions begin to mount. One index of the present ideology-reality gap can be seen in the contrast between current opinion polls that register growing acceptance of women as mainstream members of society and the continuing grim realities of occupational segregation, educational barriers, and salary and pension differentials between the genders.

The disparity between the ideology of a democracy that offers equality to all and the existential reality of the subordination of women and other minority groups creates a tension not easily dismissed. As women form political coalitions among themselves and with other subordinate groups, the tensions undoubtedly will mount. But so too will the chances for resolving these tensions. As the tensions escalate and crisis conditions develop, both women and men will begin to realize that the explanations embodied in the ideology underpinning major social institutions are providing inadequate or irrelevant, even false, answers to current problems. Then, as in any crisis period, new belief systems may emerge into public view and acceptance.

These budding belief systems have grown naturally, hidden like wildflowers beneath the broad leaves of the established ideology. Usually, they are recognized only by those disenfranchised individuals and groups whose daily experiences bring them in touch with a different reality that denies the validity of the prevailing ideology. During stable periods, when the status quo is not threatened, the prevailing ideology suffices, and the tension level between ideology and reality is below the level of social awareness. In such times, the ideology helps, or at least does not impede, the usual "muddling through." Beliefs about the dominant group's capacity and right to rule seem reasonable explanations of reality.

When the tension between the old, imprecise ideology and visible reality creates even small social explosions, new ideologies become visible. They offer a new explanation, even a way out of the current difficulties. As such, new ideologies inevitably present a clear threat to the prevailing belief system. Their threatening nature is intensified by the fact that previously subordinate groups may be the messengers bearing the news. The ideology of gender equality that underlies the women's movement is experienced as just such a threat by many women and men whose existence is predicated on the traditional power structure, with its dominant/subordinate, protector/protectorate gender patterns. For many others, if we are to believe the opinion pollsters, the values of the women's movement—equal access to opportunity for women and men of all social groups—have already colored the American consciousness. That the social forms we need to express these values in daily life have not yet been developed should not necessarily deter us. There is still time to act.

NEW SOCIAL FORMS

The very essence of crisis is the recognition that the old definitions and solutions are no longer viable. New definitions are required, new social forms and labels are needed. New decisions are needed about who can do what; who and what are valuable; what contributions are important; how and what resources are available to women, as well as what will constitute the new bargaining chips in the gender power negotiations. The next adjustment of the gender power balance depends on our ability to create these definitions and make these decisions.

New social inventions—new roles, relationships, and institutions—are needed in such times. New resources must be identified. Alternative distribution networks must be forged. Although the major impression left by the demographic trends predicted for the coming decades is one of crosscurrents whose ultimate direction is hard to predict, it seems reasonably certain that women will continue to accumulate considerable resources. It is somewhat less clear that this development will be as rapid as some might wish, or as unimpeded as others previously thought. Three steps forward and one backward—somewhat better than the historical two forward and one backward pattern—is probably a safe guess. But the ingredients for a power shift are definitely there.

WILL THE RULED BECOME RULERS?

Some fear to ask the dreaded question: "Will the ruled become rulers?" For the ruled to exchange places with their rulers often requires nothing short of a revolution. And some would argue that the demographic trends just described do, in fact, constitute a substantial, if nonviolent, revolution. But as students of power remind us, for the ruled to cast off subjugation, several important conditions must obtain. The most important condition is the ruled's perception that the odds are no longer overwhelming. And for the odds not to seem insurmountable, the ruled must have access to substantial resources.

As we have argued earlier, institutions amass substantial resource reserves. These institutions, controlled until now by the powerful male homosocial network, distribute resources through informal systems. Rewarded by institutional resources, those in power are able to sustain their dominant position. The ruled, rewarded mostly by trivial or incidental, less valuable resources, have difficulty amassing sufficient reserves to capitalize an effective revolt. In addition, when the powerless are fragmented through negative stereotypes of one another into still smaller, less capitalized groups, they fail to build the necessary resources to impose their own will on the powerful. If the powerless not only fear contamination through coalescing with other powerless groups, but also believe both in the inevitability of their own subordination and the benign authority of the powerful, it is unlikely that any but the most desperate or demented will revolt.

As our demographic overview attests, recent decades have witnessed both subtle and dramatic changes in the actual and potential resource base available to women as the subordinate group. First, education, particularly higher education, is a radicalizing force, as we have seen. It provides the tools for men and women alike to examine physical and social realities. At the very least, it challenges the acceptance of those crippling control myths by which women and men prevent themselves and one another from stepping beyond the stereotypes of sex and gender roles. Education also helps dispel the stereotypes of other groups that serve to keep the powerless separated from one another.

That women are now receiving the institutional credentials that higher education can bestow provides the basis for a previously unthinkable level of resource accumulation as individuals and groups. Such formal certification by higher educational institutions opens the way for women to enter the occupational structure and struggle through the morass of career opportunities and barriers to economic and professional self-sufficiency.

Women's march beyond the home into higher education and the paid labor force has brought them a new understanding of their power and place in the stratification system. Through the radicalizing influence of higher education, which offers new understanding and the possibility of rejecting outdated concepts and belief systems, women have acquired the tools for examining their existence in all social and political domains. With this clarified understanding of the dialectic between "what is" and "what must be," women are entering the mainstream.

In the last few decades, as women moved beyond the segregation of the home into the paid labor force, they observed the structural and ideological barriers other women confronted. Through their observations of other women whom they could recognize as able but institutionally blocked, women began to realize that the limitations they themselves had experienced and interpreted as personal were instead political. This awareness that the fault was "neither in their stars, nor in themselves," but in the very structure of society, allowed women to take important steps toward joining forces to seek equity. The degree to which women's segregation within the home, away from other non-kin women, impeded their bonding and co-alescing with women from other groups has not been sufficiently studied. The ghettoization of women within the paid labor force—that is, occupational segregation—has taught women the lessons the ghetto teaches its inhabitants so cruelly but well.

Beset in recent years by repeated national crises, from the civil rights movement to Vietnam, Watergate, and a serious economic recession, American society has experienced shock waves that threaten its philosophical moorings. Control myths, previously an unnoticeable part of the background, have emerged as foreground. As such, they have come under severe scrutiny. Control myths explaining ability, temperament, and the right to rule have begun to come apart. Understanding the pernicious effect of control myths that label women dependent, self-sacrificing, and less intelligent has enabled women to shed centuries of reluctance about asking for their own due—even when it means moving to courts of law to seek redress; even when they knew that such action would achieve only a slight adjustment in the gender power balance. Men too have begun to recognize the lethal trap that the dominant role has become for males.

For men and women, as individuals and groups, the coming decades pose a serious challenge. For policymakers and voters of both genders, the sex-gender system and the power struggle it symbolizes are top agenda items. Policymakers and voters alike will be forced to take a more complex view of social policy, from abortion and childcare to nuclear arms and other weapon systems.

The sex-gender system is a social form that in the past enabled us to deal with the uncertainties of the human condition. Over the centuries, we used it as the blueprint for all the other power relationships that we constructed to create an illusion of existential control. Rapidly changing conditions now require us to revise the blueprint to meet the demands of the twenty-first century. To respond to this challenge, women and men, through personal relationships and public policies, will need to create new social forms—a new blueprint. These new social forms will inevitably determine the next configuration of the gender power balance and all related power relationships. The design of the blueprint will direct our course, even shape our destiny in the coming years. Created with foresight and sensitivity to human issues, this new blueprint could lead us safely through the threatening social storm.

NOTES

1. Max Weber, *The Theory of Social and Economic Organization* (New York: Oxford University Press, 1922).

2. Max L. Carey, "Occupational Employment Growth through 1990," *Monthly Labor Review*, 104, no. 8 (August 1981), 42–55.

3. "Persons at Work in Non-Agricultural Industries, By Full and Part-Time Status, Sex, and Race, 1968–1981," *Labor Force Statistics Derived from the Current Population Survey: Data Book I*, Bulletin 2096, Table B-22, p. 687.

4. Dana V. Hiller and William W. Philliber, "Relative Occupational Attainments of Spouses and Later Changes in Marriage and Wife's Work Experience" (paper presented at American Sociological Association, seventy-seventh annual meeting, September, 1982, San Francisco, California).

INDEX

NAME INDEX

Acker, Joan, 178, 195
Alper, Thelma G., 146, 153
Archer, Dana, 68, 97
Atkinson, G. W., 142, 153

Bales, Robert F., 100, 116
Bandura, A., 67
Barash, David, 100, 116
Barnard, Chester, 91, 97
Barron, Deborah Durfee, 163, 174
Barthes, Roland, 75, 97
Beecher, Catharine, 136
Benston, Margaret, 132
Berkov, B., 42
Berman, Phyllis W., 68
Bernard, Jessie, 42, 67–68, 98, 103, 107, 116–17
Best, Raphaela, 68, 102, 116, 139, 154
Bies, Robert J., 68
Blanchard, E. B., 67
Blau, Peter, 176, 195
Blaustein, Rachel, 182
Boulding, Kenneth, 23, 26
Bridenthal, Renate, 132
Bronfenbrenner, Urie, 153
Bronson, G. W., 66

Caldwell, Steven B., 42
Campbell, Joseph, 69
Chafe, William H., 42, 156–57, 174, 178, 195

Clark, R. A., 142, 153
Clarke, Edward H., 94, 98, 137
Coser, Rose Laub, 131, 133
Costa, Mariarosa Dalla, 132

Daniels, Arlene, 129, 133
Datan, Nancy, 66
de Beauvoir, Simone, 135, 153
Degler, Carl N., 42, 97, 135, 137, 153, 157, 174–75, 195
de Tocqueville, Alexis, 173
Dublin, Thomas, 158, 174
Durkheim, Emile, 155, 168–72, 174, 194
Dye, Nancy Schrom, 127, 132

Edelman, M., 67
Edwards, Carolyn Pope, 68
Ehrhardt, A. A., 67
Epstein, Cynthia Fuchs, 189, 196
Erikson, Erik H., 67–68

Feldman, S. S., 67–68
Fennema, Elizabeth, 141, 153
Feshback, N. D., 139, 153
Field, W. F., 146, 154
Fox, Lynn, 141, 153
Freeman, Jo, 187
Freeze, Karen Johnson, 145, 153
French, Marilyn, 124, 132
Freud, Anna, 61
Freud, Sigmund, 103

SUBJECT INDEX